EDUCATION FOR ECONOMIC SURVIVAL

How is educational provision changing? In what ways should it change to meet the economic challenges and opportunities of the 1990s?

This collection reviews debates and reforms in education in the light of recent theories of post-fordism. There has been a globalization of economic markets and competition and an end to the 'cold war'. Apart from capitalism itself, everything seems to be 'up for grabs'. However, much of the current debate about education, economy and society has failed to rise above the cut and thrust of domestic social policy. Given the current attack on the foundations of welfare capitalism in a number of industrial societies such debates are of great importance. However, they urgently need to be complemented by discussion about the future of industrial societies and the role of education in economic and industrial policy. Indeed, when one begins to consider these wider questions one is forced to rethink much of what is currently taken for granted about educational and training systems. Therefore the aim of this volume is to take a tentative step towards a 'new agenda', as well as to examine the nature and consequences of existing education and training policies.

Administrators, policy makers, and practitioners will find the book of considerable interest as will students in the fields of sociology, labour economics, education, social policy, and youth studies.

'This is a valuable and timely collection, penetrating beneath the mountain of rhetoric that has accompanied much of the debate about vocationalism and training in education in Britain. It will be welcomed by educationalists and sociologists, and should provide food for thought for planners and politicians'.

Professor David Jary, Staffordshire Polytechnic

Phillip Brown is Lecturer in Sociology at the University of Kent, England; and **Hugh Lauder** is Professor in Education at the University of Victoria, Wellington, New Zealand.

EDUCATION FOR ECONOMIC SURVIVAL

From fordism to post-fordism?

Edited by

Phillip Brown and Hugh Lauder

London and New York

First published in 1992
by Routledge
11 New Fetter Lane, London EC4P 4EE

Simultaneously published in the USA and Canada
by Routledge
a division of Routledge, Chapman and Hall Inc.
29 West 35th Street, New York, NY 10001

Typeset by J&L Composition Ltd, Filey, North Yorkshire
Printed and bound in Great Britain by
Billings & Sons Limited, Worcester

British Library Cataloguing in Publication Data
Education for economic survival.
1. Economic conditions. Role of education
I. Brown, Phillip 1957- II. Lauder, Hugh
338.4737

Library of Congress Cataloging in Publication Data
Education for economic survival: from Fordism to post-Fordism? / edited by Phillip Brown and Hugh Lauder.
p. cm.
Includes bibliographical references and index.
1. Education—Economic aspects—Congresses. I. Brown, Phillip, 1957– . II. Lauder, Hugh.
LC65.E318 1991
338.4′737—dc20 91-11175
CIP

ISBN 0-415-04901-6

CONTENTS

CONTRIBUTORS

David N. Ashton is Professor of Sociology and Director of Research of the Labour Market Studies Group, University of Leicester. He has published widely on labour markets and the school-to-work transition. His latest book, in collaboration with Malcolm Maguire and Mark Spilsbury, is entitled *Restructuring the Labour Market: The Implications for Youth* (Macmillan, 1990).

Shane Blackman is a Research Officer in the Department of Educational Studies, University of Surrey. He has previously taught at Thames Polytechnic, and at the Institute of Education, University of London. He has published papers on vocationalism, youth training, and equal opportunities.

Phil Brown is a lecturer in Sociology at the University of Kent at Canterbury. He previously worked at the Institute of Criminology, University of Cambridge, and as a craft apprentice at British Leyland, Cowley, Oxford. His publications include *Schooling Ordinary Kids* (Tavistock, 1987) and a number of edited volumes. The most recent is *Poor Work: Disadvantage and the Division of Labour* (Open University Press, 1991) edited with Richard Scase.

Clyde Chitty was formerly a lecturer in the Curriculum Studies Department at the Institute of Education, University of London, he is now a lecturer in the School of Education, University of Birmingham, and a member of the University's Centre for Education Management and Policy Studies. He is co-editor of the journals, *Forum* and *Comprehensive Education*, and the author of *Towards a New Education System: The Victory of the New Right?* (Falmer Press, 1989).

Mike Hickox is a lecturer in Politics at the Polytechnic of the South Bank. His interests are in the areas of education and industrial society, politics, and the economy.

Krishan Kumar is Professor of Social Thought at the University of Kent at Canterbury. He has been a BBC Talks Producer, and also a Visiting Fellow at Harvard University and a Visiting Professor at the University of Colorado at Boulder. Main publications: *Prophecy and Progress: The Sociology of Industrial and Post-Industrial Society* (1978); *Utopia and Anti-Utopia in Modern Times* (1987); *The Rise of Modern Society* (1988); and *Utopianism* (1990).

Hugh Lauder is Professor of Education at the Victoria University of Wellington, New Zealand. He has co-edited *Education: In Search of a Future* (Falmer Press, 1988) (with Phillip Brown); *Towards Successful Schooling* (Falmer Press, 1990) (with Cathy Wylie), and published many papers on educational inequality and on the economics of education.

Malcolm Maguire is a Research Fellow in the Labour Market Studies Group at the University of Leicester. He has published numerous articles on education, the school-to-work transition, and training. He is also a co-author of a number of research monographs on youth and the labour market. His most recent publication (with D.N. Ashton and M. Spilsbury) is *Restructuring the Labour Market: The Implications for Youth* (Macmillan, 1990).

Susan Maguire is a Research Assistant in the Labour Market Studies Group at the University of Leicester. Her main areas of research have been developments in 14–19 education and training provisions, a European comparison of the transition to adulthood, and the development of standards of competence. Prior to this she worked as a Careers Officer for six years.

Rob Moore lectures in the Sociology of Education at Homerton College, Cambridge. His interests are in the areas of education and the economy, the curriculum, and the theory of knowledge. He has published many papers on these topics.

Gareth Rees is a lecturer in Sociology in the School of Social and Administrative Studies at the University of Wales College of Cardiff. He has published widely on urban and regional development and labour market change.

Teresa Rees is a lecturer in Sociology and Director of the Social Research Unit in the School of Social and Administrative Studies at the University of Wales College of Cardiff. She has conducted numerous studies on labour market issues.

Richard Scase is Professor of Sociology at the University of Kent at Canterbury. He is the author of *Social Democracy in Capitalist Society* (1977) and co-author (with Robert Goffee) of *The Entrepreneurial Middle Class* (1982), *Women in Charge* (1985), *The Real World of the Small Business Owner* (1987), and *Reluctant Managers* (1989); and (with Howard Davis) *Western Capitalism and State Socialism* (1985). He has edited four volumes and written numerous papers for academic and non-academic books and journals.

Harry Torrance is a lecturer in Education at the University of Sussex. He previously worked at the Centre for Applied Research in Education, University of East Anglia, and in the Assessment and Evaluation Unit at Southampton University. Recent publications include *The Changing Face of Educational Assessment* (co-author with Roger Murphy) (Open University Press, 1988) and *Changing Educational Assessment: International Perspectives and Trends* (co-editor with Patricia Broadfoot and Roger Murphy) (Routledge, 1990).

Sarah Vickerstaff is a lecturer in Industrial Relations in the Canterbury Business School at the University of Kent. She is joint author of *The History of Industrial Training in Britain*. Her current research interests include the provision of training opportunities in the Kent economy and the problems of designing effective national training strategies and policies.

PREFACE

In the late twentieth century the social and economic world has been transformed in a number of significant ways. Advances in new technology and mass communications have made it increasingly plausible to talk about the rise of the 'information' society. There has been a globalization of economic markets and competition and an end to the 'cold war'. Apart from capitalism itself, everything appears to be 'up for grabs'. However, much of the current debate about education, economy, and society has failed to rise above the cut and thrust of domestic social policy. Given the current attack on the foundations of welfare capitalism in a number of industrial societies such debates are of great importance, as the contributors to this volume will make clear. However, they urgently need to be complemented by discussions about the future of industrial societies and the role of education in the year 2000 and beyond. Indeed, when one begins to consider these wider questions one is forced to rethink much of what is currently taken for granted about educational and training systems. Therefore, the aim of this volume is to take a tentative step towards a 'new agenda', as well as to examine the nature and consequences of existing education and training policies.

We are greatly indebted to all the contributors who attended a workshop at the University of Kent at Canterbury to think about a future vision for education and training. We are also indebted to Chris Rojek from Routledge and Roger Dale from Auckland University (formerly of the Open University, UK), for their advice and encouragement, and to Nicola Kerry for her help with the preparation of the manuscript. Finally, we are indebted to Liz Brown and Karen O'Connell for their support and patience which has been frequently tested since the editors decided to collaborate from opposite ends of the world.

Phil Brown, Canterbury, UK
Hugh Lauder, Wellington, New Zealand

1

EDUCATION, ECONOMY, AND SOCIETY: AN INTRODUCTION TO A NEW AGENDA

Phillip Brown and Hugh Lauder

INTRODUCTION

The social and economic world has been transformed in a number of significant ways during the closing decades of the twentieth century. Advances in new technology and mass communications have made it increasingly plausible to talk about the rise of the 'information' society. The technological ability to condense time and space has also been accompanied by an extension of global economic markets. Increasingly, industrial societies are being forced to look beyond their own back yards in order to address the issue of sustainable economic growth. In Western Europe, such concerns have led to arguments in support of the creation of a 'United States of Europe'. The social revolutions which are taking place in Eastern Europe and the Soviet Union equally have profound implications for global politics and economics. In the West we are also confronted with issues concerning the growing economic power of the Pacific Rim and Latin America (Harris 1987), the relationship between rich and poor countries (World Bank Development Report 1990), and the need to develop international strategies to deal with the environmental destruction of our planet (Brundtland Report 1987).

A TRANSFORMATION AT WORK?

In these 'new times' the ability to compete in the global market has significant implications for existing patterns of work and education, as well as for the production of goods and the distribution of services. The nature and significance of these changes can be described in a number of ways and are discussed by Krishan Kumar in Chapter 2. There is, for instance, considerable speculation as to whether the emergence of more flexible modes of capitalist production represent shifts in surface appearance or signs of the emergence of some entirely new post-capitalist or post-industrial society (Harvey 1989).[1]

Our argument is not dependent upon an entirely new post-capitalist or post-industrial conception of the Western world, indeed we want to argue that the future organization of work and employment is open to political negotiation and struggle. Indeed, it would be naive to believe that the inherent logic of capitalist development will inevitably improve the work conditions for the majority, it will not.[2] But we do assume that the intensification of global economic competition (and growing concern about the environment) will have profound implications for the way capitalist production is organized and for the way human resources are deployed.

Piore and Sabel (1984) have argued that the deterioration in economic performance of a number of Western capitalist societies is the result of a largely redundant model of industrial development based on the mass production of standardized goods. This 'fordist' system of mass production is premised on Frederick Taylor's principles of 'scientific management':

> Taylor's idea was for management to secure the most efficient possible use of labor by codifying craft knowledge and deciding by scientific means the one right way to do a particular job. Workers were then to be forced to execute this plan exactly through the promise of high wages and the threat of sanctions for disobedience. The extreme routinization of work that Taylor implied, however, presupposes the fixity of markets and the production process characteristic of mass production.
>
> (Sabel 1984: 236)

A broader version of this debate turns on the claim that bureaucratic organizations are no longer appropriate to the conditions of the late twentieth century:[3]

> Bureaucracy thrives in a highly competitive, undifferentiated, and stable environment, such as the climate of its

> youth, the Industrial Revolution. A pyramidal structure of authority, with power concentrated in the hands of few with the knowledge and resources to control an entire enterprise was, and is, an eminently suitable social arrangement for routinized tasks. However, the environment has changed in just those ways which make the mechanism most problematic. Stability has vanished.
>
> (Bennis 1972: 111)

In both these quotations it is suggested that advanced Western economies (and this would equally apply to the Soviet Union) now confront a choice between maintaining the rigid hierarchical division of labour, and the low-skill and low-trust relationships characteristic of fordism, or shift to a system based on adaptable machinery, adaptable workers, flatter hierarchies, and the breakdown of the division between mental and manual labour and learning.

The main dimensions and trends believed to be involved in the shift from fordism to post-fordism are summarized in Table 1.1.[4]

The dimensions and trends presented in this table have also given rise to much controversy. There is, for instance, disagreement about whether the shift from fordism to post-fordism offers an adequate description of current organizational and economic trends, and disagreement about how to interpret the significance of these changes for the future of capitalist societies.

The description of a shift from fordism to post-fordism is obviously presented in ideal-typical terms, and as a consequence it tends to highlight change rather than continuity. It also tends to assume that countries can be characterized in terms of one or the other. It is true to say that some countries, such as Germany and Sweden, come closer to the model of post-fordism than Britain, France, or the USA. But we should not ignore clear examples of 'uneven development' where some organizations have adopted flexible organizational structures while others, within the same country, remain firmly locked into hierarchical systems of managerial control and surveillance. Despite such difficulties, the willingness of industrial societies to restructure along the lines of post-fordism and their success in doing so is increasingly seen to be a key factor in the capacity to survive economically in the wake of global competition in the 1990s.

Table 1.1 Characteristics of fordism and post-fordism

Fordism	*Post-fordism*
Economy competition and production process	
Protected national markets	Global competition
Mass production of standardized products	Flexible production systems/small batch/niche markets
Bureaucratic hierarchical organizations	Flatter and flexible organizational structures
Compete by full capacity utilization and cost-cutting	Compete by innovation, diversification, sub-contracting
Labour	
Fragmented and standardized work tasks	Flexible specialization/ multi-skilled workers
Low-trust/low-discretion Majority employed in manufacturing sector/'blue collar' jobs	High-trust/high-discretion Majority employed in service sector/'white collar' jobs
Little 'on the job' training Little formal education required for most jobs	Regular 'on the job' training Greater demand for 'knowledgeable' workers
Small managerial and professional elite	Growing managerial and professional class/service class
Fairly predictable labour market histories	Unpredictable labour market histories due to technological change and increased economic uncertainty
Politics and ideology	
Trade union solidarity	Decline in trade union membership
Class-based political affiliation	Declining significance of class-based politics
Importance of locality/class/ gender-based lifestyles	Fragmentation and pluralism 'global village'
Mass consumption of consumer durables	Individualized consumption/ consumer choice

EDUCATION AND GLOBAL ECONOMIC CHANGE

Given the increasing limitations on individual nation states to control the terms of economic competition, they have had to look to their own institutions and human resources to meet the challenge of economic competition. Consequently the educational system has increasingly taken on the significance of a secular religion promising spiritual and material progress.

This faith in the efficacy of the education system has a long history (Williams 1961; Lazerson and Grubb 1974). Capitalist and state socialist societies alike have invested massively in formal educational systems in order to fashion their 'products' to the demands of a modern industrial society. All such societies have developed techniques for selecting and training their members to fill occupational positions in a hierarchical division of labour. In industrial societies, those techniques have become increasingly specialized and organized within educational and training institutions. Therefore, the Enlightenment aim of 'perfecting' human nature has at best served as a sub-plot in the development of state education, and although genuine attempts to extend educational opportunities to most children were evident in the 1960s, the general contours of modern educational systems have been more decisively shaped by the relentless appetite for more efficient forms of production and control. However, social research conducted in many countries has shown that despite the massive investment in educational provision many of the jobs students were destined to enter required little more than the performance of routine tasks which permitted the large-scale wastage of talent and individual creativity. This wastage was particularly noticeable among the working class, ethnic minorities, and women.

The increasing tendency for the faith bestowed in the educational system to take the form of a secular religion is manifest in the flood of complaints from politicians and employers about the failure of the educational system to serve the needs of an advanced economy, especially at a time of high youth unemployment. Recently, the source of anxiety has shifted to fears about the declining number of young people entering the labour market at a time when there is a shortage of educated labour for 'knowledge'-based jobs (OECD 1989). It is also manifest in the attempt by national governments to make the curricula more vocationally relevant, and in those policy reforms aimed at creating 'free market' systems of education.[5]

The appeal to economic imperative as a rationale for educational reform should not obscure the fact that educational questions are always social questions, which invariably involve winners and losers. It is equally important to note that decisions concerning the structure and content of education and training programmes are never simply technologically determined, but always involve a choice between alternative policies.

Max Weber observed some seventy years ago that:

> Behind all the present discussions of the foundations of the educational system, the struggle of the 'specialist type of man' against the older type of 'cultivated man' is hidden at some decisive point. This fight is determined by the irresistibly expanding bureaucratization of all public and private relations of authority and by the ever-increasing importance of expert and specialized knowledge. This fight intrudes into all intimate cultural questions.
>
> (quoted in Gerth and Mills 1948: 243)

The question of the 'specialist' versus 'generalist' is not only one about the most efficient way of training for one's future role in the technological society. It is a question which is intimately linked to cultural definitions of what is to count as 'education' and one's subsequent position in the system of social stratification.

We will argue that sytems of education, training, and employment can be organized in different ways depending upon decisions taken by employers, politicians, and trade union representatives, among others (Block 1990). Moreover, it is those industrial societies which remain locked into fordist principles of bureaucratic organization which will find it increasingly difficult to create high trust relations and a skilled labour force.

Fox (1974) argues that the highly developed division of labour which characterizes bureaucratic organization is based on low-discretion work roles and assumes low-trust relations. As a result employees have responded by demonstrating minimum levels of commitment. In such circumstances it is extremely difficult for employers and managers to achieve open communications, high personal involvement, and the high-trust relations upon which corporate life is increasingly seen to depend. In a world of accelerating change, the success of the modern corporation:

> is said to depend on high-trust attitudes and behaviours on the part of rank and file. Yet given the low-discretion roles allocated to them they can only offer such attitudes and behaviours if they fully and actively legitimize and endorse

> their place in the total structure, the purposes of that structure, and the wider societal values which it embodies. Neither the organization nor the wider society, however, has been able to provide them with a frame of reference which leads them to offer this active legitimation (as opposed to passive acquiescence). They have found that neither the self-help exhortations of Samuel Smiles, nor the Social Darwinism said to justify the victor in his spoils, nor the social formula of the modern meritocrat (I.Q. + Effort = Merit; Young, 1961) has disposed them to transcend the low-trust responses which low-discretion roles tend to generate.
>
> (Fox 1974: 336)

Central to our thesis is the view that low-trust organizations and societies gravitate towards 'low-ability' systems of education and training in terms of the collective pool of skills, knowledge, and know-how which an organization or society is able to deploy.

In low-ability societies the concerns of the powerful focus predominantly on the top 20 per cent of the school population. Educational excellence is defined in terms of this section of the school system rather than the whole. In educational terms this has made little sense, and for the majority of pupils the offer of a few modest certificates which could be exchanged in the market for skilled manual and routine non-manual jobs was the only thing which secured their often grudging compliance (Brown 1987). Nevertheless, this massive wastage of talent has been 'affordable' because the majority of jobs required little more than the execution of a set of easily learned routines.

Of course, there has been an expansion of professional and managerial jobs in the post-war period, but this has not affected the basic structure of bureaucratic work. Hence, despite the 'technocratic' (Kerr *et al.* 1973) assumption that economic survival has depended upon the rigorous implementation of meritocratic criteria of recruitment, designed to ensure that only the most talented 'get to the top', there has remained a great deal of 'slack' within both private and public sector organizations, especially at managerial and executive levels. However, in the future a great deal of this slack will need to be removed as organizations try to improve existing levels of performance (Kanter 1984; Scase and Goffee 1989).

In the next section we will argue that, although a system of bureaucratic education is fairer than one based upon the principles of social ascription, and the reproduction of lesson notes and a diligent preparation for examinations is well suited to the production of 'smart conformists' for successful role performance in the public and private sector corporate bureaucracies,[6] these characteristics of bureaucratic education are increasingly symptoms of low-trust and low-ability societies in the 1990s.[7] Therefore, the economic changes which are already taking place on a global scale will require major changes in the areas of education and training.

In the final section, we will argue that a redefinition of commonsense notions of intelligence and educational excellence is required if Britain or the USA is to become a 'high-ability' society. Instead of assuming that there are severe limits on the pool of talent, societies will need to recognize the wealth of talent which exists throughout the whole population irrespective of class, gender, or race, and concentrate on harnessing this wealth of talent to empower the population for active citizenship as well as for their future occupational roles. This view is based on the belief that it is often 'social hierarchy and the world views associated with it that restrict the unfolding of human capacity, and not the limitations of natural endowment' (Sabel 1984: 224). We will argue that the development of 'collective intelligence' will be central to the establishment of sustainable economic growth (Brundtland Report 1987; Block 1990).

There is also a need to stop thinking about excellence in elitist terms. Excellence should be defined in terms of the collective skills, knowledge, and know-how which can be deployed within a society as a whole. To achieve the latter, it is necessary to end our obsession with the 'great man' and 'token woman' view of history. Sustainable economic growth will increasingly depend on the collective efforts of executives, managers, researchers, teachers, child carers, shopfloor workers, etc., because significant technological advances are rarely the result of the efforts and insights of any one person. It is, therefore, equally important to challenge the excessive individualism which is endemic in Britain and the USA (Marquand 1989) which, among other things, leads employers to be more concerned with poaching skilled labour from each other than developing a mutual social obligation to train.

In the drive to release talent there can be no justification for unwarranted privilege as exemplified by private schools. They are a manifestation of societies whose powerful and privileged groups use their privileges to monopolize the best educational resources in order to ensure the success of their children at the expense of others. But of course it does not stop there, because the reproduction of these educational elites subsequently reproduces the elites within government, large City firms, and multinational companies. The problem with this system of privilege is that it prevents the development of new structures for the promotion of talent which are vital if creativity and innovation are to flourish.

It will therefore come as little surprise that we view current educational policies in countries like the USA and Britain as hopelessly inadequate in the attempt to activate the changes we are describing here. The creation of a 'free market' for education and training is likely to reinforce, if not intensify, the rigidities and inequalities which already exist in these societies. Free market reforms in education are neither in the interests of the vast majority of people, despite the rhetoric of freedom and choice, nor are they in the national economic interest. They are geared to preserving the privileges and power of the minority at a time of profound social and economic change. In what follows we will argue that the 'trained capacity' of different social groups into predictable and clearly demarcated positions in the hierarchical division of education, training, and employment is increasingly a source of 'trained incapacity'.[8]

THE RISE OF BUREAUCRATIC EDUCATION

Since its inception mass schooling has been shaped by a variety of competing interests and interpretations of its purpose. It has never resembled a simple 'correspondence' to the requirements of the economy as suggested by neo-marxists such as Bowles and Gintis (1976). In the 'first wave' of socio-historical development,[9] which occurred in the industrial nations of the nineteenth century, the educational system was seen primarily as a means of differentiating elites from the masses. Education for the privileged few provided entry into a select, culturally superior world. It was a badge, distributed according to an accident of birth, which represented and reaffirmed the privileges of the economically and politically powerful. Education was also organized to reinforce the patriarchal relations which existed in both the public and private spheres of social life. However, as industrial societies developed the reproduction of the non-manual workforce could not be achieved by restricting 'education' exclusively to middle-class men. The demand for the complex and varied skills required by industrial societies could not be satisfied by existing elites and the ruling classes they were recruited from. The perceived nature and consequences of the rapid social and economic changes which confronted all Western industrial societies, especially following the Second World War, had a powerful impact on the direction of educational change, because the need to provide a suitably trained and motivated labour force has proved a powerful argument for removing educational barriers to working-class mobility. In Britain the educational barriers which have perpetuated gender inequalities have only recently been linked to the question of economic efficiency (Weiner 1989).

It was commonly assumed that the structure of education had to be transformed radically in order to impart the basic skills, select the necessary talent, and promote the appropriate attitudes required by modern industrial societies. As Halsey and Floud noted:

> Education is a crucial type of investment for the exploitation of modern technology. This fact underlies recent educational development in all the major industrial societies ... education attains unprecedented economic importance as a source of technological innovation.
>
> (1961:1)

The intensification of efforts to make the educational system reap economic returns for the society as a whole, as well as for its recipients, coupled with a growing concern to provide greater equality of opportunity for all, created the foundation for a 'second wave' in the socio-historical development of educational systems in industrial societies, which involved a shift from the provision of education based upon what Dewey called the 'feudal dogma of social predestination' to one organized on the basis of individual merit and achievement. The most conspicuous consequence of these ideas was the shift to 'comprehensive' systems of education.

Yet, because the educational system is an institutional expression of societal attitudes and power relations, its organization and development have been shaped by the more general processes of bureaucratization, which has been the dominant form of social organization throughout this century. Indeed the growing importance attached to systems of education has partly been a result of the need for a formal system of 'socialization' and 'selection':

> The bureaucratization of the high school is . . . a manifestation of the general trend toward the rationalization of daily activities in all spheres of contemporary life. With the progressive differentiation and specialization of functions in modern society, we expect an intensification of attempts to maximise the efficiency of identifying and developing the talent within the population.
>
> (Cicourel and Kitsuse 1963: 139)

The second wave in the socio-historical development of education systems in industrial societies has, therefore, been premised on a set of rules, procedures, and practices which conform to the principles of bureaucratic organization. Weber described the characteristics of bureaucracy in terms of a 'form of organization that emphasizes precision, speed, clarity, regularity, reliability, and efficiency achieved through the creation of a fixed division of tasks, hierarchical supervision, and detailed rules and regulations' (quoted in Morgan 1986: 24–5). At the turn of the century, Weber viewed bureaucracy as a reaction against the personal subjugation, nepotism, cruelty, and subjective judgement which passed for managerial practices in the early days of the Industrial Revolution (Bennis 1972: 107). He also argued that 'if these principles of bureaucracy are followed it is possible to attain a high degree of efficiency and an organizational structure which is superior to any other form in its precision, stability and reliability'.[10]

As well as providing a social technology which can create a set of predictable outcomes, bureaucracy is intimately related to the idea of a 'meritocracy' because it treats individuals according to 'objective' criteria. In education this means that individuals are, in principle, treated according to ability rather than on the basis of ascribed characteristics such as social class, gender, or race.

The organization of formal educational systems according to

bureaucratic criteria therefore provided a rational means of social selection for expanding public administrations and capitalist corporations. School and college credentials provided a useful screening device for employers who were concerned that future employees should be inculcated into the appropriate forms of rule-following behaviour, as well as having the appropriate knowledge and skills for their place in the techno-structure. However, given the demand for large numbers of low-skilled workers with little room for individual autonomy, the educational system, throughout its second wave of development, has had to confront the problem of offering greater equality of opportunity whilst limiting the aspirations and ambitions of the majority by defining them as academic failures. This contradiction at the heart of bureaucratic education – of seeking to promote a 'talented' few while attempting to 'cool out' the majority – has consistently presented a problem of legitimation and resulted in various forms of working-class resistance.

BUREAUCRATIC EDUCATION: DILEMMAS AND TENSIONS

The bureaucratic nature of education has been shaped by a number of factors which deserve further elaboration. However, we will limit this discussion to three areas which are germane to our argument, these are: (a) the view of intelligence as unchangeable, as measurable, and as a scarce resource; (b) the use of formal academic qualifications as a means of recruitment to the hierarchical division of labour; and (c) the structure and consequences of schooling.

Notions of intelligence

The idea that individual intelligence is relatively fixed and unchangeable represents an attempt to shackle our understanding of human abilities to bureaucratic demands. Such ideas have been used throughout the twentieth century in both capitalist and state socialist societies to support the early selection of educational talent, which has consistently operated to the advantage of the socially privileged. A system of bureaucratic education needs a way of identifying and grading its inputs; IQ tests provide just such a mechanism – a single score which summarizes the potential range of an individual's achievements. Such a test is quick to administer and economic in the way it communicates the results.

It is significant that the original IQ test developed by Binet was never intended to 'fix' individuals' intelligence in this way. Indeed he saw the test as a means of establishing a benchmark for future progress. In other words, the IQ test was rather like having a physical fitness exam before being given a conditioning programme.[11] However when Binet's concept of the IQ test was translated into English it came to be interpreted quite differently. It was assumed that the test could be used as a way of predicting an individual's intellectual capability and subsequent occupational level.

In 1923 the American psychologist Terman wrote that IQ tests could be used to predict the level of work that an individual could accomplish:

> preliminary investigations indicate that an IQ below 70 rarely permits anything better than unskilled labor: that the range from 70 to 80 is preeminently that of semi-skilled labor, from that of 80 to 100 that of the skilled or ordinary clerical labor, from 100 to 110 or 115 that of the semi-professional pursuits; and that above all these are the grades of intelligence which *permit* one to enter the professions or the larger fields of business. ... This information will be of great value in planning the education of a particular child and also in planning the differentiated curriculum here recommended.
>
> (1923: 27–8)

A similar view was taken by the English psychologist Burt in his 1943 paper 'Ability and income', in which he argued that measured ability could be used to predict subsequent income. Both Terman and Burt and the psychometric tradition they represent have been largely discredited and their work revealed as little more than an apology for the interests of the middle classes in the societies from which they came (Kamin 1977). Yet while their work had the effect of maintaining the position of the already rich and powerful it gained its potency from the wider bureaucratic mechanisms of which it was a part, because it provided a rational basis for social selection into a rigid hierarchical division of labour. Despite the declining scientific credibility of this view of intelligence, its legacy has been to create a deeply embedded cultural myth which will remain as long as bureaucratic education is considered the best means of promoting rationality and efficiency.

When we come to examine the content of so-called 'intelligence' tests we find a further sense in which they can be considered the servant of bureaucratic education. For as Lacey has pointed out, IQ tests represent an attempt to measure skill and talent but:

> Skills and talents are concerned with solving problems 'within' already existing paradigms and systems of knowledge. Intelligence has to do with understanding the relationships 'between' complex systems and making judgements about when it is appropriate to work within existing paradigms and when it is appropriate to create new courses of action or avenues of thought.
>
> (1988: 93–4)

As we shall see, the content and context of bureaucratic education lays down predetermined conditions for what is to count as knowledge, largely through the medium of the textbook. Textbooks, as Kuhn (1970) has pointed out, indoctrinate students into a particular paradigm or theory. Hence the kinds of judgements Lacey considers integral to intelligence are simply not valued or required.

Bureaucratic education is based on a rational linkage between intelligence, subject choice, academic credentials, and suitability for particular occupations. Consistent with the point Terman made above, bureaucratic education has always assumed that the curriculum should be differentiated according to ability because 'intelligent' people will choose or be directed into taking subjects such as physical science, mathematics, and foreign languages which are deemed more difficult and demanding. Less 'intelligent' people will take the less demanding subjects such as home economics, typing, and woodwork. It is further assumed that proficiency in the 'difficult' subjects reflects a more general ability to engage successfully in professional and managerial work so that restricting entry to the prestigious and highly paid jobs to those with high credentials is a rational process. We can depict this model as follows.

Table 1.2 Model of bureaucratic education

High IQ	→	Academic subjects	→	High credentials	→	Professional/ managerial jobs
Low IQ	→	Practical subjects	→	Low credentials	→	Semi-andunskilled jobs/unemployment

There are a number of problems with this model including the fact that even when IQ scores have been taken into account social origins continue to play an important part in determining educational performance and occupational destinations.[12] Other problems include the possibility that tests may harbour a gender or cultural bias and the assumption that 'bright' male students will choose the 'harder' physical science subjects, while equally able female students will feel more comfortable (sic) with the 'softer' social sciences.

Several hypotheses have been developed as to why schools have failed large numbers of working-class students, including many of those with high IQs. The curriculum, school organization, teacher expectations, and methods of selection, have all been advanced as causes of working-class failure. Over the past thirty years considerable research time and effort has been devoted to testing these hypotheses, yet the evidence clearly shows that despite important changes and improvements, there has not been a *substantial* reduction in the wastage of working-class talent.[13] This is because problems of inequality and wastage cannot be blamed on, or resolved within, the confines of the educational system. Some Western researchers in the sociology of education have found it useful to incorporate theories of capitalist development and class culture to explain why students from working-class backgrounds remain 'disadvantaged' with respect to social destinations relative to their counterparts from professional and managerial backgrounds.[14] They have concluded that schools cannot compensate for the inequalities created by the nature and rewards of work in capitalist societies. More recently the problem of sexual and racial inequalities in education has also received sustained analysis. Much of this work has arrived at a similar conclusion, that although there is decisive room for improving the educational performance of female and ethnic minority students, the success of reforms in schools must be part of a broader campaign to combat sexism and racism which exists within the wider social structure (Arnot and Weiner 1987; Cole 1989).

The strong implication to be drawn from this research is that the social division of labour has a decisive influence on IQ and educational attainment, which is why we concur with Sabel's (1982) view that it is often social hierarchy and the world views associated with it that restrict the unfolding of human capacity, and not the limitations of natural endowment. For instance, the more autonomy workers have in their job and the more cognitively complex it is, the more they are likely to pass on the norms and values necessary for a successful educational career to their children. This is a point to which we shall return when we come to discuss the nature of collective intelligence.

Academic qualifications and the division of labour

If IQ tests came to determine the way individuals were to be 'processed' as inputs into the education system, credentials have come to symbolize the quality of the output. Moreover, academic credentials are the counterpart to the IQ score in the labour market. Credentials also provide a simple summary score of an extraordinarily complex set of cognitive and social processes. Like the IQ score, the gaining of a credential is often based on the outcome of one performance in an examination, hence it is relatively quick to administer and straightforward for employers to understand. However, the credential as a bureaucratic device has only gained currency due to its adoption by profession groups as a means of screening and controlling the supply of new recruits (Collins 1979).

Over the past century human capital (the ability to develop skills for economic return), has increased in importance within industrial societies. Perkin (1989) has noted that it has become as important to contemporary society as land was to pre-industrial society, and industrial capital to early industrial society. It has been estimated that whereas in 1867 the returns to skilled labour accounted for between 5 and 25 per cent of national income, a century later they amounted to between 46 and 58 per cent of pre-tax household income (Perkin 1989: 428). The widespread development of professions has occurred largely as a result of this shift in the importance of 'skilled' labour.

Of course, the notion of a profession and a professional

person is difficult to define, especially at a time when more or less everyone from a footballer to a brain surgeon can be described as a professional. Perhaps the best way of defining professional work is to follow Collins who argues that:

> not all occupations can become professions in the strong sense of the term. What we have instead is a continuum. . . . A strong profession requires a real technical skill that produces demonstrable results and can be taught. Only thus can the skill be monopolised by controlling who will be trained. The skill must be difficult enough to require training and reliable enough to produce results. But it cannot be too reliable, for then outsiders can judge work by its results and control its practitioners by their judgements. The ideal profession has a skill that occupies the mid-point of a continuum between complete predictability and complete unpredictability of results.
>
> (1979: 132–3)

This account is helpful in linking the notion of professions to credentials in that it points to the need for a standardized measure by which entrants to a profession can be judged: after all, professionals, as Collins suggests, need to be reliable enough in their performance to consistently produce adequate results, hence it is necessary to ensure that new entrants have the potential to perform reliably. By the same token, since professional work can rarely be judged by outsiders, the legitimation of a profession rests on the level of credentials demanded at the point of entry. The entry requirements specified by different professional groups are therefore used as a way of controlling the supply of entrants.

Collins's notion of a continuum also suggests how credentials have been coupled with a particular hierarchical ordering of occupations. An example is skilled craft jobs where the credentials needed to enter them are often judged to be lower in the status hierarchy than those credentials required for jobs conducted by professional workers, whose competency cannot be so easily or widely judged. The essence of the ordering of credentials lies in their comparability. The reason why doctors can command the wealth and status they do is in part because the entry credentials to the profession can be *ranked* as superior to those needed for a craft apprenticeship.

However, the link between credentials and productivity is problematic in at least four ways. First, it is not at all clear how a formal academic education serves as a preparation for economic productivity. This is especially so for more qualified workers. As Berg (1970) has noted, there is no necessary connection between engaging in a complex cognitive job such as that done by air traffic controllers and their level of formal education. Possibly even more damaging is Berg's finding, which he and others have subsequently confirmed, that there is considerable under-utilization of education in the workplace.[15] This under-utilization of education in the workplace is often the result of introducing technology which is designed to maximize managerial control rather than job satisfaction (Braverman 1974).

Second, as Murphy (1988) notes, the predominant effect of credentials has been that of exclusion, domination, and inequality. The idea that employers use credentials as a convenient device for regulating the supply of labour should not obscure the fact that, for those in skilled trades and professions, credentials have been used as a weapon of exclusion. Murphy sees contemporary professions as having developed the guild principle:

> (a) by employing formal educational credentials dispensed by the state-school system as state sanctioned exclusionary barriers, and (b) by employing the state legal system to mitigate regulation and evaluation of the work of members. ... Corporatist credentialled groups, and in particular the professions, are distinct from guilds only in that they have gone further in formalizing and rationalizing through the state their means of monopolization.
>
> (1988: 187)

One method of doing this is outlined by Collins above – to ensure a reasonable and predictable standard of competence in performance without those outside the profession being able to make an expert judgement of that performance.

Third, in matching individuals to specific kinds of jobs credentials have become a form of currency used by employers to regulate the demand for the jobs they have available. As the supply of educated labour has increased, so employers have increased the level of credentials they demand for any specific job. Collins (1979) argues that although a significant proportion of jobs in the USA have been upgraded in terms of their entry requirements, this is often the result of credential inflation rather than significant changes in the demand for technical knowledge.

The high rates of youth unemployment in most industrial nations over the last decade have also served to fuel the diploma disease (Dore 1976) and to intensify concerns about the relationship between education, certification, and employment. Grubb (1985) has noted that there has been a world-wide trend for nation states to view the cause of youth unemployment as the absence of an appropriate education and training. Although this has led to calls for students to study for more vocationally relevant qualifications, the main cause of unemployment over the last decade has been a collapse in the demand for young workers (Coombs 1985; Ashton *et al.* 1990).

Fourth, as a consequence of credentials becoming an increasingly important commodity which can be exchanged in the labour market, the 'certificate' has been seen by a large number of students and their parents to be more important than what is taught or learnt. Dore (1976) has pointed out that this is self-defeating because when everyone is playing the same game it leads to a decline in the exchange value of qualifications. But whereas, in the past, a willingness to engage in the competition for qualifications exhibited the virtue of being willing to 'stay the course' for extrinsic rewards (which was an asset in the preparation for a bureaucratic career), the growing demand for employees capable of being creative and innovative has intensified the contradictions inherent in the certification process. Moreover, Fallows argues that we need to distinguish between an entrepreneurial society and a professionalized society, which he considers we now have in the USA:

> an entrepreneurial society is like a game of draw poker you take a lot of chances, because you're rarely dealt a pat hand and you never know exactly what you have to beat. A professionalised society is more like blackjack and getting a degree is like being dealt a nineteen. You could try for more but why?
>
> (1985: 64)

In our view the crucial point Fallows is making here is not so much a plea for an entrepreneurial society, whatever that may mean, but rather that bureaucratic education tied to the development of the professions has served as a way of reducing the risk of children from professional backgrounds experiencing downward social mobility. Paradoxically, the shift to free market systems of education will not increase the entrepreneurial energies of middle-class students, but increase the potential use of the education system as an instrument for reducing such risks because middle-class parents are being encouraged to 'buy out' their children from having to compete with those from less affluent backgrounds. In this sense, a high level credential carries with it the whiff of a contemporary sinecure.

So far we have argued that systems of bureaucratic education produce a standard 'product' that can be ranked and which is symbolized by the credential. In both the case of the IQ test score and the credential, judgements are made about individuals which are apparently impersonal – the bureaucratic hallmark of the treatment of individuals. By what processes are IQ test scores converted into credentials? It is time to look at the structure and some of the consequences of schooling.

The structure and consequences of schooling

Weber argued that the administrative power of bureaucracy has at least two sources. The first concerns knowledge:

> The primary source of bureaucratic administration lies in the role of technical knowledge. ... This is the feature of it which makes it specifically rational. ... Bureaucracy is superior in knowledge, including both technical knowledge and knowledge of the concrete fact within its own sphere of interest.
>
> (quoted in Henderson and Parsons 1947: 337–9)

The second source of power is derived from discipline:

> The content of discipline ... is nothing but the consistently rationalised, methodically trained and exact execution of the received order, in which all personal criticism is unconditionally suspended and the actor is unswervingly and exclusively set for carrying out the command.
>
> (quoted in Gerth and Mills 1948: 254)

When we look at the conduct of education for most of the twentieth century we see that these two bureaucratic principles have informed its conduct. Levin captures the essence of these aspects of bureaucratic education in the following terms:

> Teachers supervise a work process that is relatively uniform and usually organised according to grade levels. The work process for teacher and student has been set out well in advance of the implementation of the schooling activity and without the involvement of the major participants. The design and planning of the curriculum, pedagogy, sequence of courses, selection of textbooks and methods of evaluation are usually set out by a political and administrative process with the help of specialists. . . . Each course is generally divided into units and subunits which are followed sequentially and often learned by rote to enable success on standardized tests of the units. Students have little control over the use of their time and little input into the learning process.
>
> (1987: 148)

Knowledge is therefore inculcated according to the epistemologically arbitrary division of subjects and the delivery of these subjects has been regulated by the division of time into discrete periods. In this way knowledge and discipline are fused into an indivisible set of bureaucratic rules, rituals, and procedures governed by that masterplan – the timetable. In this context the textbook provides the means for standardizing knowledge and its content is largely determined by the demands of the system of assessment and professional training.[16]

At the heart of these processes is the educational exchange in which student compliance is traded for knowledge which in turn can be converted into credentials to be traded in the market for jobs. It is when the selection processes of the educational system are considered that the extraordinary power of bureaucratic procedures described by Weber can be fully appreciated. It is no easy task to obtain student compliance when the system is designed to confer success on a minority. However, despite the resistance shown to result from these processes, especially by those defined as school failures, the reproduction of educational inequalities has rarely been seriously threatened. The power of bureaucratic education is neatly captured by Meyer who says it

> has a network of rules creating public classifications of persons and knowledge. It defines which individuals belong to these categories and possess the appropriate knowledge. And it defines which persons have access to valued positions in society. Education is a central element in the public biography of individuals, greatly affecting their life chances. It is also a central element in the table of organisation of society, constructing competencies and helping create professions and professionals. Such an institution clearly has an impact on society over and above the immediate socialising experiences it offers the young.
>
> (1978: 55)

How does education maintain this power? It socializes students into compliance through a series of myths, routines, and inducements. The myths of intelligence and ideologies of professional competence create an appropriate climate of awe and mystification. The book that has most clearly captured the subjective impact of these myths and the way they legitimize the inequalities created by bureaucratic education in the USA is *The Hidden Injuries of Class*. In this book Sennett and Cobb (1977) argue that the key notion legitimizing inequalities in Western societies is the idea of individual ability. They suggest that because qualifications are commonly seen to reflect individual ability, they represent a badge of individual worth which, in turn, creates an image of an elitist society in which a few individuals stand out from the masses. Moreover, due to the fact that successful academic performance is the passport to upward social mobility, it provides a personal sense of dignity and self-worth which is reinforced by teachers in an attempt to maintain pupil compliance.

The political and moral effect of this ideology is that it perpetuates the inequalities of the world of nineteenth-century capitalism on new terrain:

> just as the material penalties of the old capitalism fell hardest on the workers, despite the fact that both rich and poor might be alienated by the work, so now the moral burdens and the emotional hardships of class are the thorniest and most concentrated among manual labourers.
>
> (Sennett and Cobb 1977: 76)

They illustrate this claim through a series of interviews with working-class men. The complex way in which the interviewees respond to their exclusion from the club of 'badge'-holders provides an insight into the way compliance is gained, and inequalities are legitimated. They comment on Frank Rissarro's (one of their interviewees) attitudes to the educated in the following terms:

> Educated men can control themselves and stand out from the mass of people ruled by passions at the bottom of society; the badge of ability earns the educated dignity in Rissarro's eyes. Yet the content of their power – their ability considered in essence rather than in relation to his personal background and memories – this he finds a sham, and repugnant. Still, the power of the educated to judge him, and more generally, to rule, this he does not dispute. He accepts as legitimate what he believes is undignified in itself, and in accepting the power of educated people *he* feels more inadequate, vulnerable and undignified.
>
> (Sennett and Cobb 1977: 78)

The consequences of such 'injuries' for a high-trust and high-ability society are likely to be serious because bureaucratic education generates a large population of 'failures' who are profoundly wounded by the system. At the same time it sells those who are successful short because they rarely have the opportunity to gain the transferable social and conceptual skills which are increasingly required by employers.[17] Equally, in a high-ability society the system of bureaucratic education which we have outlined above is no longer appropriate precisely *because* it is a drain on human resources which, for social and economic reasons, can no longer be squandered. But before we can address the question of educational reform in the 'third wave' we need to examine the current popularity of seeking to expose formal systems of education and training to the discipline of the 'free market'.

EDUCATION AND THE FREE MARKET: THE RIGHT APPROACH?

In countries including Britain, the USA, Australia, and New Zealand there is evidence of a significant shift in educational policy towards 'free market' solutions, given an implicit recognition that bureaucratic education is inappropriate for the social and economic context of the 1990s. Consequently, the 'new right' (Gamble 1988) have initiated fundamental changes under the rubric of promoting greater freedom and choice for parents and making the educational system at all levels more responsive to market forces as a means of improving educational standards and maximizing the economic returns accruing from educational investments.

Briefly stated, the right have argued that the ideology of meritocracy and its manifestation in the move towards comprehensive state systems of education have not only generated a schooling which is inappropriate to the 'needs' of most students but has generated a state-sponsored professional regime which has been designed to further the interests of the providers (teachers) rather than those of the consumers. One consequence of this, so it is argued, has been the inculcation of anti-industrial attitudes and a disregard for the realities of economic life. Such arguments have been eagerly supported by the popular press as accounts of why educational standards have declined and why Britain and the USA are faltering in the global economic competition. Despite the intellectual poverty and paucity of empirical support for these ideas they are real in their consequences.

The essence of the new right response to the educational crisis can be characterized in terms of the *ideology of parentocracy* where the education a child receives must conform to the wealth and wishes of parents rather than the abilities and efforts of pupils (Brown 1990: 65).[18] Therefore the ideology of parentocracy is based on a quite different set of assumptions to that which has driven bureaucratic schooling during the second wave. Bureaucratic schooling was developed partly as a means of ensuring that through their abilities and efforts students were given the opportunity to achieve in a meritocracy, irrespective of their social circumstances. However, in the market-led reforms of the new right, parental choice rather than the ability and motivation of pupils is placed at a premium in the way school systems are organized. Yet despite the popularity of new right thinking on education and other elements of the welfare state, there are a number of reasons for believing that the current direction of educational reform will do little to meet the future conditions for sustainable economic growth or for achieving social justice.

Despite the rhetoric of 'freedom' and 'choice', free market solutions to educational and training problems are low-trust and low-skill solutions (see also Finegold and Sockice 1988). When the proponents of the free market talk about educational freedom and choice they are talking about consumer freedom, and in relation to educational decision-making it is not the individual child but his or her parents who will do the deciding. In a high-trust system children and their parents cannot be lumped together and assumed to be of one mind. Parents have a tendency to bring up their children in their own image, which, socially and educationally, may prove to be disastrous for the child. Educational selection in the recent past has, despite its faults, been organized by a third party, a teacher, who is asked to use her or his objective professional judgement about a given child. A high-trust system of education recognizes that, because children do not have the knowledge to decide their futures at an early age, the educational system must be organized in such a way that all children are given a good broad-based education at least until the age of 18, when they are more able to make their own 'educational' decisions. A high-trust system must also be premised on the belief that the vast majority of children are capable of benefiting from advanced studies given sufficient motivation to undertake them. Therefore, no attempt is made to select a minority of pupils at an early age and groom them for academic success while the majority are contained and controlled in second-rate institutions.

Another reason why systems of free market education will fail to create a high-ability society is because in such a system one may have formal equality before the law but not substantive equality. The problem with this approach can be illustrated in terms of a game of 'Monopoly'. In this game everyone begins with the same amount of money and chance to win, depending on a combination of choice, skill, and luck. Life chances in capitalist societies do not begin with this kind of substantive equality, but begin close to the end of the game with a few players owning hotels on expensive streets such as 5th Avenue in New York or Mayfair in London. The rest of the players may have a few houses but they cannot hope to compete because the logic of this 'free market' game does not lead to an equalization of resources, but a winner who ends up with a monopoly! Of course 'Monopoly' is not like real life in another sense, because when the game is over you can start again on equal terms. In real life those who own property and the accruing advantages are able to pass these advantages on to future family members. Therefore when education is treated as a commodity the economic power of parents, or lack of it, becomes an increasingly important determinant of educational and life chances.

In educational terms schools, credentials, and the status attached to them are likely to become more sharply differentiated, creating elite schools for the rich and a gradation of less prestigious and less 'successful' schools beneath them. A major consequence of these developments is that the economic problem of wastage of talent will become even more acute than it is now. In our view the free market solution in education will simply serve to create the personalities and skills for a low-skill, low-trust society.

The educational realities of a free market equally reveal that rather than generating more entrepreneurial attitudes on the part of students, which is often stated as an aim, what we find is an entrepreneurial response from middle-class parents who perceive educational credentials as a way of reducing the social risks of downward social mobility for their children. In the free market, education will be increasingly a means to translating material capital into cultural capital, and will not increase the level of entrepreneurial activity on the part of those with the financial resources and know-how to engage in such activity.[19] Parents who can afford to will invest increasing amounts of their money on private education as a way of reducing the risk of their children failing in an open system of competitive achievement.

THE THIRD WAVE: EDUCATION IN THE AGE OF THE SMART MACHINE[20]

In this section we examine how to generate 'high-ability' systems of education. Such systems are necessary in order to provide the intellectual, technical, and creative resources which will be required to achieve sustainable economic growth and for individuals to participate actively in a more complex, information-rich world, which is rapidly transforming existing patterns of social and economic life.

In an earlier section we argued that formal educational systems in industrial societies (both capitalist and socialist) are distinguished by their organization on bureaucratic principles. There are of course significant variations in the way industrial societies have organized systems of education in the second wave, and the popularity of free market solutions to educational problems in the late twentieth century testifies to the absence of any economic imperative or 'hidden hand' forcing educational institutions to be restructured in a way which best serves an efficient high-tech economy (Ainley and Corney 1990).

A viable 'third wave' in the socio-historical development of education cannot be premised on the 'free market' because it represents an inadequate response to the historical challenge confronting industrial societies. This assertion invites the challenge of attempting to describe the principal features of educational organization in its third wave of development. Fortunately, some of what will be outlined in this section is inspired by elements of existing progressive educational and organizational practice.

Table 1.3 offers a summary of the major changes we are advocating in the third wave. Taken together the application of these principal features of educational organization would mean the end of bureaucratic education as we have defined it. We make no claim to know all the questions, let alone all the answers to the issues raised here, but we do seek to generate interest in new areas of enquiry. Some of the latter will be briefly outlined in the following discussion.

COLLECTIVE INTELLIGENCE

We have shown that the foundations of systems of education and training in most industrial societies have been based on the underlying assumptions of fordism, and that the idea that there is a limited 'pool of talent' in a sea of mediocrity is part of the myth of bureaucratic notions of intelligence which ignore the important ways in which intelligence is collectively

Table 1.3 Characteristics of second and third wave education

Educational Change	
Second Wave	*Third Wave*
Early differentiation/selection/ specialization	Late differentiation/selection/ specialization
Teacher 'economy of respect' based on academic attainment/ cultural uniformity	Teacher 'economy of respect' based on rounded individual/ cultural diversity
Low-trust relations between teacher/pupil and teacher/ parents	High-trust relations between teacher/pupil and teacher/parents
Low-ability system: tap the pool of ability	High-ability system: harness the wealth of talent
Emphasis on individual intelligence/achievement	Emphasis on both individual and collective intelligence/ achievement
End of year or course examinations	More emphasis on continuous assessment/Records of achievement
Emphasis on educational standards of a minority	Emphasis on educational standards of all
Rigid subject divisions	Integrated core studies
Education and training complete during 'teens'	Life-long education and training
Distinction between academic and vocational studies	Academic/vocational distinction no longer appropriate
Selective/comprehensive school organization	Comprehensive school/college organization
State funded/private schools	All schools state funded/no private schools
Human Ability and Motivation[21]	
Second Wave	*Third Wave*
The average human being has a dislike of work and will avoid it if possible	The expenditure of physical and mental effort in work is as natural as play or rest
People must be coerced, controlled, directed, threatened with punishment to fulfil organizational goals	People will exercise self-direction and self-control to fulfil aims to which they are committed
Most people avoid responsibility, have relatively little ambition, and above all want security	Under the right conditions most people will both accept and seek responsibility
Intelligence is a scarce resource, but can be 'scientifically' identified among children at an early age	Unfolding of human capacity limited by social hierarchy and cultural attitudes
The organization of education and employment corresponds to the normal distribution of talent	The capacity to exercise imagination, ingenuity, creativity, etc., is widely distributed in the population

structured by the form of production (Kohn and Schooler 1983).

Intelligence – the ability to solve problems, to think critically and systematically about the social and natural worlds, and the ability to apply new skills and techniques – is usually seen as an attribute of individuals. However, there is a clear sense in which it is determined by forms of production and the social systems they create. In a period of work that now extends over thirty years Melvin Kohn and his associates[22] have found that many of the psychological dispositions that are key ingredients in the functioning of intelligence are determined by job conditions. In particular they have found that the cognitive complexity and responsibility associated with a job has an impact on individuals' values, conception of reality, and ideational flexibility. The more complex the job, the more likely workers are to be self-directed, to believe that they can act on the world rather than merely have its conditions imposed on them, and be more flexible in their ideas.

There are two aspects to Kohn's research programme which are particularly significant: through longitudinal study he has been able to establish that while there is a reciprocal causal relationship between job conditions and the psychological dispositions he has studied, the link from job conditions to psychological dispositions is strong. In addition, with respect to the variables 'self-directedness' and 'conception of reality' he has found that there is an inter-generational link – parents' world views and associated attitudes are frequently passed on to their children. At root, what Kohn is describing are psycho-social aspects of the material basis on which different class cultures arise. Where societies have adopted fordist forms of production it is not surprising to find a massive wastage of talent, precisely because the ability to act on the world is given to so few – the elite at the top of bureaucratic organizations who make all the key operational and policy decisions.

Clearly if forms of production can have an impact on intelligence in the ways described by Kohn then we need to dispense with the notion of a 'pool of talent' and all that it has meant for the way education has been structured as a system of 'talent spotting' society's future corporate managers and executives. Indeed, in a modernized post-fordist society, the elimination of the notion of a pool of talent and its corresponding education system is necessary in order for the collective intelligence of society to be used to greatest effect. Advanced economies will require a much larger proportion of employees to contribute to the decision-making process and to be more self-directed, regardless of their position within the organization. In such a context the current notions of intelligence and bureaucratic schooling would simply be inappropriate because it is designed to 'create' failures – people who do not believe they have the capacity to think creatively or have the capacity to influence decisions about the world in which they live. Hence the unfolding of human capacity and creativity has been artificially limited by social hierarchy and a division of labour which has necessitated a large proportion of low-trust and low-discretion work roles.

An emphasis on collective intelligence would mean that education would no longer be geared to selecting the talented few. The implications for education of this change in emphasis would be enormous for the related processes of socialization and selection. It was previously assumed that the economic benefits of gearing schools to the task of selecting a 'talented' minority had few costs. However, Meyer (1978) makes the point that the economic gains of selecting a few to be highly educated may simply occur with an equivalent loss for the under-educated.[23]

The majority of students would no longer be socialized to believe that they do not have the 'brains' to benefit from formal education because far greater emphasis would be placed on empowering students to believe that they can have an impact on the world around them. An education for empowerment must include providing students with the 'power tools' of personal confidence and the intellectual skills required to interpret the wealth of information and ideological dogma to which we are all exposed, in order to make considered judgements in both the public and private spheres of everyday life.

It would follow fairly quickly that schools would need to discard streaming in favour of mixed ability teaching. In general selection for the various routes into industry would be delayed as long as possible in order to provide the greatest opportunity for students' intelligence and creativity to flourish. A corollary of the principle of delayed selection is that as far as possible there should be open access to all forms of tertiary education and training. This will become increasingly important given that formal learning is a life-long process involving periods of re-training for employment purposes and given a growing demand for self-development.[24]

Underlying these principles is the aim of developing a common educational culture. If a general aim of educating for a high-trust society is to foster teamwork and co-operation then, just as the hierarchies and differential cultures distinctive of fordist production would have to be discarded, so would the differential cultures which inhabit contemporary schooling.[25] This can only be achieved by breaking down the class, gender, and racial barriers within systems of education and training. Students soon learn their relative standing with respect to others, and it is only when genuine opportunities for social and personal advancement are available that students, for instance, from a working-class background, will contemplate the social cost of seeking social mobility (Turner 1964). This is because student understandings of being at school are closely connected to class-cultural understandings of becoming a working-class adult. Equally, if we are genuinely concerned to produce the labour force of the future, the educational and training systems must break down sexist (and racist) practices which operate against both girls and boys and foster the development of narrow gender-specific occupational preferences and skills by, among other things, reinforcing the processes through which boys enter metalwork, woodwork, and technical design courses and the girls get channelled into home economics, childcare, and office practice. The reason why these social inequalities require serious attention results from the fact that all educational and training innovations confront the real acid test of how they shape future life chances. Although there is nothing inherently superior about receiving a narrow and intensive 'academic' education, it is favoured because it has the most 'cultural capital' and 'exchange value' in the school and labour market. It is for this reason that virtually all programmes of vocational education have failed to provide a 'parity of esteem' because they deny access to the real vocational prizes (Watts 1983; Kantor and Tyack 1982). There are consequently strong social and educational grounds for developing a broad based curriculum of academic, technical, and practical study for all students at least during the compulsory school years.

Moreover, the creation of a high-ability society will need to continue to structure opportunity on the basis of individual effort and ability, but the 'ideology of meritocracy' will need to be strongly reinforced. It has too often been a tool of 'administrative convenience' for both teachers and employers to explain why some (usually from a middle-class background) make it, and why others (usually from a working-class background) do not. Official assessments of this kind are extremely difficult to argue against as a student or as a parent because even if teachers are unable to produce a low IQ score as a 'cause' of low achievement, they will point to the other half of the meritocratic equation, that poor achievement must be the result of a failure to work hard or as a consequence of poor parental motivation. The *coup de grâce* of this form of ideological justification is reserved for those who prove the system wrong by achieving later as a 'mature' student. These are imaginatively labelled the 'late developers' on the assumption that had they been capable of earlier achievement they would obviously have attained it. However, the growing need for knowledgeable and empowered citizens is heightening concern about a system which incapacitates and alienates large numbers of young people. There is strong evidence to suggest that the education system must be organized on the premise that all rather than a few are capable of significant practical and academic achievements, of creative thought and skill, and of taking responsibility for making informed judgements. The role of education and training in this context must become one of nurturing this wealth of talent. We will need to re-direct our attention away from the attributes of individual students as the cause of low-ability systems of education, to the institutional context in which the learning process takes place. Instead of pointing to the fact that their 'failing' students are usually working class or black, teachers and trainers would be forced to examine the institutional context and their professional practices for explanations of trained incapacity. This strategy would certainly help to overcome the existing 'brain drain' and lead to a more integrated system of education and training involving teachers, parents, trade unionists, employers, etc.

This would also be a far more sensible way of tightening the bond between education and employment than trying to tailor the school curriculum to the often out-dated and ill-defined 'needs' which employers habitually report themselves requiring. The importance of a new division of learning in the workplace as well as in formal educational and training institutes is recognized by Zuboff (1988) in her account of technological innovation in the USA (see also Hirschhorn 1984). She distinguishes between technology which *automates* from that which *informates*. Automation simply involves the replacement of the human body with a technology that enables the same processes to be performed with more continuity and control. In other words, it conforms to the principles of fordism. Rather than decrease the dependence on human skills, technology which has the capacity to informate can enlarge job tasks and the room for individual discretion given that activities, events, and objects are translated into and made visible by information:

> Under these circumstances, work organization requires a new division of learning to support a new division of labor. The traditional system of imperative control, which was designed to maximize the relationship between commands and obedience, depended upon restricted hierarchical access to knowledge and nurtured the belief that those who were excluded from the organization's explicit knowledge base were intrinsically less capable of learning what it had to offer. In contrast, an informated organization is structured to promote the possibility of useful learning among all members and thus presupposes relations of equality. However, this does not mean that all members are assumed to be identical in their orientations, proclivities, and capacities; rather, the organization legitimates each member's right to learn as much as his or her temperament and talent will allow. In the traditional organization, the division of learning lent credibility to the legitimacy of imperative control. In an informated organization, the new division of learning produces experiences that encourage a synthesis of members' interests, and the flow of value-adding knowledge helps legitimate the organization as a learning community.
>
> (Zuboff 1988: 394)

In terms of education and training this raises important issues about the way employers and managers make decisions about how they deploy new technology in the workplace, and the need to break down low-trust and low-discretion relations which often existed in the past and which many employers and managers seek to preserve.

This final point should serve as a reminder that those who argue for the progressive reform of education *solely* in terms of its beneficial consequences for economic productivity do so at their peril because, despite the fact that in the future the possible shift to post-fordism may offer a powerful justification for progressive educational reform, the demand that such changes be introduced on the principles of democratic rights will become more important, due to the fact that high rates of unemployment and under-employment are likely to remain a feature of advanced societies. Moreover, given the trend towards shorter working hours and working lives, the education system must seek to provide the intellectual and practical 'power tools' needed to empower people to participate in *all* spheres of social life.

Therefore an important aim of education in the third wave is to provide students with the ability and creativity to make critical judgements and to develop alternative modes of thought. Clearly, given the current pace of technological change there is little point in teaching students specific skills which are non-transferable and may rapidly become obsolete. As Kanter has noted, single-skilled people are unable to function in the kinds of cross-disciplinary teams that produce innovation, and are less adaptable when circumstances change (Kanter 1984: 368).

IN SEARCH OF EXCELLENCE

We also argued in an earlier section that the notion of standards has come to be defined in terms of standardization: the selection and packaging of knowledge into discrete subject areas, the labelling of students with an IQ score, and badges of ability gained by amassing qualifications. The mass production of standardized products, given a stable market for bureaucratic competence, may still appeal to conservatives as a symbol of educational excellence, but it can command little educational or economic justification in the late twentieth century.

The overriding organization of the curriculum into subject specializations militates against fostering the kind of intelligent judgements that are required in everyday life. Judgements made in the 'real' world are typically of an inter-disciplinary nature. As electronic communications increasingly integrate the global political economy, the demands mad on decision-makers at all levels will become more challenging. Moreover such judgements cannot be divorced from fundamental human problems, such as the destruction of non-renewable ecological resources. Yet it is a damning corollary of subject specialization that, for the most part, schools do not educate students to understand, let alone help solve, such fundamental human problems. In this respect collective intelligence means more than simply increasing the pool of knowledgeable and technically competent people. It also needs to be understood as a measure of our ability to face up to the problems that confront us collectively and to develop collective solutions (Lacey 1988: 94). Therefore an education which does not examine the issues of the day, or help students to make connections between different aspects of their studies, renders students less 'intelligent' than they need be. A nation state which, for example, denies its youth the opportunity to examine issues concerning the causes and consequences of environmental pollution, the nature of the HIV and AIDS virus, or offer political education, is symptomatic of a low-trust and low-ability society.

Clearly, then, greater emphasis needs to be placed on inter-disciplinary problem solving. In doing so, the class and gender tagged nature of school subjects will need to be eradicated (Hughes and Lauder 1990), thereby helping to create a common educational culture. In the process of developing problem-solving skills which encourage students to make judgements about when it is appropriate to work within existing paradigms and when it is appropriate to create new courses of action or avenues of thought, the emphasis on textbooks will have to give way to group project work – which, to encourage initiative, will have to be negotiated rather than imposed.

In this context the notion of standards and educational excellence would have to be redefined. Of course the textbook and subject specialization would still have a place, but alongside them the ability to work in an inter-disciplinary way, the initiative to engage in independent research, to organize and execute projects, and the ability to work co-operatively would all become part of what an excellent education would mean for *all levels of the education system.*

Such an education would not only break the chain of bureaucratic demands by giving students and teachers far greater freedom to pursue knowledge but it would necessitate quite different responses from students and teachers. Having been through a bureaucratic education system ourselves we tend to forget just how constraining it is in training its participants to behave in ways which would be inimical to the exercise of the kind of initiative necessary in an 'advanced' democratic society.

Moreover, as the bureaucratic hold over the curriculum and educational selection is loosened, it makes less sense to maintain a narrow range of skill-based tests at various stages of schooling. The curriculum outlined above would actually demand the development of far wider competencies than could be captured in narrow skill-based tests. There are, of course, alternatives now being developed centring on the ideas of continuous assessment, records of achievement, and student participation in the process of assessment.[26]

In our view, excellence in education is also best achieved through a state provided comprehensive system. The fact is that in the third wave education differentiated according to privilege and status would militate against the promotion of collective intelligence. Moreover, the evidence suggests that the better the social mix of schools the better the performance of the majority of students. There is a small cost to the performance of the most able – judged by conventional 'intelligence' tests – but not so much as to impede their academic progress.[27] In other words, far from a proliferation of school types in competition, what is required is a well-maintained comprehensive state system. Parents would have some choice of school, but the general thrust of policy would be to generate high-trust relations between teachers and parents, given that schools would become a truly community resource, used daily by people of all ages.

Our final point is that it will be necessary to challenge the increasingly instrumental attitudes of students and their parents to formal education because it is turning the 'diploma disease' into an epidemic. Moreover, while complying to school rules for long periods of time in order to get through examinations clearly contributed to the trained capacities of middle managers in bureaucratic organizations, the growing demand for creative and innovative people runs counter to the dictates of an increasingly competitive pursuit of credentials, because the overriding concern with grades tends to inhibit rather than develop the power tools required in high-trust and innovative organizations (Kanter 1984). This problem has serious consequences for the future and makes a nonsense of claims that educational excellence can be measured in terms of numbers of credentials. What employers thought they wanted in the past, and which was measurable by certificates, may be precisely what they do not want in the future. The only way of reducing the severity of this problem is by adopting a broader view of educational excellence; and employers should reflect this broader understanding in their recruitment practices.

CONCLUSION

In this chapter we have argued that the transformation of social and economic life has profound implications for systems of education and training. A failure to register the importance of these changes, and to act upon them, will have serious consequences because of an increasing need for industrial societies to organize social relations in employment, education, and training on the base of high trust and high ability. We have described these changes in terms of a shift from fordism to post-fordism, while recognizing the absence of a more precise vocabulary and the fact that many of the changes we describe remain in their nascent form.

It was suggested that so long as industrial production is distinguished by the routinized tasks symbolized by the assembly line, where the majority need only to conform to the demands of the task in hand and a minority conceive and develop policy, a rigid division of labour based on bureaucratic procedures proves a reliable technology for the administration of production. The aim of education in this context is to 'process' the raw material of human abilities into workers who are then fed into the appropriate level of the productive hierarchy.

Consequently, despite the shift to a fairer system of educational selection during the twentieth century and major gains in economic efficiency (achieved in the context of mass production of standardized products), the way in which systems of education and training have been organized in industrial societies – on the principles of machine bureaucracy – has resulted in a massive 'brain drain'.[28] Usually the latter term refers to images of well educated and trained people waiting at airports destined for other countries which they believe will offer them a better quality of life. This image represents the tip of the iceberg. The real brain drain is far less exotic and far more serious. It is taking place in virtually every school and college in the everyday production and reproduction of school 'failure'. Indeed, we also argued that even those who end up as winners in the battle for qualifications have frequently sacrificed much of their creative talent in order to amass an ever increasing number of intrinsically meaningless pieces of paper. Therefore, in one way or another, the educational system is incapacitating the vast majority of students. We also argued that whereas class, gender, and racial inequalities did not lead to severe economic penalties in the past this seems to be less so now. The following quotation from Tawney is particularly apt in the present context:

> Capricious educational inequalities which make it impossible for the nation to develop the full power of all its children, are not merely, as they always were, offensive to humanity and good sense; they are an economic burden which we cannot afford to carry.
>
> (quoted in Carter 1966: 11)

In the final section of this chapter we attempted to outline the guiding principles which would need to be followed in order to transform the trained incapacities of young people today into the trained capacities required for tomorrow. In Britain and the USA we are aware that the opportunity to generate a 'new deal' for young people which would combine the bid to generate a high-trust and high-ability society, with a programme of democratic and social reforms, has so far been squandered. The right-wing administrations of Thatcher/Major and of Reagan/Bush seem more interested in preserving the vested interests of the powerful and privileged. Indeed the 'free market' has contributed to the failure of both countries to maintain their relative positions in the world industrial super league, while there has been a significant increase in poverty, inequality, crime, and drug addiction. It is ridiculous to assume that, in isolation, the education system can solve socio-economic problems. It has never been able to compensate for the problems of the wider society of which it is a part. But it is equally true to say that wider institutional change will also be limited unless the formal systems of education and training are geared to meet the challenges which industrial societies are now confronting.

ACKNOWLEDGEMENT

We would like to thank Pat Ainley, Fliss Carlton, and Krishan Kumar for their comments on an earlier draft of this chapter. All errors and confusions are the exclusive property of the authors, whose names are listed alphabetically to reflect an equal amount of responsibility for what is presented.

NOTES

1 These issues will be discussed in detail by Krishan Kumar in Chapter 2.

2 The evidence to date reveals marked differences between nation states (Lane 1989), but there are genuine reasons to fear that some capitalist societies are becoming increasingly polarized into what Therborn (1989) has called the 'two-thirds, one-third society', where one-third of the population are becoming marginalized from the rest of society. There is also empirical evidence in countries such as Britain and the USA to show that some employers are organizing their labour force in ways which permit maximum numerical flexibility, but little evidence of flexible specialization (Lane 1989). The former involves the establishment of a small elite 'core' of expert (usually male) workers who are indispensable, and a 'peripheral' workforce of contract or part-time labour which consists of women, young people, and ethnic minorities, organized to respond to fluctuations in the supply and demand for labour (see Brown and Scase 1991).

3 This immediately raises problems about what is understood by Weber's concept of bureaucracy as Gouldner makes clear in his case history of the bureaucratization of a gypsum factory in the USA (1954).

4 In many respects this terminology is inadequate because it is questionable whether fordist principles ever gained domination over the organization of production. See Kumar in Chapter 2. Table 1.1 draws upon a number of sources including: Lash and Urry (1987), Harvey (1989), Lane (1989), and Phillimore (1989).

5 The question of privatization in education and training colleges is addressed by Clyde Chitty in this volume.

6 As Whyte (1960) noted in his classic study of organizations, even within higher education there was little enthusiasm for views which questioned the system, given that the overriding concern was to learn how to become 'the technicians of the society, not innovators'

(p. 66). This quotation is from an economics professor who clearly viewed the lack of concern among his students to change the system with approval.

7 In arguing this case we are aware of the tradition initiated by 'human capital' and 'political arithmetic' theorists who linked the argument for eliminating the wastage of talent to the question of economic efficiency in order to advocate a comprehensive system of education.

With hindsight we can see that their arguments, although effective in the short term, were limited in ways which have now assumed importance. For example, they had no analysis of the form of production for which the pool of untapped talent was to be used. They also underestimate the importance of the relationship between equality and democracy (Lauder 1988), and underplay the importance of class, gender, and ethnic divisions.

8 The concept of 'trained incapacity' is outlined in Merton's (1949) classic account of bureaucratic structure and personality.

9 For a more detailed account of the three waves of socio-historical development of state education in England see Brown (1990).

10 This claim has been contested because Weber tended to downplay the dysfunctions of bureaucratic organizations (Merton 1949).

11 See Fallows (1985) for a discussion of Binet and his reception in the USA.

12 This wastage is documented in Bowles and Gintis (1976), Jencks *et al.* (1979), Halsey *et al.* (1980) and Hughes and Lauder (1991).

13 See Halsey (1972) for a discussion of the failure of liberal reforms in education, and Lauder and Hughes (1990) for a discussion of the limits to schools' capacity to promote equality of opportunity.

14 See for example Willis (1977), Griffin (1985), Brown (1987), Walker (1988), Jones (1989).

15 See the discussion of the evidence on this point in Levin (1987).

16 See Lauder, Scott, and Freeman-Moir (1986) for a discussion of the historically arbitrary division of knowledge into subjects and their relationship to capitalism. See Scott (1982) for a discussion of the partitioning of school time into discrete periods and Kuhn (1970) for a perceptive analysis of the role of the textbook in the training of scientists.

17 The impact of corporate reorganization on the demand for highly educated labour is discussed by Richard Scase in Chapter 3 of this volume.

18 It is important to note that the ideology of parentocracy has not emerged as a result of a groundswell of popular demand for radical educational reform among a majority of parents, and does not imply an increase in 'parent power' over the school curriculüm. On the contrary, it has been the state and not parents which has strengthened its control over what is taught in school (see Gamble 1988, Dale 1989, Brown 1990: 66).

19 The question of education for enterprise is addressed in Chapter 5, by Rees and Rees.

20 The idea of a 'third wave' is of course lifted from Toffler's (1981) book *The Third Wave* and *In the Age of the Smart Machine* is the title of an interesting book by Zuboff (1988).
21 The first three dimensions are adapted from McGregor (1960).
22 See Kohn (1977) and Kohn and Schooler (1983).
23 The artificial limitations on 'talent' within the educational system is also noted by Cicourel and Kitsuse (1963: 139–40).
24 These ideas are developed in more detail in a number of subsequent chapters.
25 See Hickox and Moore, Chapter 4 in this volume.
26 See Chapter 7 this volume, by Torrance.
27 See McPherson and Willms (1987), Lauder and Hughes (1990).
28 The improvements in economic efficiency throughout the industrialized world have not been 'achieved' without exacting considerable damage to the environment and seriously threatening the world's natural resources (Brundtland Report 1987; Kumar 1988: 66).

REFERENCES

Ainley, P. and Corney, M. (1990) *Training for the Future: The Rise and Fall of the Manpower Services Commission*, London, Cassell.

Arnot, M. and Weiner, G. (eds) (1987) *Gender and the Politics of Schooling*, London, Hutchinson.

Ashton, D.N., Maguire, M.J., and Spilsbury, M. (1990) *Restructuring the Labour Market: The Implications for Youth*, London, Macmillan.

Bennis, W. (1972) 'The decline of bureaucracy and organisations of the future', in J.M. Shepard (ed.) *Organizational Issues in Industrial Society*, Englewood Cliffs, Prentice-Hall.

Berg, I. (1970) *Education and Jobs: The Great Training Robbery*, New York, Praeger.

Block, F. (1990) *Postindustrial Possibilities: A Critique of Economic Discourse*, Berkeley, University of California Press.

Bowles, S. and Gintis, H. (1976) *Schooling in Capitalist America*, London, Routledge & Kegan Paul.

Braverman, H. (1974) *Labor and Monopoly Capitalism: The Degradation of Work in the Twentieth Century*, New York, Monthly Review Press.

Brown, P. (1987) *Schooling Ordinary Kids*, London, Tavistock.

—— (1990) 'The "third wave": education and the ideology of parentocracy', *British Journal of Sociology of Education* 11, 65–85.

Brown, P. and Scase, R. (eds) (1991) *Poor Work: Disadvantage and the Division of Labour*, Milton Keynes, Open University Press.

Brundtland Report (1987) *Our Common Future*, World Commission on Environment and Development, Oxford, Oxford University Press.

Burt, C. (1943) 'Ability and income', *British Journal of Educational Psychology* 13.

Carter, M. (1966) *Into Work*, Harmondsworth, Penguin.

Cicourel, A.V. and Kitsuse, J.I. (1963) *The Education Decision-makers*, New York, Bobbs-Merrill.

Cole, M. (1989) (ed.) *The Social Context of Schooling*, Lewes, Falmer Press.
Collins, R. (1979) *The Credential Society*, New York, Academic Press.
Coombs, P.H. (1985) *The World Crisis in Education*, Oxford, Oxford University Press.
Dale, R. (1989) *The State and Education Policy*, Milton Keynes, Open University Press.
Dore, R. (1976) *The Diploma Disease*, London, Allen & Unwin.
Fallows, J. (1985) 'The case against credentialism', *The Atlantic Review*, December, 49–67.
Finegold, D. and Sockice, D. (1988) 'The failure of training in Britain: analysis and prescription', *Oxford Review of Economic Policy* 4 (3), 21–53.
Fox, A. (1974) *Beyond Contract: Work, Politics and Trust Relations*, London, Faber & Faber.
Gamble, A. (1988) *The Free Market and the Strong State*, London, Macmillan.
Gerth, H. and Mills, C.W. (1948) *From Max Weber*, London, Routledge & Kegan Paul.
Gouldner, A.W. (1954) *Patterns of Industrial Bureaucracy*, New York, Basic Books.
Gramsci, A. (1971) 'Americanism and fordism', in Q. Hoare and G. Howell-Smith (eds) *Selections from the Prison Notebooks of Antonio Gramsci*, London, Lawrence & Wishart.
Griffin, C. (1985) *Typical Girls? Young Women from School to the Job Market*, London, Routledge & Kegan Paul.
Grubb, W.N. (1985) 'The convergence of educational systems and the role of vocationalism', *Comparative Education Review* 29, 526–48.
Halsey, A.H. (1972) *Educational Priority*, London, HMSO.
Halsey, A.H. and Floud, J. (1961) 'Introduction', in A.H. Halsey, J. Floud, and J. Anderson (eds) *Education, Economy and Society*, New York, Free Press.
Halsey, A.H., Heath, A., and Ridge, J. (1980) *Origins and Destinations*, Oxford, Clarendon Press.
Harris, N. (1987) *The End of the Third World*, Harmondsworth, Penguin.
Harvey, D. (1989) *The Conditions of Postmodernity*, Oxford, Blackwell.
Henderson, A. and Parsons, T. (eds) (1947) *Max Weber: The Theory of Social and Economic Organisation*, New York, Oxford University Press.
Hirschhorn, L. (1984) *Beyond Mechanization*, Cambridge, MIT.
Hughes, D. and Lauder, H. (1990) 'Public examinations and the structuring of inequality', in H. Lauder and C. Wylie (eds) *Towards Successful Schooling*, Lewes, Falmer Press.
—— (1991) 'Human capital theory and the wastage of talent', *New Zealand Journal of Educational Studies* (forthcoming).
Jencks, C. *et al.* (1979) *Who Gets Ahead*, New York, Basic Books.
Jones, A. (1989) 'The cultural production of classroom practice', *British Journal of Sociology of Education* 10, 19–31.
Kamin, L.J. (1977) *The Science and Politics of IQ*, Harmondsworth, Penguin.
Kanter, R. (1984) *The Change Masters*, London, Allen & Unwin.
Kantor, H. and Tyack, D. (eds) (1982) *Youth, Work and Schooling*, Stanford, Stanford University Press.

Kerr, C., Dunlop, J., Harbison, F., and Myers, C. (1973) *Industrialism and Industrial Man*, Harmondsworth, Penguin.

Kohn, M. (1977) *Class and Conformity*, Chicago, University of Chicago Press.

Kohn, M. and Schooler, C. (1983) *Work and Personality: An Inquiry into the Impact of Social Stratification*, New Jersey, Ablex Publishing Co.

Kuhn, T. (1970) *The Structure of Scientific Revolutions*, Chicago, University of Chicago Press.

Kumar, K. (1988) *The Rise of Modern Society*, Oxford, Blackwell.

Lacey, C. (1988) 'The idea of a socialist education', in H. Lauder and P. Brown (eds) *Education: In Search of a Future*, Lewes, Falmer Press.

Lane, C. (1989) *Management and Labour in Europe*, Aldershot, Edward Elgar.

Lash, S. and Urry, J. (1987) *The End of Organized Capitalism*, Cambridge, Polity Press.

Lauder, H. (1988) 'Traditions of socialism and educational policy', in H. Lauder and P. Brown (eds) *Education: In Search of a Future*, Lewes, Falmer Press.

Lauder, H. and Hughes, D. (1990) 'Social inequalities and differences in school outcomes', *New Zealand Journal of Educational Studies* 23, 37–60.

Lauder, H., Scott, A., and Freeman-Moir, J. (1986) 'What is to be done with radical academic practice?', *Capital and Class*, 29 (summer), 83–110.

Lazerson, M. and Grubb, W.N. (1974) *American Education and Vocationalism: A Documentary History 1870–1970*, Columbia, Teachers College Press.

Levin, H. (1987) 'Work and education', in G. Psacharopoulous (ed.) *Economics of Education: Research and Studies*, Oxford, Pergamon.

Marquand, J. (1989) *The Sources of Economic Growth*, Brighton, Harvester/Wheatsheaf.

McGregor, D. (1960) *The Human Side of Enterprise*, New York, McGraw-Hill.

McPherson, A. and Willms, J.D. (1987) 'Equalisation and improvement: some effects of comprehensive reorganisation in Scotland', *Sociology* 21, 509–40.

Merton, R.K. (1949) *Social Theory and Social Structure*, New York, Free Press.

Meyer, J. (1978) 'The effects of education as an institution', *American Journal of Sociology* 83, 55–77.

Morgan, G. (1986) *Images of Organization*, London, Sage.

Murphy, R. (1988) *Social Closure: The Theory of Monopolization and Exclusion*, Oxford, Clarendon Press.

OECD (1989) *Education and the Economy in a Changing Society*, Paris, OECD.

Perkin, H. (1989) *The Rise of Professional Society*, London, Routledge.

Phillimore, A.J. (1989) 'Flexible specialisation, work organisation and skills: approaching the "second industrial divide"', *New Technology, Work and Employment* 4, 79–91.

Piore, M.J. and Sabel, C.F. (1984) *The Second Industrial Divide: Possibilities for Prosperity*, New York, Basic Books.
Sabel, C.F. (1984) *Work and Politics: The Division of Labor in Industry*, Cambridge, Cambridge University Press.
Scase, R. and Goffee, R. (1989) *Reluctant Managers*, London, Unwin Hyman.
Scott, A. (1982) 'School time as ideology: from period bell to factory hooter', *Delta* 31, 33–44.
Sennett, R. and Cobb, J. (1977) *The Hidden Injuries of Class*, Cambridge, Cambridge University Press.
Terman, L. (1923) *Intelligence Tests and School Reorganisation*, New York, World Book Co.
Therborn, G. (1989) 'The two-thirds, one-third society', in S. Hall and M. Jacques (eds) *New Times: The Changing Face of Politics in the 1990s*, London, Lawrence & Wishart.
Toffler, A. (1981) *The Third Wave*, London, Pan Books.
Turner, R.H. (1964) *The Social Context of Ambition*, San Francisco, Chandler.
Walker, J. (1988) *Louts and Legends*, Sydney, Allen & Unwin.
Watts, A.G. (1983) *Education, Unemployment and the Future of Work*, Milton Keynes, Open University Press.
Weiner, G. (1989) 'Feminism, equal opportunities and vocationalism: the changing context', in H. Burchell and V. Millman (eds) *Changing Perspectives on Gender*, Milton Keynes, Open University Press.
Whyte, W.H. (1960) *The Organization Man*, Harmondsworth, Penguin.
Williams, R. (1961) *The Long Revolution*, Harmondsworth, Penguin.
Willis, P. (1977) *Learning to Labour*, Farnborough, Saxon House.
World Bank Development Report (1990) *Poverty*, Oxford, Oxford University Press.
Zuboff, S. (1988) *In The Age of the Smart Machine: The Future of Work and Power*, New York, Basic Books.

2

NEW THEORIES OF INDUSTRIAL SOCIETY

Krishan Kumar

THE REVIVAL OF POST-INDUSTRIAL THEORY

Labels, like rumours, can take on a life of their own. The labels of intellectual discourse are no exception. Once sufficiently established, they can govern reality, at least scholarly reality. They inspire conferences, books, television programmes. They can create a whole climate of critical enquiry which, especially in these days of academic entrepreneurship and the multinational scholarly enterprise, feeds on itself. 'The lonely crowd', 'the affluent society', 'the technological society', 'the hidden persuaders', 'the power elite': these are all well-known examples of labels which in recent decades have generated much activity of this sort.

This is not to say that all this intellectual activity is simply self-indulgent. Genuine hypotheses can often be formed out of it; it gives rise to reflections which can be illuminating even and especially in disagreement. But as elements of self-regarding publicity inevitably surround their utterance we need to guard ourselves against that in assessing their worth.

During the 1960s and early 1970s, several prominent sociologists elaborated a view of contemporary society that they labelled the theory of post-industrial society. The best-known proponent of this was the Harvard sociologist Daniel Bell, especially as expressed in the book which summed up his thinking, *The Coming of Post-industrial Society* (1973). Bell himself, in international conferences and in semi-popular journals such as *The Public Interest*, was an active and able propagator of his views. But the theory of post-industrialism gained even wider currency through some vivid popularizations, notably in such books as Peter Drucker's *The Age of Discontinuity* (1969) and Alvin

Toffler's *Future Shock* (1970). In such works the educated public of the West was asked to prepare itself for the possibly uncomfortable transition to a new society, one as different from industrial society as that had been from agrarian society.

The post-industrial idea has been intensively debated. Its shortcomings, as well as the stimulating questions it raises, have been widely noted (see e.g. Gershuny 1978; Kumar 1978). Partly as a result of that, partly as the result of the changed climate of feeling – not to mention a world-wide recession – in the Western world following the 1973 oil shock, one had the distinct impression that 'post-industrialism' had had its day. The debates of the later 1970s all seemed to be about 'the limits to growth', about containing not exploiting the dynamic potential of industrialism. They were about the revival of distributional conflicts as industrial societies ceased to be able to make pay-offs from increased growth (see e.g. Hirsch 1977). A mood of crisis replaced the optimism of the 1960s. Right-wing parties capitalized on this mood, preaching a return to 'Victorian' values and practices of self-help and *laissez-faire*. They called for the abandonment of central planning and state intervention, the most obvious features of the post-1945 settlement and a key premise of the post-industrial idea.

Whatever the future of industrial societies, then, they still seemed to be preoccupied by the same difficulties and dilemmas that had beset them for the past hundred years. In the history of industrialism it was the post-war era of continuous growth that now looked like the exceptional episode, the happy accident. Its ending had restored some of the classic conflicts and debates of industrialism. The past had reasserted itself. At a time when 'deindustrialization' and economic decline became issues to grapple with, visions of a post-industrial society were bound to appear fanciful, if not irresponsible.

Malcolm Bradbury has called the 1970s 'the decade that never was'. But the 1980s of course came out of the 1970s (just as the 1960s came out of the 1950s). We can now see that during that decade various new forms of post-industrial theory were in the making. They lack on the whole the confident optimism of the 1960s varieties. They do not look forward to the 'super-industrial' society so euphorically anticipated by Alvin Toffler. As the product of left- as much as right-wing thinking, they foresee great stresses and conflicts ahead. But they are as insistent as earlier post-industrial theorists that industrial societies have crossed a divide. Classic industrialism, the kind of society analysed by Marx, Weber, and Durkheim, the kind of society inhabited by most Westerners for the past century and a half, is no more.

The greatest continuity with earlier post-industrial theory is shown in the view of contemporary society as 'the information society'. Daniel Bell is here again the most prominent exponent. His post-industrial idea had already singled out 'theoretical knowledge' as the most important feature – the source of value, the source of growth – of the future society. In his later writing he has come to identify this more firmly with the development of the new information technology and its potential application to every sector of society. The new society is now defined, and named, by its novel methods of acquiring, processing, and distributing information. Bell is as confident now as in his earlier analysis that this amounts to a revolutionary transformation of modern society.

The concept of the information society fits in well with the liberal, progressivist tradition of Western thought. It maintains the Enlightenment faith in rationality and progress. Its current exponents belong generally to the centre of the ideological spectrum. To the extent that knowledge and its growth are equated with greater efficacy and greater freedom, this view, despite its pronouncement of a radical shift in societal arrangements, continues the line of thought inaugurated by Saint-Simon, Comte, and the positivists.

More unexpected is the view of the new society that has emerged from the left side of the ideological spectrum. Marxists had been among the most vigorous denouncers of the original post-industrial idea, as the clearest demonstration of late bourgeois ideology (see e.g. Ross 1974). Now some of them have come up with their own version of post-industrial theory. It has most commonly been expressed under the banner of 'post-fordism'. As mostly marxists of a kind, they still generally hold to some concept of capitalist development as the engine of change. But so struck are they by the differences between the old and the new forms of capitalism that they feel forced to speak of our times as 'new times', or as the era of 'the second industrial divide'. For many of them Marx, as the supreme theorist of capitalism, remains a relevant thinker. But the changes in society in the latter part of the twentieth century are regarded as so momentous, and constitute so sharp a break with earlier capitalist patterns and practices, that it is clear to these writers that severe revisions will be needed to Marxist theory if it is to remain serviceable.

A third strand of post-industrial theory has a less familiar provenance. This is the theory of 'post-modern' society. Post-modernism is the most comprehensive of recent theories. It includes in its generous embrace all forms of change, cultural, political, and economic. None is seen as the privileged 'carrier' of the movement to post-modernity. What others see as the evidence for 'post-fordism' or 'the information society' it smoothly subsumes as components of its own ambitious conceptualization of current developments. As eclectic – and elusive – in its ideological make-up as the eclecticism it sees as the principal feature of the contemporary world, post-modernism is the most difficult of contemporary theories to assess. Its terms can lead one into a bewildering circle of self-referentiality.

Post-modernism is a beguiling topic which I shall deal with elsewhere (for a good account, see Harvey 1989). Here there is room only to examine the first two theories. They are in any case the ones most relevant to the themes of this volume.

THE INFORMATION SOCIETY

The earlier statement of the post-industrial idea received extensive publicity through its popularization in the press and broadcasting media, as well as in books by professional journalists. So too its later evolution into the concept of the information society has been accompanied by journalistic bestsellers such as Alvin Toffler's *The Third Wave* (1981) and John Naisbitt's *Megatrends* (1984). Works such as these make helpfully explicit what are often understated or over-qualified arguments in the writings of more cautiously-minded academics.

'My basic premise', says Bell, 'has been that knowledge and information are becoming the strategic resource and transforming agent of the post-industrial society ... just as the combination of energy, resources and machine technology were the transforming agencies of industrial society' (Bell 1980a: 531, 545; see also Bell 1980b; 1987: 34). The central symbol and 'analytical engine' of the change is the computer (Bell 1980a:

509). As Naisbitt puts it, 'computer technology is to the information age what mechanization was to the industrial revolution' (Naisbitt 1984: 22).

It is not the computer by itself however but its convergence with telecommunications that has produced the explosive mix (a mix that some have blessed with the unlovely name 'compunications'). This has broken down the long-standing distinction between the processing and the communication of knowledge (Bell 1980a: 513). Marshall McLuhan had looked to television to bring into being the 'global village'; far more effective in linking the world has been the communications satellite. 'The real importance of Sputnik is *not* that it began the space age, but that it introduced the era of global satellite communications' (Naisbitt 1984: 2). The combination of satellites, television, telephone, fibre optic cable, and microelectronic computers has meshed the world together into a unified knowledge grid. It has 'collapsed the information float. Now for the first time we have on the planet instantaneously shared information' (Naisbitt 1984: 57).

The new info-sphere operates in a global context. No need to move; the information can be brought to your home or local office. A world-wide electronic network of libraries, archives, and data banks comes into being, accessible in principle to anyone, anywhere, at any time. The information technology revolution compresses space and time into a new 'world *oikoumene*' oriented towards the future. Past societies, says Bell, were primarily space-bound or time-bound. They were held together by territorially based political and bureaucratic authorities and/or by history and tradition. Industrialism confirmed space in the nation state but replaced the rhythms and tempo of nature with the pacing of the machine. The clock and the railway timetable are the symbols of the industrial age. They express time in hours, minutes, seconds. The computer, the symbol of the information age, thinks in nanoseconds, that is, almost instantaneously. Its conjunction with the new communications technology thus brings in a radically new space–time framework for modern society.

As with his earlier exposition of the post-industrial idea, Bell is meticulous in giving statistical flesh to the structural bones of the information society. Knowledge does not simply govern, to an unprecedented extent, technical innovation and economic growth; it is itself fast becoming the principal activity of the economy and the principal determinant of occupational change.

In his earlier account Bell had relied for his assessment of the 'knowledge factor' in the economy on the celebrated calculations of Fritz Machlup (1962). Latterly he has come to rely on the more sophisticated and widely-regarded calculations by Marc Porat (1977) of the extent of the US 'information economy'. Bell combines Porat's calculations (centred on the year 1967) of the 'primary information sector' – industries which directly produce marketable information goods and services – with his calculations of the 'secondary information sector' – information activities in the 'technostructure' of both public and private organizations which contribute indirectly (through planning, marketing, etc.) to output but which are not formally counted as information services in the national accounts. Together these suggest that the information economy in the US amounts to about 46 per cent of GNP and more than 50 per cent of all wages and salaries earned, that is, more than half of the national income. 'It is in that sense that we have become an information economy' (Bell 1980a: 521; see also Stonier 1983: 24).

This remarkable degree of information activity – and Bell assumes it to have grown considerably since 1967 – is matched by the rapid growth of information workers in the occupational structure. Separating out an 'information sector' from the more general tertiary category of services, Bell shows that by the mid-1970s information workers in the US had come to constitute the largest group of workers – almost 47 per cent – in the civilian workforce (industrial workers accounted for a further 28 per cent, service workers for 22 per cent, and agricultural workers for 3 per cent). Using what he calls a more 'inclusive definition' Bell claims that already 'by 1975 the information workers had surpassed the noninformation groups as a whole' (Bell 1980a: 523–4).

'We now mass-produce information the way we used to mass-produce cars ... this knowledge is the driving force of the economy' (Naisbitt 1984: 7). The information society, according to its proponents, brings about change at the most fundamental level of society. It initiates a new mode of production. It changes the very source of wealth-creation and the governing factors in production. Labour and capital, the central variables of the industrial society, are replaced by information and knowledge as the central variables. The labour theory of value, as classically formulated by a succession of thinkers from Locke and Smith to Ricardo and Marx, must give way to a 'knowledge theory of value'. Now 'knowledge, not labour, is the source of value' (Bell 1980a: 506).

Bell is cautiously optimistic about the new society. But in the hands of Tom Stonier (1983) and Yoneji Masuda (1985) the information society takes on positively utopian dimensions. The information society, says Stonier, eliminates 'the primary social need for war, the need to expand resources to match growing populations'. It also enhances democracy, as it diffuses information throughout society, making for a more alert and educated public. Information is 'the new coin of power'. Unlike money or land in former times, it is widely distributed. 'No dictator can survive for any length of time in communicative society as the flows of information can no longer be controlled from the centre.' Orwell's *Nineteen Eighty-Four* was wrong: television, and *a fortiori* the newer media, liberate, they do not enslave. A 'consensus democracy' is coming into being (Stonier 1983: 202–3).

It is in the work of Yoneji Masuda that the information society takes on an almost mystical cast. Masuda offers a vision of 'computopia', the information society of the twenty-first century. It will be a 'universal society of plenty'. Individuals, largely freed by automation from the need to labour, will form themselves into voluntary communities for the fulfilment of diverse ends. 'The future information society ... will become a classless society, free of over-ruling power, the core of society being voluntary communities.' Computer-communications technology will make it possible to do without centralized politics and administration. Instead there will be participatory democracy and local 'citizen management systems' (Masuda 1985: 625–32).

OLD AND NEW

It would be perverse and foolhardy to deny the reality of much of what the information society theorists assert. The common experiences of daily life alone are enough to confirm that. Automatic tellers in banks, automatic billing at supermarket check-outs, the virtual disappearance of cheques along with cash in most monetary transactions, word processors and fax machines, direct on-line hotel and airline bookings, direct broadcasting by satellite from any part of the world: all these are facts of everyday life for most sections of the population in the advanced industrial countries.

The linking of information world-wide for scholars and specialists is also fast becoming a reality. The catalogues of the major libraries and archives can be scanned from a multitude of points by means of a computer terminal. Much of the material deposited in these libraries can also be read locally on microfilm or microfiche. The principal stock markets of the world are electronically linked, allowing for instantaneous adjustment of stock prices in response to minute-by-minute information conveyed by the computer screens. Round-the-clock trading becomes for the first time a possibility and increasingly the practice.

The information society has most clearly invaded our homes. Television is still the most obvious symbol of this, enhanced now by the additional facility of the videocassette recorder and the variety provided by cable and satellite. But 'telebanking', 'teleshopping', and 'teleworking' are also now making considerable inroads into our lives (see e.g. Olson 1987; Hakim 1988). 'Tele-education' may turn out to be an even more significant development. At the younger ages collective institutionalized provision would still seem to be desirable, for social as much as educational reasons. But the Open University in Britain already provides a model for home-based higher education. The potential for expansion into something like a World University of the Air is evident.

Still, the acceptance of the growing importance of information technology, even an information revolution, is one thing; the acceptance of the idea of a new industrial revolution, a new kind of society, a new age, is quite another. Here the criticism has been voluminous, sharp, and largely persuasive. It has also been, to a somewhat wearisome degree, familiar. This is not surprising. Since the concept of the information society has evolved smoothly out of the earlier idea of a post-industrial society, since the two share many of the same analytical features, and since they are propagated in both cases by much the same people, we should expect that the objections to the thesis of the information society would substantially repeat those levelled against the earlier idea of the post-industrial society (for which see Kumar 1978).

Such is the case. The information society theorists can be attacked, first, for their short-sighted historical perspective. As with the post-industrial theorists, they attribute to the present developments which are the culmination of trends deep in the past. What seems to them novel and current can be shown to have been in the making for the past hundred years. James Beniger, for instance, accepts the correctness of the designation of present-day society as the information society. But his detailed historical study shows this to be merely the current manifestation of a much more profound change in the character of industrial societies that took place over a century ago. This change he labels 'the Control Revolution' (Beniger 1986).

The Industrial Revolution, Beniger argues, so speeded up 'the material processing system' of society that it precipitated a crisis of control. Information-processing systems and communication technologies lagged behind those of energy generation and use. The application first of steam power and later of electricity forced innovations in communication and control in every sphere of society. Fast-moving steam trains had, for urgent reasons of safety, to be carefully monitored and controlled. The speeding up of commercial distribution as a result of steam trains and steam boats imposed wide-ranging changes in wholesale and retail organization. The pace of material throughput in factories called forth the moving assembly line (fordism) and the 'scientific management' of labour (Taylorism). Overarching all these, and modelled as often as not on the centralized, systematized railway system that was the pioneering response to the control crisis, was the growth of a formal Weberian bureaucracy in business and governmental organization. By 1939 at the latest, Beniger convincingly shows, the structural elements of the Information Society – including the basic principles of the computer – were all firmly in place. Post-war developments were largely extensions and applications of the control techniques – the Control Revolution – that were elaborated by an immensely creative group of scientists, technologists, and marketing specialists in the period from the 1880s to the 1930s.

A similar charge of historical short-sightedness is made by those, such as Kevin Robins and Frank Webster (1987, 1989), who see the information society as essentially the further application of Taylorism. Taylorism, the principles of 'scientific management' advocated by Frederick Winslow Taylor in the early years of this century, is best thought of as a powerful system of work organization capable of more or less indefinite application in a variety of industrial contexts. This means that what Taylorism connotes – the radically refined division of labour, the rigid separation of conception and execution, the standardization and splitting of tasks into the simplest possible form – might well continue apace even though many of Taylor's practical recommendations have fallen into disfavour (Littler 1978).

In response to the earlier thesis of the post-industrial 'service society', Harry Braverman (1974) had already shown that much service work is as 'Taylorized' as work in manufacturing industries. The office, it turned out, could be industrialized as readily as the workshop; much white-collar work was subjected to the same routinization, fragmentation, and de-skilling as blue-collar work. The belief in the spread of some new principle of work, some new ethic of professionalism as services grew in industrial economies, was, Braverman concluded, therefore misguided.

Taylorian organization can of course be adapted not just to routine white-collar work but to the work of many professionals and skilled technicians, new and old. The computer has been hailed by many as an instrument of liberation. It will automate the tedious and tiring work and free workers to engage in more interesting and creative tasks (see e.g. Hyman 1980). This remains, currently at least, a hope or a promise rather than widespread practice. For many information workers, the application of the new technology has continued the 'dynamic of deskilling' (Littler 1978: 189) intrinsic to Taylorian principles, complemented as these were by the tighter technical control made possible by the moving assembly line of the fordist factory (Edwards 1979: 111–29).

In manufacturing, computer numerically controlled (CNC) machines are already replacing 'some of the most highly skilled and satisfying work on the shop floor, such as jig boring, milling, universal turning and highly skilled workshop practices' (Barker 1981: 7; see also Noble 1979; Evans 1982: 162–4). In the printing trade, previously skilled typesetters and compositors may have hung on to their high wages, but for many their work has been reduced by computerized typesetting to the skill level of a typist (Webster and Robins 1986: 139). Architects and industrial designers have had their work 'simplified' – i.e. deskilled – by Computer Aided Design (CAD) (Cooley 1981), while many other professionals – in medicine and education, for instance – are having their work monitored and their expertise challenged by 'Expert' systems of artificial intelligence (Cooley 1982; Rosenbrock *et al.* 1985: 640–1; Forester 1987: 45–9).

Most notably of all, the continuing development of computers has Taylorized the computer professionals themselves. Computer work has followed the familiar pattern of the separation and splitting of tasks, leading to increasingly routinized work for the mass of workers and highly specialized work for a small group of designers and researchers. First systems analysts were separated from programmers, marking a significant distinction between those who conceived and those who executed software programmes. Later programmers were themselves distinguished from a more routine class of operators who were concerned largely with the repetitive task of coding. The development of computer languages – Cobol, Fortran, etc. – and 'structured programming' have further polarized software production along skill lines. All the creativity goes into the design and preparation of programme 'packages' – such as those for payroll calculations – which are then capable of simple implementation by programmers. The de-skilling of computer programmers in particular, taken with the general de-skilling of white-collar work in automated offices, has led Morris-Suzuki to single out the 'semi-skilled computer worker' as the typical worker of the future (Morris-Suzuki, 1988: 124).

Knowledge, according to information society theorists, is progressively supposed to affect work in two ways. One is the upgrading of the knowledge content of existing work, in the sense that the new technology adds rather than subtracts from the skill of workers. The other is the creation and expansion of new work in the knowledge sector, such that information workers come to predominate in the economy. Moreover it is assumed that it is the more skilled, more knowledgeable, information workers who will come to constitute the core of the information economy.

We have already had reason to doubt, on general grounds, that the workforce is increasing in skill and autonomy. In so far as Taylorism remains the master principle, information technology has a greater potential for proletarianization than for professionalization. This process can be quite effectively disguised by occupational statistics that suggest a more educated and better trained workforce. The growth of credentialism – i.e. demanding higher qualifications for the same jobs – and the familiar process of the inflation of job labels and occupational self-advertisement, can all given a quite misleading impression of the growth of a more 'knowledgeable' society (Kumar 1978: 211–19).

Most of the growth in jobs in the last two decades has indeed come from a quite different quarter: not from the knowledge sector, but from the lower levels of the tertiary economy, where the extent of skill and knowledge is not notably high. For instance, in the US between 1973 and 1980 almost 13 million new jobs were created. Most of these were in the private sector, and most – over 70 per cent – in services and the retail trade. The typical new workers were in 'eating and drinking' establishments, including fast-food restaurants; in 'health services', mainly nurses and ancillary staff in private hospitals and private nursing homes; and in 'business services', mainly routine information workers concerned with data processing, copying, and mailing. Many of the new workers were women, many of them part-time or temporary. Pay levels were low, job security and career prospects virtually nil. This pattern continued during the 1980s (Rothschild 1981: 12–13, 1988: 46; Walker 1985: 45; Leadbeater and Lloyd 1987: 31).

THE POLITICS OF THE INFORMATION SOCIETY

It is clear from this account of developments in the information economy that there is a distinct politics, as well as a political economy, of the information society. The growth of knowledge work, for instance, has evidently been directly affected by recent governmental policies. Knowledge workers in the public sector – especially those in human services – have declined while those in the private sector – especially those in business service – have increased. But state involvement in the information economy also operates at a far deeper structural level. Governments have taken a leading role in promoting and disseminating the idea of an information society – including vigorous attempts to encourage a 'computer culture' in schools and universities (Robins and Webster 1989). In Britain, not notably in the forefront of the information technology (IT) revolution, more than half of all research and development (R & D) in IT is funded by the government; the government is responsible, as customer, for more than half of the total market in electronics; and it absorbs more than a third of all computer capacity (Webster and Robins 1986: 273).

But it is in the military connection that we can perhaps most intimately see the link between government and the information society. From the very first development of the semi-conductor industry at the Bell Laboratories in New Jersey in the 1940s, to the 'Star Wars' and 'Strategic Computing' projects of the US Department of Defense in the 1980s, it has been obvious that military ('defence', 'space', etc.) requirements have in nearly all societies been the main engine of growth of the IT industries (Japan and Germany are partial, and perhaps temporary, exceptions). Military R & D, on one estimate, is responsible for 40 per cent of total world expenditure on research, and absorbs the activities of 40 per cent of the world's research scientists and engineers. Since it is microelectronics that has revolutionized military technology – especially in missile and intelligence systems – in the past twenty years, it is not surprising to find that a large part of this vast military expenditure on R & D is devoted to work in information technology (Barnaby 1982: 243–4; see also Lyon, 1988: 26–30).

Political and military actors, though they have their own motivations and interests, do not operate in a social vacuum. That social space is forcibly occupied, to a good extent, by large private multinational corporations that have their own pressing need for the most comprehensive development of information technology. The growth in the scale and complexity of organizations, their bursting of their national boundaries, have necessitated a degree of co-ordination and communication that has itself been a major force in the expansion of information technology.

The big commercial organizations, like government departments, have developed an appetite for IT which other companies, old and new, have hurried to satisfy. In the process a powerful new group of IT multinationals has risen to prominence. These then not only further the growth of IT by their own organizational needs but are active in generating and pressing new services on other giants. These others, also partly out of their own necessities and partly to get a share of the rich pickings, begin to move in on the act. A spiral develops whose main effect is the continuous creation of IT goods, services, and workers (Douglas and Guback 1984: 234–5; Traber 1986: 3; Webster and Robins 1986: 219–56).

The names of the IT multinationals have become household: IBM in computers, AT & T and IT & T in telecommunications, Xerox and Olivetti in office equipment, Philips and Siemens in electronics. But the original bases in particular products and services are fast becoming irrelevant. All these companies, and the many others that are in or trying to enter the field, aim to become 'integrated information' concerns. The goal, substantially achieved in several cases, is to exploit economies of scale and mutual dependencies so as to offer the complete IT package: computers, telecommunications, electronic goods and components, cable, satellite and broadcast systems, TV and video goods and programming services, film and photography. The bulk of IT has so far been developed for the state or business user. This is where expansion has been easiest and the profits greatest. But the home has also already been firmly targeted, along with leisure and entertainment. From the point of view of information technology, distinctions between office and home, work and leisure, are largely unimportant. Indeed IT is in the business of making them unimportant.

Taken with the military and political motives noted earlier, the clearly capitalist character of much IT activity has led to a widespread questioning of the whole theoretical underpinning of the idea of an information society. There is no new age, no new revolution comparable to the Industrial Revolution of the nineteenth century (Nowotny 1982: 101; Rosenbrock *et al.* 1985: 641). The information society is a myth developed to serve the interests of those who initiate and manage the 'information revolution': 'the most powerful sectors of society, its central administrative elites, the military establishment and global industrial corporations' (Hamelink 1986: 13). It is no more than the latest ideology of the capitalist state. 'Capitalism is still the name of the game' (Arriaga 1985: 294).

This is not however the whole story of the information society. To call the information society an ideology, and to relate that ideology to the contemporary needs of capitalism, is to begin, not to end the analysis. Capitalism has had many ideologies over the past two hundred years – *laissez-faire*, managerialism, welfarism, even, arguably, varieties of fascism and communism. Each has had its own kind of relation to capitalist society; each has contained its own distinctive contradictions. What kind of ideology is the ideology of the information society, and what are its particular contradictions? Ideologies, as many people have pointed out, are not just ideas in the head but real practices, as real as any other social practices. They are lived realities. They constrain our thinking about ourselves and our world, and thus have practical consequences. 'The information society' may be a partial and one-sided way of expressing the contemporary social reality, but for many people in the industrial world it is now an inescapable part of that reality. To describe this as 'false consciousness' misses the point.

POST-FORDISM

The different theories of post-industrialism – the information society, post-fordism, post-modernism – overlap one another. The differences are more than those of emphasis, certainly; but certain themes and figures recur. Information technology, for instance, which more or less defines the information society idea, is also central to the analysis of the other two theories. Globalization is another common denominator. Decentralization and diversity feature prominently in all accounts of the new era.

What distinguishes these accounts is therefore not so much the particular development they single out as the frameworks they use to examine them. Information society theorists tend to adopt an optimistic, evolutionary approach that puts all the emphasis on major new clusters of technological innovations. The information revolution is the latest, and by so much the most progressive, step in the sequence of changes that have transformed human society since earliest times (history is 'a succession of rolling waves of change' Toffler 1981: 13). Like the agricultural and industrial revolutions before it, its basis is in new techniques and new types of energy, new forms and forces of production (both Bell and Toffler are ex-marxists and seem reluctant to throw off all the errors of a misspent youth). The new technology determines, in a more or less regular way everywhere, new forms of life. Work, play, education, family relationships, and structures of feeling gradually adapt or succumb to the pressures and opportunities of the new technical forces.

If the theory of the information society emphasizes the forces of production, post-fordist theory emphasizes the relations of production. Technology loses its neutral or inherently progressive character and is put instead within a matrix of social relations that determines its use and application. This does not, it must be stressed, necessarily entail a gloomy view of current developments. Post-fordists tend to be left-wing radicals of various sorts; but this can lead them to view the new state of things with optimism as much as disquiet. The contrasting attitudes to recent changes in Italy illustrates this very well. Italy is also a good example because it was developments there that first gave rise to post-fordist theory. The Italian case can therefore provide us with the elements of post-fordist analysis.

THE THIRD ITALY

During the 1970s and 1980s, Italian and other observers began to document and discuss a phenomenon that they came to call *la Terza Italia*, the Third Italy. The Third Italy was distinguished from, on the one hand, the First Italy of large-scale mass production, concentrated in the industrial triangle of Turin, Milan, and Genoa; and, on the other hand, the Second Italy of the *mezzogiorno*, the economically undeveloped South. The Third Italy was, by contrast, a dynamic area of small firms and workshops in the central and north-eastern regions of the country: Tuscany, Umbria, Marche, Emilia-Romagna, Veneto, Friuli, Trentino-Alto Adige.

The main features of production in the Third Italy were what one of its leading students has called 'productive decentralization and social integration' (Brusco 1982). This is another way of stating the principles of the industrial district, as classically expounded by Alfred Marshall in his account of the industrial districts of nineteenth-century Birmingham and Sheffield (Bellandi 1989). But it would be wrong if this reference to the past were to make us think of the Italian industrial districts as somehow traditional and old-fashioned. There were indeed artisanal and even, in agriculture, co-operative traditions in this area. But most of the workshops and factories were brand new. They were 'high technology cottage industries' employing the latest numerically controlled tools. Their products were sophisticated and design-conscious, enabling them to penetrate international as well as national markets. Their workers were as well-paid as workers in the large plants in the north; unemployment rates in the area were generally lower than elsewhere in Italy. Transport, housing, education, and social security benefits were all of a markedly high standard, thus providing an additional 'social wage'.

Social relations within the firm, between firms, and between the firms and their surrounding community were certainly on the pattern of the classic industrial district. Most workers were highly skilled, and there was little sense of distinction between them and their supervisors. It was easy to move from being an artisan to being an entrepreneur. The aim of designing new products, and of exploiting gaps in the market, meant that there was constant collaboration between entrepreneurs, designers, engineers, and workers. Taken with the small size of enterprises, this made for a flexible division of labour and flattened hierarchies within the firm. Conception and execution, separated in the Taylorist and fordist practices of the large firms, were here to a good extent reunited.

The collaborative, collective character of relations within the firm was reproduced in its relation with other firms. As with the industrial district elsewhere, a 'monocultural' area emerged. Firms had a low degree of vertical integration and depended on each other for a wide range of specialized activities. A dense system of sub-contracting lay at the heart of the local economy. The 'extraordinarily rich and complex relationship' (Brusco 1986: 261) between clients (producers of finished goods) and sub-contractors (producers and designers of parts and services) kindled innovation and enhanced adaptability. Clients, it was often said, arrived to ask not that a product be made but that a problem be solved (Sabel 1984: 223).

There is lastly the role of the local community as a whole, in its social and political aspects. The financial and political institutions of the region did not just respond positively to the individual or collective approaches of firms, for loans and other forms of support. Banks and city and regional political authorities themselves took an active part in promoting and sustaining the small-firms economy in their area (Triglia 1989).

To some theorists the pattern of the Third Italy belongs not just to the past but the future of industrialism. Dualism, the coexistence of economic organizations with different principles of work and different relations to the community, is not an aberrant or outmoded feature of industrialism but one intrinsic to its very development. The fordist pattern of mass production, where unskilled labour is put to work on single purpose machines to produce standard goods, is only one part of the story of industrialism. Alongside mass production there has always co-existed craft production, where skilled labour works on multi-purpose or universal machines to make specialized products, in limited quantities, for a variety of customers (Samuel 1977; Berger and Piore 1980; Brusco 1982: 179–80).

Historically mass production has come to overwhelm craft production, in the sense of setting the pace and determining the purpose of production. But this was not because of some technological imperative or for reasons of economic efficiency. The dominance of mass production in the twentieth century was the result of social choices and political decisions (including those prompted by world war). That being so, social choice and political will can bring about a revitalization of small firms and industrial districts, especially in the conditions of the late twentieth century. This could mean a recovery of skill in work and, as in the past, a stronger tie between economic life and valued social purposes (Sabel and Zeitlin 1985).

'NEW TIMES'?

Sebastiano Brusco notes, as an observable cause of the movement towards productive decentralization in Italy, 'the emergence since the mid-1960s of a significant demand for more varied and customized goods, produced in short series ...' (Brusco 1982: 171). This points to one of the most important sources of post-fordist production everywhere (Piore and Sabel 1984: 183–93). Fordism was unparalleled in its ability to deliver standardized goods cheaply and on a mass scale. This was all right so long as there were sufficient groups in the population still awaiting their turn to enjoy the fruits of mass production. But what when these new groups of mass consumers were exhausted? What when demand significantly changes? What when the dictates of fashion, new styles of life, ceaseless technological innovation all call out for rapid turnover and swift changes of production? What when the mass market fragments into a diversity of consumer groups, each pursuing different things, each restlessly and rapidly discarding current patterns of consumption in search of new ones? And what, too, if this suits the requirements of contemporary capitalist firms, seeking to find ever new ways of exploiting and expanding markets? A novel pattern – novel at least in its scale – of production and consumption emerges, the pattern of 'flexible specialization'.

Flexible specialization depends on the new information technology (thus highlighting the interpenetration and overlap of current theories of social change). Numerically controlled machine tools allow for the economic production of small batches of goods – capital as well as consumer – directed to specialized sections of the market. The new tools make possible speedy changes of output, in response to new opportunities and new needs. New products do not require new tools, or the expensive and lengthy readjustment or reassembly of old ones. Numerically controlled tools are non-specialized, universal machines. New designs and new products are the result of relatively simple changes in the computer controlled programmes that direct the tools.

Flexible technology gives rise to flexible specialization. New ideas can be quickly turned into new products, newer ideas into newer products. Production is customized, geared to highly specific wants and needs in a constant state of flux. And since, as Adam Smith insisted, the division of labour is limited by the extent of the market, the segmentation of markets and their rapidly shifting patterns can lead to a lowering of the division of labour in enterprises. Customized, short-run production neither requires the large-scale plant and technology necessary to achieve economies of scale (which can be justified only by production in long series), nor can it depend on the unskilled or semi-skilled detail worker common in the industrial establishments of the fordist kind. Flexible specialization calls for skill and flexibility in the worker as much as in the machines. It is this that has led some observers to hail the new developments as heralding a renaissance of craft production (Piore and Sabel 1984: 258–80).

Flexible specialization clearly works to the benefit of small firms, at least to the extent of offsetting the competitive advantages of economies of scale traditionally enjoyed by large firms. The rise of flexible specialization as a significant, not merely peripheral or 'interstitial', phenomenon in contemporary industrial economies is undoubtedly partly responsible for the strong revival of small firms, as widely observed and documented (e.g. Lash and Urry 1987: 104, 115, 133, 148).

But there is no reason why large firms should not also benefit from flexible specialization, and considerable evidence that they are embracing it with conspicuous success. Economies of scale are replaced by 'economies of scope' – that is, the use by large plants of flexible manufacturing technologies to produce for several relatively small or segmented markets (Perez 1985: 449). Accompanied by the judicious use of sub-contracting this can allow large firms to flourish in the new environment. The Italian clothing firm Benetton, and IBM, the giant American computer firm, are in their different ways conspicuous examples of this.

For all thinkers, flexible specialization has been at the heart of the theory of post-fordism. It combines the capability of the new technology with the idea of a fundamental shift in the nature of the market in late twentieth-century industrial society. For some, it points to the way out of the global economic crisis of the 1970s and 1980s. In their much-discussed book, *The Second Industrial Divide*, Michael Piore and Charles Sabel argue that 'we are living through a second industrial divide' in our time, a transition comparable to the first industrial divide that saw the rise of mass production in the later nineteenth century (Pioe and Sabel 1984: 5, 251–80). The way ahead is not certain – alternative strategies are possible – but they see some real hope in the current revival of craft production. Craft production, the suppressed alternative to mass production and for long a minor current in its stream, is once more showing itself to be a real possibility. Its return in more propitious circumstances could mean not just economic but social and political gains.

The computer, Piore and Sabel claim, 'is a machine that meets Marx's definition of an artisan tool: it is an instrument that responds to and extends the productive capacities of the user'. Put to the purposes of flexible specialization, it 'restores human control over the production process' (Piore and Sabel 1984: 261). The advent of flexible specialization thus means greater involvement and work satisfaction for the bulk of workers. Flexible specialization puts a premium on craft skills and it also depends on collaboration between all grades of workers in the enterprise. Moreover, as in the industrial districts of the Third

Italy, it can also bring about a closer integration between economic production and the general life of the local community. Deliberately searching for the brightest prospect, Piore and Sabel speculate on the revival of a 'yeoman democracy' in the West, a form of 'collective individualism' that they see as the 'political analogue' of the 'cooperative competition' that characterized craft production in the nineteenth century. 'In the end, then, if we are right, the future refers to the past' (Piore and Sabel 1984: 306).

Other thinkers, while accepting the reality of flexible specialization, are less sanguine about its impact. For Scott Lash and John Urry, the crisis of mass production is central to what they call 'the end of organized capitalism'. Capitalism, they argue, achieved an 'organized' state in most Western societies in the period from the 1870s to the Second World War. Organized capitalism – which follows 'liberal capitalism' – consisted of some familiar features of industrial society: the concentration, centralization, and regulation of economic enterprises within the framework of the nation state; mass production along fordist and Taylorist lines; a corporatist pattern of industrial relations; geographical and spatial concentration of people and production in industrial towns; cultural modernism.

'Disorganized capitalism', a still continuing process whose onset varied in different countries but which essentially started in the 1960s, reverses or modifies many of these central features. The development of an integrated world market has led to a decartelization and deconcentration of capital, as seen from the perspective of the nation state. Flexible specialization and flexible forms of work organization increasingly displace mass production. The mass industrial working class contracts and fragments, leading to a decline of class politics and the dissolution of the national corporatist system of industrial relations. A distinctive service class, originally an effect of organized capitalism, in its later development becomes a source of new values and new social movements that increasingly disorganize capitalism. Industrial deconcentration is accompanied by spatial deconcentration, as people and work move out of the older industrial cities and regions and as production is decentralized and dispersed globally ('de-industrialization'), much of it to the Third World. Pluralism and fragmentation increase in all spheres of society. The culture of post-modernism replaces that of modernism (Lash and Urry 1987: 3–7, 300–13; see also Offe 1985).

'Disorganized capitalism' evidently takes in rather more than the flexible specialization that is the main plank of Piore and Sabel's theory. Moreover, despite its name, it is not meant to suggest a system in a state of dissolution, or even necessarily of disorder. Disorganized capitalism, unfortunate as the choice of term might be, is simply counterposed to organized capitalism; it is a new phase of capitalism, a systematic process of restructuring in the face of new circumstances (Lash and Urry 1987: 8). It is unstable, but that has been the condition of capitalism for most of its existence. We might even say, with Marx, that that has been capitalism's very principle (Berman 1983; Kumar 1988). The chief novelty, according to Lash and Urry, is the demise – forever? – of the (putative) working-class project to reshape history.

Post-fordist theories – following in the footsteps of Antonio Gramsci's influential treatment of fordism in the *Prison Notebooks* – usually have a left-wing provenance. They are attempts by radical theorists to come to terms with what are seen as fundamental and far-reaching changes in the nature of contemporary capitalism. Many thinkers remain hopeful that, despite what these changes might suggest about capitalism's capacity to renew itself, there may still be some scope for the realization of socialist aims, as historically conceived. But a basic ambivalence remains. Post-fordist capitalism is still, after all, capitalism. It is driven as insistently as ever before by the motor of the accumulation process. The restructuring implicit in post-fordism is intended to strengthen, not weaken, capitalism. There may be some unexpected bonuses for radicals – the revival of craft skills, a service class not necessarily wedded to capitalism and willing to challenge it at certain points – but these clearly have to be assessed in the context of a global economic system whose outstanding feature is dominance by transnational corporations of unprecedented wealth and power.

This ambivalence is most acutely felt in the variety of post-fordist theory presented by British Marxists under the banner of 'New Times'. First stated in a series of articles in the journal *Marxism Today*, the perspective was later substantially adopted by the executive committee of the British Communist Party and published by them as *The Manifesto for New Times* (June 1989).

Subsequently many of the original articles, accompanied by extracts from the *Manifesto*, together with critical responses, were brought out as a book, *New Times* (Hall and Jacques 1989a).

Gramsci, in his 'Americanism and Fordism', had defined fordism in the broadest possible terms. Fordism had introduced a new epoch in capitalist civilization. It marked the passage to a 'planned economy'. But it was not just production that was planned, it was also the person. Fordism did not stop at the factory gates but invaded the home and the most private and intimate spheres of the worker's life (Gramsci 1971: 302).

Post-fordists of the 'New Times' school have been similarly wide-ranging in their accounts of the new times. As with other post-fordists, they single out flexible specialization as the force that is 'orchestrating and driving on the evolution of the new world'. But in the spirit of Gramsci they argue that 'diversity, differentiation and fragmentation' – the hallmarks of post-fordism – are replacing 'homogeneity, standardization and the economies and organizations of scale' in more than simply the economic sphere (Hall and Jacques 1989b: 12).

Various attempts have been made to express schematically the differences between fordism and post-fordism, in all their various dimensions (see e.g. Harvey 1989: 174–9; Rustin 1989: 56–7; the editors' introduction to this volume, ch. 1). Put simply, the changes are generally said to be as follows. In the *economy*: the rise of a global market and of global corporations, and the decline of national enterprises and the nation state as effective units of production and regulation; flexible specialization and the dispersal and decentralization of production, replacing mass marketing and mass production; flatter hierarchies and an emphasis on communication rather than command in organizations; vertical and horizontal disintegration, and an increase in sub-contracting, franchising, internal marketing within firms, and the hiving-off of functions; rise in the number of flexi-time, part-time, temporary, self-employed, and home workers.

In *politics and industrial relations*: the fragmentation of social classes, decline of national class-based political parties and class voting, and rise of social movements and 'networks' based on region, race, or gender, or on single-issue politics (e.g. anti-nuclear movement); 'peripheral' sub- and supra-national movements; decline of mass unions and centralized wage bargaining and rise of localized, plant-based bargaining, and a labour force divided into core and periphery; end of the class compromise of corporatism; break-up of standardized, collectivist welfare provision, and rise of consumer choice and private provision in welfare.

In *culture and ideology*: the rise and promotion of individualist modes of thought and behaviour; a culture of entrepreneurialism; the end of universalism and standardization in education, and the rise of modularity and pupil- and parent-choice; fragmentation and pluralism in values and lifestyles; post-modernist eclecticism, and populist approaches to culture; privatization in domestic life and leisure pursuits.

New Times theorists admit that post-fordist changes have benefited the right more than the left; or, at least, that the right has been quicker to capitalize on the changes than the left. Reaganism and Thatcherism have been the principal beneficiaries of post-fordist developments. Left-wing thinkers and parties have been slow to throw off the heritage of theories and policies conceived within the framework of national, organized capitalism. The Keynes–Beveridge managerial/welfare state has been for them the premise of all their thinking about the future; they have found themselves floundering when the ideas and institutions that underpinned that system have crumbled.

Nevertheless, New Times theorists have accepted the challenge of post-fordism – even if largely in the Carlylean spirit of 'you'd better'. They refuse to give way to pessimism in the face of the failure of certain historical outcomes as classically predicted by marxism. The world has changed, but that is what any good marxist should have expected. Capitalism remains in place, is indeed, in its global phase, more deeply entrenched than ever before; but in both East and West new opportunities for challenging it are opening up. A marked feature of New Times, say Hall and Jacques, is 'the proliferation of the sites of antagonism and resistance, and the appearance of new subjects, new social movements, new collective identities – an enlarged sphere for the operation of politics, and new constituencies for change' (Hall and Jacques 1989b: 17). The *Manifesto* gives, as examples from Britain, the Green movement, 'local campaigns' against housing policies and in defence of local industries, 'consumer campaigns' on such matters as health services, transport, and food hygiene, and 'anti-inequality campaigns' over the poll tax and in defence of child benefit (*Manifesto for New Times* 1989: 27). Others have championed social movements structured around the 'collective identities' of gender, sexuality, and race, or strategies designed to foster a culture of 'socialist individualism' around the concept of citizenship (Brunt 1989; Leadbeater 1989; Weeks 1989).

INDUSTRIAL AND POST-INDUSTRIAL SOCIETY

It would be easy to condemn post-fordism, especially in its New Times form, as a 'Thatcherism (or Reaganism) of the Left'. It has been accused of promoting 'designer socialism', of being, indeed, 'the socialism of designers', a vision of the future as it looks to the new service class based in the media, the universities, and the information technology industries (Rustin 1989: 63). The language it uses, the language of individualism, choice, and diversity, can be said to pay excessive homage to the vocabulary of the new right. When a New Times theorist speaks of 'consuming as a source of power and pleasure', and of 'the hyper-eroticisation of a visit to the shops' (Mort 1989: 161–2), it is difficult not to feel that even where the language is used ironically there has been a considerable shift towards the perspective of the left's traditional antagonists (see also Murray 1989: 44). 'For socialists', as Michael Rustin says, 'there has to be more to life than shopping ...' (Rustin 1989: 68).

This may be thought largely a matter for left-wingers to debate. More serious is the accusation that post-fordist theory mistakes effects for causes, that what it sees as primary facts are derivative or dependent products of less visible processes. Post-fordism has for example made much of the rise or revival of localism and particularism, the cultivation of identity through attachment to place and to local cultures and traditions. It not merely picks out but celebrates the ethnic revival, the rise of 'peripheral nationalisms', the struggles to conserve local ways and local histories.

But to what extent are localism and pluralism autonomous phenomena, the self-willed responses of individuals to mass production and mass centralized politics? To what extent are they rather the consequences and outcomes of far-reaching changes in the strategies of multinational corporations seeking to make the most effective mix of economies of scale and scope?

The cultivation of local differences, the celebration of ethnicity, and the stimulation of consumer preference for a variety of exotic, 'authentic' cultural objects and experiences make good sense to 'flexible transnationals' in search of new market niches to exploit (Harvey 1989: 141–97; Robins 1989). The global standardization of *Dallas* (and the global products of Sky and other satellite companies) can co-exist quite happily with the (artificial) diversity of Disneyland and the (manufactured) localism of the heritage industry. All are of course big business, among the biggest and fastest growing today. To acknowledge this is to see in 'localism' and 'diversity' a motive and a force not very different from those that have propelled capitalism for most of its history. At the very least it is to accept that fordism as a global strategy can readily consort with post-fordism in the West and 'peripheral' as well as substantial fordism in the Third World (Lipietz 1987).

Here we come to the nub of the problem. Post-fordists are of course aware of globalization and its consequences. They know that it is part of a massive restructuring of contemporary capitalism. They are not therefore so naive as to judge its effects by their face value. They fully accept that continuity as much as change is inscribed in the practices of post-fordism.

But they feel keenly the need to throw the emphasis on the subjectivity and self-understanding of individuals and groups. Both socialism and sociology, for much the same reasons, have tended to disparage this emphasis. What has mattered are the objective structures, the immanent logic, the dynamic and impersonal forces of social sytems. When people do not act according to the expectations derived from this kind of analysis, the tendency is to shift the terms of the analysis rather than to attend to the felt experience and expressed attitudes of individuals in concrete situations.

It is possible that, for all the criticisms that have justly been made of the theories of the information society, post-fordism, and post-modernism, the strength and appeal of these theories might lie in their responsiveness to the textures of everyday life in our times, in Western societies at least. Pluralism and fragmentation – in politics, in work, in family life – do seem to be the real experiences of many people. Swiftly changing lifestyles and a sense of the instability (or plurality) of identities are another constant. In this flux the singling out of place, ethnicity, sexuality, or gender as the bedrock of identity might be simply a way of finding a relatively secure anchorage or vantage point from which to take on the rest of the world on its own mobile and shifting terms.

The same thing may be true of the strong impulse towards privatization that is readily discernible in contemporary Western society. Work matters to the extent that having a job is the passport to other opportunities – mainly by providing the financial means to enjoy those opportunities. Politics too is largely an instrumental matter for the vast majority of citizens, a question of nicely judging where to put one's vote so as to secure the maximum return at least cost to oneself. For the rest there is private life, which means largely home life. This is not necessarily the same thing as family life, for the family does not so much involve its members as provide a place, a physical space where individuals make their lives in varying combination with other individuals. For this they can draw upon all the resources of the new information technology. The symbol of the future is a house sprouting wires to which are attached a myriad of components and facilities for living the private life – whether at work, play, or prayer.

Is this what post-industrialism tends towards? It is an extreme version, certainly, of what current post-industrial theory asserts. Post-industrialism sees new forms of community, new collective identities, being formed beyond the workplace and beyond the formal sphere of politics. Its hopes for the future lie in these new forms, both as sites of resistance and as the source of new kinds of sociability. Where its critics may be right is in pointing to the fragility and vulnerability of these new forms, as compared with the old.

Industrialism, as classically conceived and practised, is changing in many respects. But the main feature of what has emerged so far is the ever greater concentration of power at the top. It is in the global reach of the multinational corporations, their ability to shape the economic and political environment, that the post-industrial order most clearly reveals itself. New Times to that extent shows continuity with old times. The dominant principle remains, the principle of capitalist industrialism. It is at the level of its working out, in its impact on societies, communities, and individuals, that the new features appear. But the marriage of global structures with micro-political and micro-social movements is one between very unequal partners. Divorce cannot be ruled out – but at what cost, and to whom?

REFERENCES

Arriaga, P. (1985) 'Toward a critique of the information economy', *Media, Culture and Society* 7, 271–96.

Barker, J. (1981) 'Technological change and quick obsolescence of qualifications', paper presented to FAST seminar, 'Attitudes to Work', 23–6 November, Marseilles.

Barnaby, F. (1982) 'Microelectronics in war', in G. Friedrichs and A. Schall (eds) *Microelectronics and Society: For Better or for Worse*, Oxford, Pergamon Press.

Bell, D. (1973) *The Coming of Post-industrial Society*, New York, Basic Books.

—— (1980a) 'The social framework of the information society', in T. Forester (ed.) *The Microelectronics Revolution*, Oxford, Basil Blackwell.

—— (1980b) 'Teletext and technology', in D. Bell, *Sociological Journeys: Essays 1960–1980*, London, Heinemann.

—— (1987) 'The world in 2013', *New Society*, 18 December, 31–8.

Bellandi, M. (1989) 'The industrial district in Marshall', in E. Goodman, J. Bamford, and P. Saynor (eds) *Small Firms and Industrial Districts in Italy*, London, Routledge.

Beniger, J.R. (1986) *The Control Revolution: Technological and Economic Origins of the Information Society*, Cambridge, MA, Harvard University Press.

Berger, S. and Piore, M.J. (1980) *Dualism and Discontinuity in Industrial Societies*, Cambridge, Cambridge University Press.

Berman, M. (1983) *All That Is Solid Melts Into Air: The Experience of Modernity*, London, Verso.

Braverman, H. (1974) *Labor and Monopoly Capitalism: The Degradation of Work in the Twentieth Century*, New York, Monthly Review Press.

Brunt, R. (1989) 'The politics of identity', in S. Hall and M. Jacques (eds) *New Times*, London, Lawrence & Wishart.

Brusco, S. (1982) 'The Emilian model: productive decentralization and social integration', *Cambridge Journal of Economics* 6, 167–84.

—— (1986) 'Small firms and industrial districts: the experience of Italy', in D. Keeble and E. Wever (eds) *New Firms and Regional Developments in Europe*, London, Croom Helm.

Cooley, M. (1981) *Architect or Bee? The Human/Technology Relationship*, Slough, Langley Technical Services.

Cooley, M. (1982) 'Computers, politics and unemployment', in P. Sieghart (ed.) *Microchips with Everything: The Consequences of Information Technology*, London, ICA/Comedia.

Douglas, S. and Guback, T. (1984) 'Production and technology in the communication/information revolution', *Media, Culture and Society* 6, 233–45.

Drucker, P. (1969) *The Age of Discontinuity*, London, Heinemann.

Edwards, R. (1979) *Contested Terrain: The Transformation of the Workplace in the Twentieth Century*, London, Heinemann.

Evans, J. (1982) 'The worker and the workplace', in G. Friedrichs and A. Schaff (eds) *Microelectronics and Society: For Better or for Worse*, Oxford, Pergamon Press.

Forester, T. (ed.) (1980) *The Microelectronics Revolution*, Oxford, Basil Blackwell.

—— (ed.) (1985) *The Information Technology Revolution*, Oxford, Basil Blackwell.

—— (1987) *High-tech Society: The Story of the Information Technology Revolution*, Oxford, Basil Blackwell.

Gershuny, J.I. (1978) *After Industrial Society? The Emerging Self-service Economy*, London, Macmillan.

Gershuny, J.I. and Miles, I. (1983) *The New Service Economy: The Transformation of Employment in Industrial Societies*, London, Frances Pinter.

Gill, C. (1985) *Work, Unemployment and the New Technology*, Cambridge: Polity Press.

Gramsci, A. (1971) 'Americanism and Fordism', in Q. Hoare and G. Nowell-Smith (eds) *Selections from the Prison Notebooks of Antonio Gramsci*, London, Lawrence & Wishart.

Hakim, C. (1988) 'Homeworking in Britain', in R.E. Pahl (ed.) *On Work: Historical, Comparative and Theoretical Approaches*, Oxford, Basil Blackwell.

Hall, S. and Jacques, M. (eds) (1989a) *New Times: The Changing Face of Politics in the 1990s*, London, Lawrence & Wishart.

—— (1989b) 'Introduction' to S. Hall and M. Jacques (eds) *New Times*, London, Lawrence & Wishart.

Hamelink, C.J. (1986) 'Is there life after the information society?', in M. Traber (ed.) *The Myth of the Information Society: Social and Ethical Implications of Communications Technology*, London and Beverley Hills, CA, Sage Publications.

Harvey, D. (1989) *The Condition of Post-modernity: An Enquiry into the Origins of Cultural Change*, Oxford, Basil Blackwell.

Hirsch, F. (1977) *Social Limits to Growth*, London, Routledge & Kegan Paul.

Hyman, A. (1980) *The Coming of the Chip*, London, New English Library.

Jones, B. (1982) *Sleepers, Wake! Technology and the Future of Work*, Brighton, Wheatsheaf.

Kumar, K. (1978) *Prophecy and Progress: The Sociology of Industrial and Post-industrial Society*, Harmondsworth, Penguin.

—— (1988) 'The limits and capacities of industrial capitalism', in K. Kumar, *The Rise of Modern Society*, Oxford, Basil Blackwell.

Lash, S. and Urry, J. (1987) *The End of Organized Capitalism*, Cambridge, Polity Press.

Leadbeater, C. (1989) 'Power to the person', in S. Hall and M. Jacques (eds) *New Times*, London, Lawrence & Wishart.

Leadbeater, C. and Lloyd J. (1987) *In Search of Work*, Harmondsworth, Penguin.

Lipietz, A. (1987) *Miracles and Mirages: The Crises of Global Fordism*, London, Verso.

Littler, C.R. (1978) 'Understanding Taylorism', *British Journal of Sociology* 29, 185–202.

Lyon, D. (1988) *The Information Society: Issues and Illusions*, Cambridge, Polity Press.

Machlup, F. (1962) *The Production and Distribution of Knowledge in the United States*, Princeton, NJ, Princeton University Press.

Manifesto for New Times (1989) Special issue, *Marxism Today*, June.

Masuda, Y. (1985) 'Computopia', in T. Forester (ed.) *The Information Technology Revolution*, Oxford, Basil Blackwell.

Miles, I. and Gershuny, J. (1986) 'The social economics of information technology', in M. Ferguson (ed.), *New Communication Technologies and the Public Interest*, London and Beverley Hills, CA, Sage Publications.

Morris-Suzuki, T. (1988) *Beyond Computopia: Information, Automation and Democracy in Japan*, London and New York, Kegan Paul International.

Mort, F. (1989) 'The politics of consumption', in S. Hall and M. Jacques (eds) *New Times*, London, Lawrence & Wishart.

Murray, R. (1989) 'Fordism and post-fordism', in S. Hall and M. Jacques (eds) *New Times*, London, Lawrence & Wishart.

Naisbitt, J. (1984) *Megatrends: Ten New Directions Transforming Our Lives*, New York, Warner Books.

Noble, D. (1979) 'Social choice in machine design: the case of NC Machine Tools', in A. Zimbalist (ed.) *Case Studies in the Labor Process*, New York, Monthly Review Press.

Nowotny, H. (1982) 'The information society: its impact on the home, local community and marginal groups', in N. Bjorn-Anderson, M. Earl, O. Holst, and E. Mumford (eds) *Information Society: For Richer, for Poorer*, Amsterdam, North-Holland Publishing Company.

Offe, C. (1985) *Disorganized Capitalism*, Cambridge, Polity Press.

Olson, M.H. (1987) 'Teleworking: practical experience and future prospects', in R.E. Kraut (ed.) *New Technology and the Transformation of White-Collar Work*, Hillside, NJ, Lawrence Erlbaum Associates.

Perez, C. (1985) 'Microelectronics, long waves and world structural change: new perspectives for developing countries', *World Development* 13, 441–63.

Piore, M.J. and Sabel, C.F. (1984) *The Second Industrial Divide: Possibilities for Prosperity*, New York, Basic Books.

Porat, M. (1977) *The Information Economy: Definition and Measurement*, Washington, DC, US Department of Commerce.

Robins, K. (1989) 'Global times', *Marxism Today*, December, 20–7.

Robins, K. and Webster, F. (1987) 'Information as capital: a critique of Daniel Bell', in J.D. Slack and F. Fejes (eds) *The Ideology of the Information Age*, Norwood, NJ, Ablex Publishing Corporation.

—— (1989) *The Technical Fix: Education, Computer and Industry*, London, Macmillan.

Rosenbrock, H. *et al.* (1985) 'A new Industrial Revolution?', in T. Forester (ed.) *The Information Technology Revolution*, Oxford, Basil Blackwell.

Ross, G. (1974) 'The second coming of Daniel Bell', in R. Miliband and J. Saville (eds) *The Socialist Register 1974*, London, Merlin Press.

Rothschild, E. (1981) 'Reagan and the real America', *New York Review of Books*, 5 February, 12–18.

—— (1988) 'The real Reagan economy', *New York Review of Books*, 30 June, 46–53.

Rustin, M. (1989) 'The politics of post-fordism: or, the trouble with "New Times"', *New Left Review* 175, 54–77.

Sabel, C.F. (1984) *Work and Politics: The Division of Labor in Industry*, Cambridge: Cambridge University Press.

Sabel, C. and Zeitlin, J. (1985) 'Historical alternatives to mass production: politics, markets and technology in nineteenth-century industrialization', *Past and Present*, 108, 133–76.

Samuel, R. (1977) 'Workshop of the world: steam power and hand technology in mid-Victorian Britain', *History Workshop Journal* 3, 6–72.

Stonier, T. (1983) *The Wealth of Information: A Profile of the Post-industrial Economy*, London, Thames Methuen.

Toffler, A. (1970) *Future Shock*, New York, Random House.

—— (1981) *The Third Wave*, New York, Bantam Books.

Traber, M. (1986) 'Introduction' to M. Traber (ed.) *The Myth of the Information Revolution*, London and Beverley Hills, CA, Sage Publications.

Triglia, C. (1989) 'Small-firm development and political subcultures in Italy', in E. Goodman, J. Bamford, and P. Saynor (eds) *Small Firms and Industrial Districts in Italy*, London, Routledge.

Walker, R.A. (1985) 'Is there a service economy? The changing capitalist division of labour', *Science and Society* 49, 42–83.

Webster, F. and Robins, K. (1986) *Information Technology: A Luddite Analysis*, Norwood, NJ, Ablex Publishing Corporation.

—— (1989) 'Plan and control: towards a cultural history of the information society', *Theory and Society* 18, 323–51.

Weeks, J. (1989) 'Value for many', *Marxism Today*, December, 30–5.

3

ORGANIZATIONAL RESTRUCTURING, CORPORATE NEEDS FOR CHANGING MANAGERIAL SKILLS, AND THE ROLE OF HIGHER EDUCATION

Richard Scase

INTRODUCTION

The growth of professional management and of large-scale organizations has been one of the major social trends of the twentieth century. In all of the highly industrialized capitalist societies, amalgamations and takeovers have led to the emergence of corporations that dominate not only local and national economies but also dictate, to a large extent, the character of a globally based division of labour. Alongside these developments within the privately owned sectors of capitalist-dominated economies, there has been the growth of state institutions as a result of the increasing provision of services in such areas as education, health, and social welfare. Indeed, despite the rediscovered popularity of 'enterprise' and 'entrepreneurship', state institutions in most of the advanced capitalist economies continue to shape the character of the social structure as well as the economic fabric within which profit-making corporations operate (Davis and Scase 1985). It is, then, not surprising that the dominance of large-scale institutions – both in the private and the public sectors – has attracted the attention of social scientists. The emergence of such organizational forms raises important issues about patterns of decision-making in society, ownership and control, and social accountability (Kumar 1989). Further, the growth of large-scale organizations has fundamental ramifications for the dynamics of class relationships and, coupled with these, the patterning of opportunity structures. Indeed, no analysis of social class and of mobility in society can be adequately undertaken without consideration being given to these broader processes of organizational change.

Unfortunately, there are too few studies of organizational change which are related to analyses of the dynamics of class relationships and to the distribution of opportunities and rewards in society. A number of factors account for this, not least the fragmentation of sociological research into a number of sub-divisions such as, for example, 'education', 'work and organization', 'social class and stratification', etc., so that key inter-relationships in society are neglected because they cut across what have now become *traditional* academic divisions within sociology. Thus, although sociological research within the areas of social class, stratification, and social mobility has documented historically and cross-nationally broader social trends, rarely have these been related to specific processes of organizational change and how these, in turn, lead to changing demands for different kinds of human talent. Thus, there are few studies of how organizational restructuring requires changing management *competences* with varied implications for staff recruitment and training (Handy 1989). Accordingly, there are few studies of how managers are recruited, socialized into their roles, and how they – constituting a distinctive occupational category – are key actors in the shaping of class relationships in society (Dahrendorf 1959). Thus, this chapter considers the extent to which organizational restructuring during the 1980s and 1990s is affecting the nature of managerial work and how this, in turn, is leading to changing needs in the 'quality' and 'nature' of human skills. It argues that the selection of those chosen for management positions is becoming more problematic because of the growing importance which senior corporate leaders now attach to various 'indeterminate' criteria in their management recruitment processes. The reasons for this are explained, as well as the broader ramifications for the 'providers' of potential managers such as, for instance, universities and other institutions of higher education. Hence it is argued that one of the many reasons why corporate leaders claim that higher education fails to meet the needs of industry in Britain is not because of the precise quality of technical competences which students acquire, but because of their perceived inability to provide talent that is seen to be equipped with the 'appropriate' inter-personal skills necessary for managing people in organizational forms which are 'post-bureaucratic', 'flexible', and highly decentralized.

MANAGEMENT AND ORGANIZATIONAL CHANGE

Within large-scale organizations, human, technical, and financial resources have to be co-ordinated and controlled. In addition, work tasks have to be defined and allocated to individuals whose job performance must be supervised and evaluated. In other words, organizations have to be *managed* and, as such, the responsibility for this lies with those who, within the context of different organizational settings, are variously designated as *managers* (Drucker 1974). Thus, the growth of large-scale organizations has witnessed the emergence of management as *the* core organizational activity. It is because of this that managers enjoy considerable economic and social privileges. Through their control of work processes and as a function of their positions of control, they are able to appropriate for themselves high earnings and various fringe benefits which are relatively better than those enjoyed by other employees (Regional Reward Surveys 1985). If only for this reason, relationships between managers and their subordinates within large-scale profit-making organizations are those of *class* and it is this which shapes the essentially antagonistic nature of manager–worker interactions within work settings (Salaman 1981).

During the immediate post-war decades, economic growth facilitated the expansion of business corporations and state-owned institutions. Managers could be reasonably optimistic about their career chances and, in turn, about their opportunities for enjoying steadily improving living standards. According to many commentators, managers belonged to an affluent and rapidly expanding middle class who were the product of a 'new' or more 'open' society within which academic, technical, and professional forms of meritocratic qualification were gaining ascendancy over more traditional forms of hereditary class privilege (Pahl and Pahl 1971). In other words, the growth of large-scale organizations – through their increasing need for managerial, technical, and professional skills – was bringing about the decline of traditional class relations (Bell 1974). This was a trend which was reinforced by the expansion of the welfare state which brought with it the growth of institutions in the provision of health, welfare, and education services. As with profit-making organizations, these also offered new and increasing career and job prospects for managers, professionals, and technical experts (Galbraith 1967). They also created the need for public sector management as a specialist function which incorporated its own specific principles and codes of competences. Even so, like their colleagues in large privately owned corporations, these managers worked within hierarchies where pay, promotion, security, and the associated incremental enhancements in status and responsibility were major personal incentives. Hence, in so far as they had reasonably clearly-defined careers personal progress could be measured in terms of age, experience, and achievement (Sofer 1970).

One of the many reasons why they could subscribe to these assumptions was because of the character of the organizations within which they were employed. During the immediate post-war decades the prevailing paradigm of organizational design was one which emphasized the desirability of *bureaucracy* and the *bureaucratic* mode of operation. Thus, as organizations expanded, corporate leaders developed systems of management which were largely based upon *fordist* methods and principles (Braverman 1974). As on the shopfloor, the on-going pursuit of cost-effectiveness and rationality was achieved through job fragmentation and the creation of management processes based upon a precisely defined division of work tasks. If the principles of fordism (or scientific management) enabled managers to exercise tight supervisory control over shopfloor operatives, it was the opinion of corporate leaders that similar methods could be applied to the execution of managerial and administrative work tasks. Accordingly, managerial work processes could be systematically investigated through 'scientific' enquiry and, on the basis of detailed analysis of each person's work tasks, *rational* administrative and managerial work processes could be created. It was because of this that the post-war decades witnessed the rapid growth of 'management science' as an empirical discipline, with its application of the techniques of operational research and systems analysis to management practices.

The outcome was the design of organizations according to a

number of core principles, many of which have become synonymous with the notion of *bureaucracy* as it is conventionally discussed within the sociological literature (Child 1984). Thus the rational and therefore cost-effective organization was one in which there was centralized control with hierarchical decision-making. Communication procedures were required to be vertically structured so that those vested with senior managerial authority could monitor and control the flow of information and determine the effective allocation of resources within the organization. The bureaucratic paradigm of organization stressed the need for tasks to be allocated according to strictly defined principles of *superordination* and *subordination*. Hence *obedience* and *compliance* were strongly emphasized as organizational values. But equally important was the breakdown of the total work process into precisely delineated job tasks. If this is one of the essential features of fordist forms of shopfloor organization, it was considered just as pertinent for determining the rational allocation of duties among managers. With the adoption of bureaucratic forms of control, the potential indeterminacy and ambiguity of managerial work is *routinized* into co-ordinated and precisely designated job descriptions which become the tasks and duties of individuals. Consequently, a further objective of fordism can be attained, namely, the nurturing of expert personal skills and competences. But as managers undertake their duties within a clearly designated division of tasks, bounded by systems of authority and steeped in relationships of superordination and subordination, they become not only *expert* but also *dependent* upon both the organization and *each other* for the exercise of their skills. As a result, psychological commitment is obtained since managers become not only key actors but also stakeholders in the extent to which their organizations successfully achieve their goals. At the same time, a cognitive management style emerges which emphasizes *dependency*, *conformity*, *co-operation*, and 'satisfactory' job performance (Merton 1964).

The implications of such assumptions for recruitment procedures are self-evident. The overriding goal is to select those who are prepared to undertake their tasks in a compliant, dutiful, and reliable manner. The required behaviour of managers is to perform 'satisfactorily' rather than 'outstandingly' if only because the latter can lead to uncertainties and therefore ambiguities within the work process. Management selection, therefore, focuses upon those who can demonstrate that they are able to learn the rules, who are prepared to be compliant within roles of super- and subordination, and who are able to work with others within a functionally interdependent division of labour. By contrast, they are not expected to be *exceptionally* 'creative', 'entrepreneurial', or 'individualistic' since these qualities could lead to an undermining of the bureaucratic or 'fordist' principles upon which modern management techniques were established. Thus the British university system – especially in terms of its more 'elite' institutions – was seen to be ideally suited for providing the human talent which would be appropriate for senior management positions. Such people, having been through the necessary processes of organizational socialization and training, could be relied upon to sustain and reproduce fordist, bureaucratic ideals according to which their junior and middle-level colleagues would work.

It is for these reasons that British companies continue to be characterized by a particularly distinctive feature, namely, the relatively low proportion of university graduates appointed to management positions compared with those in many other countries (Constable and McCormick 1987). If university graduates have been recruited for the most senior corporate roles – if only because they are needed for strategic decision-making – it has been considered doubtful whether this is necessary for lower managerial positions. The bureaucratic form of organization emphasizes the desirability of obedience, reliability, and duty – features which many university graduates are inclined to reject. Indeed, the experience of a higher education is likely to encourage students to think 'independently' and 'creatively' and to develop the necessary personal skills for performing tasks in a relatively unstructured, autonomous manner. In other words, university education tends to nurture those very qualities which are underplayed within bureaucratic organizations. Hence there is a reluctance to recruit graduates for lower-level managerial positions. Equally, of course, many graduates attach a relatively low priority to obtaining careers in management. For them, such a career is generally perceived to offer limited opportunities for personal creativity, as well as for personal development and self-growth. Indeed, this is often confirmed by their own experiences of corporate management development programmes. The outcome is frequently rapid job change and/or the search for employment in smaller, less bureaucratically structured companies (Scase and Goffee 1989) such as, for instance, media-based and professional organizations in which personal creativity is more highly valued. The outcome for the management recruitment strategies of large-scale bureaucratic organizations is the selection of people who have not been to university but who have enjoyed a particular pattern of family, childhood, and school socialization. Hence, they are inclined to select middle-class young people who have attended the less prestigious independent schools and who are perceived to be capable of ultimately filling 'middle' management positions. It is assumed that such trainees possess the necessary personal characteristics so that it will be possible to *trust* them to perform their duties in a compliant and routinized manner. Alongside, there is the selection of 'fast track' graduates, chosen from the more 'elite' universities and, more recently, the more prestigious business schools, who will be groomed for the more challenging, psychologically demanding, and personally creative senior management positions (Nicholson and West 1988; Scase and Goffee 1989).

The growth of large-scale organizations, then, structured on the basis of fordist or bureaucratic principles has had a number of implications for the nature of class relationships, social mobility, and for the role of higher education institutions in Britain. Certainly, throughout the twentieth century and especially during the earlier post-war decades, the structuring of organizations according to bureaucratic principles offered relatively secure career paths for large sectors of the middle class. By undertaking their work tasks according to clearly specified procedures and precisely formulated job descriptions they were able to enjoy reasonably high earnings and social status. As middle managers, they commanded 'respect' both within the workplace and the wider community (Pahl and Pahl 1971). Accordingly, the expansion of a 'new middle class', claimed to be symptomatic of the affluence of the 1960s and early 1970s, was contingent upon the development of organizational forms that required the recruitment of people for the rapidly expanding number of corporate managerial positions (Young and Willmott 1973).

However, these trends altered direction in the 1970s with

repercussions that continue today. Middle-class optimism and self-confidence was superseded by a realization that career aspirations and desires for improved living standards could not always be fulfilled. A number of factors contributed to this change in mood, but three would seem to be particularly pertinent. First, the early 1970s witnessed a series of industrial disputes which led to the development of a widespread opinion that management had lost the will and/or right to manage and that organized labour had become the dominant economic and political force. Indeed, within a corporatist framework of industrial relations there did seem to be something to such claims because of the wage increases trade union leaders were able to obtain from management and the overall fall in profit margins. As a result corporations were becoming reluctant to invest in new productive capacity and to expand their business operations in Britain. Second, the oil crisis of 1973 not only increased the production costs of British companies but also weakened the competitive position of the British economy as a whole. Finally, the increasing 'professionalization' of management, through the expansion of business schools and the development of business education, was encouraging many corporate leaders to review their business practices and to reassess the cost-effectiveness of fordist and bureaucratically based management systems (Scase and Goffee 1989).

Thus there were a number of forces in the 1970s which were compelling British companies to explore ways whereby they could reduce their managerial overheads and their overall cost structures. Such pressures were also evident within public sector organizations, such as the nationalized industries, state health, welfare, and education institutions. With the election of the 1979 Conservative government, committed to reducing the public sector borrowing requirement and overall levels of personal taxation, and to 'cutting back' the role of the state in the economy as a whole, managers in public sector organizations came under similar pressures to review their costs and to reappraise the effectiveness of their organizational and management systems. Hence the 1970s witnessed a new era for British managers, with regard to their corporate roles as well as for their broader social identities. Indeed, the trends continue today as private and public sector organizations continue to strive to be more cost-effective and efficient. Managers, accordingly, are pressurized to achieve ever higher levels of measurable performance. Demands for greater efficiency often mean they can no longer be assured of relatively secure jobs with reasonably predictable career paths. In common with other categories of employees, they are now the victims of corporate restructuring so that their jobs and duties are frequently redesigned or changed and they are often declared redundant (Handy 1989). Even those organizations which have expanded their trading activities over the past decade have often been able to do so without increasing staff levels, including the number of managers which they require. Changes in national and global markets have led corporations to implement strategies geared to the production and sales of products and services for specialist 'niches' rather than for general markets. Often, organizational restructuring has led to the adoption of smaller wholly-owned subsidiaries and 'strategic business units'. Further, corporate strategies since the late 1970s tend to be concerned with achieving profits through consolidating and contracting trading activities through investment rather than solely through high-volume growth. At the same time, the use of computer-based information systems has enabled senior management to cut overheads through reducing their need for routine clerical workers and for various categories of junior and middle managers (Jenkins and Sherman 1979). But perhaps most important of all, the economic and political pressures which have increasingly impinged upon the operation of large-scale organizations in both public and private sectors have brought about the demise of the bureaucratic organization as the basis upon which effective and rational managerial decision-making can be determined. It has been superseded by an organizational model which emphasizes quite the reverse attributes (Minzberg 1979).

THE POST-BUREAUCRATIC PARADIGM

A major objective of strategies aiming to abolish bureaucratic forms of organization is to eliminate organizational attitudes which foster risk-avoidance and conformist, 'ritualistic' forms of behaviour. As stated above, the popularity of bureaucracy rested upon the extent to which operating procedures – characterized by the clear delineation of work tasks and responsibilities – sustained reliable, predictable, and compliant forms of behaviour.

It was assumed that organizational goals could be achieved in a pre-planned and orderly fashion and with a minimum amount of ambiguity. However, in the 1990s there is an increasing recognition of the costs associated with these structures in their tendencies to mould 'bureaucratic personality types' among managers who then value role conformity and job security rather than innovation and change. As a result, senior managers – particularly those within private sector organizations – are anxious to encourage more 'entrepreneurial' and 'creative' forms of conduct among their middle-level and junior colleagues. Indeed, *intrapreneurship* is frequently used to describe the attitudes of those managers who, working within 'looser', less clearly defined organizational structures, adopt many of the attitudes and behaviours supposedly characteristic of the 'classical' nineteenth-century entrepreneurs (Minkes 1987).

There is, then, the growing ascendancy of an organizational model which is established on principles and assumptions which are in sharp contrast to those underlying more bureaucratic forms. Instead of an emphasis upon clearly defined tasks, work roles are broadly determined according to their contribution to the accomplishment of *specific* objectives. Channels of communication are deliberately encouraged to be 'open', 'flexible', and 'informal' rather than, as in bureaucratic structures, according to strictly prescribed authority roles. If, then, reliability and conformity are valued attributes within bureaucratic management systems, in more loosely structured organizations, a greater emphasis is placed upon individual creativity and the capacity to cope with ambiguity and change. Managers are expected to be psychologically immersed in their jobs and it is for this reason that so much importance is attached to fostering appropriate organizational *cultures* since it is through these, rather than through explicitly stated rules and regulations, that psychological involvement is obtained (Pascole and Athos 1982).

It is ideas of this sort which are to be found in many of the present-day panaceas advocated by management 'gurus' as prescriptions for improving organizational effectiveness. Indeed, these seem to be attaining growing popularity among senior managers in both private and public sector organizations as witnessed, for instance, in the world-wide success of Peters and Waterman's *In Search of Excellence* (1982). In this book, the authors argue that high-performing organizations have been able to reduce their dependency upon highly formalized structures and to implement *cultures* which encourage, among other things, 'a basis for action', 'autonomy and entrepreneurship', 'productivity through people', 'hands on, value driven' leadership, and 'simultaneous loose-tight' organizational properties. Similarly, other advocates of organizational change stress the desirability of 'simple structures', 'adhocracies', and 'matrices' (Minzberg 1979). Hence it is argued that small and medium-sized companies enjoy considerable competitive advantages over larger organizations because their chief executives, who are often owner-managers, are able to exercise 'direct' day-to-day control over their employees through cultivating open and informal systems of communication (Scase and Goffee 1987). Similarly, in large-scale organizations, it is claimed that the nurturing of 'matrices' and 'adhocracies', typically involving the utilization of ever-changing project teams and task forces, offers the means for overcoming more rigid departmental, functional, or divisional boundaries in order to achieve particular goals. Further, for many large-scale organizations, the need for greater responsiveness to more competitive and more rapidly changing market circumstances is expressed in the adoption of more 'devolved' and 'decentralized' structures. Hence the setting-up of 'strategic business units' and shifts towards highly autonomous divisions to which budgeting control and strategic management are delegated represent attempts to be more responsive to the changing needs of different product markets. Some large corporations have even gone so far as to abandon altogether their divisionalized structures and to substitute in their place wholly-owned subsidiary companies. The latter can enjoy almost total operating autonomy so long as they achieve a satisfactory level of performance as determined by their parent holding companies (Peters 1988).

The rejection of the bureaucratic paradigm, then, has led to the implementation of a variety of organizational forms, many of which are subsumed under the general label of the 'flexible' or 'adaptive' firm. Indeed, the extreme of this development is the organization which consists of little more than a small number of negotiators who agree trade terms with a variety of production sub-contractors and who then 'sell on' the products to wholesalers and retailers with no direct involvement in the production process itself. In such instances, 'the office and the telephone' supersede the workplace and such organizations are little more than 'brokers' in various products and services, negotiating trading terms with a broad range of sub-contracting manufacturers, franchises and others. If such forms of organization represent the 'adaptive' firm in the extreme and, hence, only a very small number of organizations, their numbers are, nevertheless, increasing (Handy 1984). They are, for instance, growing rapidly in the media industry, where production processes in television and film, which were once undertaken in an integrated manner 'in-house', are now fragmented and subdivided among a variety of 'independent', self-employed 'freelancers' who are temporarily co-ordinated into 'one-off' teams for the purposes of particular projects. As soon as a particular project is completed, the teams are dismantled and each freelance worker seeks engagement on another task with other groups of specialists.

But if the abandonment of bureaucratic rules and procedures and their being superseded by more 'adaptive forms' of organization is becoming a pronounced feature of modern economic life, it is also reinforced by senior managerial attempts to change the nature of corporate cultures. Just as organizations can vary in their structural characteristics so, too, can they differ in their predominant values and assumptions (Pascole and Athos 1982). Highly bureaucratized organizations tend to foster cultures which emphasize the *desirability* of clearly defined rules and procedures for attaining operating efficiency. These encourage the adoption of routinized behaviour and reinforce a general psychological resistance to change. Established procedures will be assumed to be both necessary and efficient and, as such, not be regarded as cumbersome 'red tape'. Role cultures also tend to sustain values which give priority to 'security' and 'promotion' as rewards for staff who perform their duties *satisfactorily* with *loyalty* and *compliance.* Within bureaucratically structured organizations, therefore, predominant structures and cultures tend to be mutually reinforcing so that employees become moulded into 'bureaucratic personalities'. Hence they develop cognitive styles which reduce their propensity to take risks. It is in response to this that, alongside the introduction of more 'adaptive' or 'flexible' forms of organization, senior managers are attempting to impose *cultures* that emphasize the value of experimentation, innovation, and creativity. They are attempting to foster values which stress goal achievement rather than the rigid adherence to routines and procedures. Informal and intensive patterns of consultation and communication among colleagues are encouraged while, at the same time, vertical or hierarchical forms of managerial control – as exercised within traditional bureaucratic cultures – are underplayed (Handy 1985).

The introduction of task-oriented ideals can reduce the need for organizational rules if senior management is able to generate a high level of organizational commitment and to create relationships of *high trust* (Fox 1974). Fewer managerial and supervisory staff are required and the associated reduction in costs can give trading advantages in highly competitive markets. Witness the success of many Japanese-owned corporations whose management has given high priority to developing 'flexible' forms of organization and, related to this, nurturing cultures which emphasize the desirability of 'high trust', commitment, and personal 'creativity' (Wickens 1987). Hand in hand with this, there is the use of various forms of subcontracting systems, Quality Management Systems, Just-in-Time Management, and other forms of operating flexibility. Through these methods, senior managers of many corporations have managed to keep their overheads low by reducing the need for supervisory staff through fostering high-trust relationships so that *all* employees – including those on the shopfloor – are *incorporated* within the decision-making process of the organization as a whole. It is, of course, such practices which the leaders of Western corporations are attempting to initiate in order to meet the 'Japanese challenge' (Ouchi 1981).

THE NEED FOR 'NEW' MANAGEMENT SKILLS AND THE ROLE OF HIGHER EDUCATION

The abandonment of the bureaucratic paradigm as a basis for effective organizational practice and its being superseded by more 'adaptive' and 'flexible' forms has clearly had important ramifications for management 'style' and the ways in which senior managers control their staff. Within bureaucratic structures, they can rely upon rules and formally prescribed procedures but in looser organizational forms there are fewer explicit guidelines governing behaviour. In the relative absence of such rules and regulations, a greater emphasis is placed upon the use of a variety of *inter-personal* skills in order to motivate staff to achieve their goals (Scase and Goffee 1989). These can best be summed up by the use of the term '*creative leadership*'. Within newly-evolving organizational forms, it is necessary for managers to *work with* their subordinates in order to achieve various specified goals. Instead of the imposition of orders and instructions through more traditional forms of 'autocratic' management, it is necessary for managers to develop leadership skills that encourage the sharing of problems and the discussion of possible solutions and strategies for achieving goals (Kanter 1989). The exercise of creative leadership skills presupposes that managers are flexible and accommodating in their attitudes and that they adopt an open-participative approach to decision-making. This is particularly necessary within the context of project teams where the successful attainment of goals is dependent upon personal compatibility, the sharing of ideas, and the commitment of highly motivated staff. Further, the leadership skills required of managers within adaptive organizations focus upon the ability to understand and empathize with staff *as individuals* – in terms of understanding their personal job needs and motivation – and to be able to communicate with them on a close, intimate, and personal basis. Hence the psychological requirements of 'competent' management within the newly emerging non-bureaucratic forms of organization are more complex and demanding than those required in traditional structures. If, within bureaucratic forms, managers could manage through rules and procedures and thereby psychologically distance themselves from their staff, this is no longer the case. The flexible firm, by contrast, demands a higher degree of psychological involvement in generating motivation and morale among staff and, hence, a greater understanding of human relations and inter-personal skills (Kanter 1983).

It is for these reasons that it is being recognized that there is a problem of management development in Britain. As stated earlier, the proportion of managers who are university graduates is low by comparison with that in most other industrial countries. One of the reasons for this is the over-dependence upon the bureaucratic form of organization with its need for 'conformist' and 'reliable' behaviour. Hence, traditionally, graduates have been recruited primarily in terms of their potential for senior management positions. However, with the development of more 'flexible' or 'adaptive' forms of organization it is necessary for the predominant mode of management – at all levels – to adopt more creative leadership skills. Hence the contemporary demand for university graduates who will be destined, in the long term, to occupy managerial positions *of all sorts and at all levels* rather than simply those at the top of organizational structures. Thus, the qualities that universities nurture among their graduates, to be creative, to be innovative, and to be enterprising, have – with the abandonment of the bureaucratic paradigm – become requirements for managers at all levels within organizational structures. Accordingly, the direction of organizational change – from the bureaucratic to the adaptive – is leading to a greater degree of 'fit' between the *supply* of educated labour by the university system and the demand for such labour by large-scale organizations; a trend that is being reinforced by developments within *both* the university system *and* large-scale corporations.

Partly as a result of government pressure, but not entirely so, universities are recognizing the need that companies have for graduates who have the potential to exercise creative leadership skills. This is reflected in the Enterprise in Higher Education Initiative through which the government's Training Agency is encouraging universities to develop programmes for students to acquire the *inter-personal* – rather than technical – leadership skills needed by more 'adaptive' organizations. The Conservative government, committed to the ideals of an enterprise culture, has been keen to encourage the shift in management style required of more adaptive organizations and, therefore, to subsidize programmes in higher education that facilitate the transition of creative talent from universities to large organizations. A consequence of this is that universities are becoming more vocational in the orientation of their curriculae. They are abandoning some of their more traditional notions of liberal education and taking on the more vocationally related attributes of universities in most other industrial countries (OECD 1989). The outcome is the rapid expansion of business studies, law, accountancy, industrial psychology, economics, and management and, with this, a rapid increase in the number of university graduates seeking careers in large-scale corporations.

Within these organizations, the 'fit' between management and university graduates is being reinforced by a number of trends. The abandonment of bureaucracy and the adoption of more 'flexible' structures are making managerial careers more attractive to university graduates because they are no longer compelled to conform to the same extent as in the past, to rules and procedures in a tightly prescribed manner. They are less likely to be constrained by hierarchical authority relationships and to be exposed to organizational cultures which emphasize role compliance, conformity, and the underplay of personal creativity. Instead, the 'flexible' organization, in the importance that it attributes to informal personal relationships, openness in patterns of consultation and communication, and the underplay of 'rank' and status orders, emphasizes attributes not unfamiliar to those which graduates experience within their various university settings. Indeed, some organizations deliberately attempt to foster such similarities. In high technology companies such as those found in the electronics and pharmaceutical industries, as well as in such areas as advertising, broadcasting, publishing, and the popular media, management often goes to great lengths to 'recreate' the cultures of universities (Peters and Waterman 1982). Work is defined as a sphere for self-fulfilment and a high value is attached to informality in dress, speech, and patterns of inter-personal relations. Through these means, senior managers are attempting to recruit and retain high quality graduates who, over time, will acquire the necessary skills for *creative* leadership. It is a pattern which is in sharp contrast to the traditional methods of graduate recruitment which were oriented to selecting small numbers for only the most senior corporate positions. In occupying these, graduates were expected to adopt leadership styles which stood in sharp contrast to the open and participative forms that are nurtured within more adaptive organizational forms.

BUT DOES IT WORK?

Although in Britain there are major shifts towards the adoption of more 'adaptive' and 'flexible' forms of organization, the magnitude of these trends should not be overstated. This chapter has focused on these but it must be recognized that bureaucratic forms of organization persist. Accordingly, the extent to which the development of new management styles, based upon creative skills and drawing on the innovative talents of university graduates, will become predominant within large-scale organizations must be seen as an open question. The major reasons for this are to do with the nature of *British* culture which, because of a range of factors, tends to associate *effective* 'leadership' with particular qualities (Bryman 1986). Traditionally, the independent schools, the military, and the higher echelons of the civil service have shaped the characteristics of what have become regarded as the necessary behavioural features of those in senior leadership positions (Scase and Goffee 1989). For these, particular patterns of conduct are required in terms of speech, dress, and personal appearance. It is further assumed that such 'leaders' subscribe to particular values, attitudes, and beliefs which can only be acquired through particular patterns of childhood, education, and class-based experience.

Such 'traditional' forms of leadership operate most effectively within bureaucratically structured organizations, since it is within such settings that there is a heavy emphasis upon rank, hierarchy, and position. Communications tend to be 'top-down' and the professed style of leadership is one which emphasizes 'moral superiority', 'distance', and 'formality' in inter-personal relationships and the enforcement of employee compliance through tight supervision, inter-personal competition, and 'stigma' for under-performers. It is a style of leadership which fosters, and is dependent upon, 'paternalistic' organizational cultures, such that women and those of ethnic and working-class origin are disadvantaged despite their competence and commitment to organizational goals (Scase and Goffee 1989). This traditional style of leadership is in sharp contrast to that which is required within 'adaptive' organizations. There is, then, a resultant confusion as to what constitutes appropriate 'leadership' and, from this, whether or not the 'adaptive' form of organization is, after all, more effective than traditional bureaucratic forms for the rational pursuit of goals.

Hence, the present attractiveness of university graduates for senior corporate leaders may be short-lived if there is a return to more bureaucratic models of organization. If so, it will merely mark a return to the more traditional strategies of corporate leaders who will recruit graduates from the more elite universities for their most senior positions and non-graduates for more middle and junior managerial posts. Indeed, the bureaucratic model of management appears to be more compatible with broader social processes. In essence, Britain is a *low-trust* society and bureaucratic rules and procedures, 'tight' methods of supervision, and an emphasis upon hierarchy and 'social distance' in inter-personal relations are consistent with this (Fox 1974). So, the application of looser, more 'adaptive' or 'flexible' forms of organization, integated by senior managerial appeals to 'shared values' and 'corporate cultures' could turn out to be little more than a 'passing fad' and, in the longer term, only pertinent for a limited range of organizational settings. In this case, rules, clearly defined procedures, and hierarchical authority relationships of the sort found within bureaucracies will continue to provide the basis for the exercise of managerial prerogatives in work contexts in which working relationships between superordinates and subordinates are characterized by suspicion. If only for this reason, attempts to encourage 'enterprise' among university students may be misplaced because of the failure to recognize that adaptive forms of organization are unlikely to flourish within a society characterized by low-trust and rigid class divisions.

REFERENCES

Bell, D. (1974) *The Coming of Post-industrial Society*, London, Heinemann.

Braverman, H. (1974) *Labor and Monopoly Capitalism: The Degradation of Work in the Twentieth Century*, New York, Monthly Review Press.

Bryman, A. (1986) *Leadership and Organisation*, London, Routledge & Kegan Paul.

Child, J. (1984) *Organisation* (2nd edn), New York, Harper & Row.

Constable, J. and McCormick, R. (1987) *The Making of British Managers: A Report for the BIM and the CBI into Management Training, Education and Development*, Corby, British Institute of Management.

Dahrendorf, R. (1959) *Class and Class Conflict in Industrial Society*, London, Routledge & Kegan Paul.

Davis, H. and Scase, R. (1985) *Western Capitalism and State Socialism: An Introductory Text*, Oxford, Blackwell.

Drucker, P. (1974) *Management: Tasks, Responsibilities and Practices*, London, Heinemann.

Fox, A. (1974) *Beyond Contract: Work, Power and Trust Relations*, London, Faber.

Galbraith, J. (1967) *The New Industrial State*, Harmondsworth, Penguin.

Handy, C. (1984) *The Future of Work*, Oxford, Blackwell.

—— (1985) *Gods of Management*, London, Pan.

—— (1989) *The Age of Unreason*, London, Business Books.

Jenkins, C. and Sherman, B. (1979) *The Collapse of Work*, London, Eyre Methuen.

Kanter, R. (1983) *The Change Masters*, London, Allen & Unwin.

—— (1989) *When Giants Learn to Dance*, London, Simon & Schuster.

Kumar, K. (1989) 'Divisions and crisis in industrial capitalism', in R. Scase (ed.) *Industrial Societies: Crisis and Division in Western Capitalism and State Socialism*, London, Unwin Hyman.

Merton, R.K. (1964) *Social Theory and Social Structure*, Glencoe, IL, The Free Press.

Minkes, A. (1987) *The Entrepreneurial Manager*, Harmondsworth: Penguin.

Minzberg, H. (1979) *The Structuring of Organisations*, Englewood Cliffs, NJ, Prentice-Hall.

Nicholson, N. and West, M. (1988) *Managerial Job Change: Men and Women in Transition*, Cambridge, Cambridge University Press.

OECD (1989) *Education and the Economy in a Changing World*, Paris, OECD.

Ouchi, W. (1981) *The Theory Z Firm*, Reading, MA, Addison-Wesley.

Pahl, R. and Pahl, J. (1971) *Managers and their Wives*, Harmondsworth, Penguin.

Pascole, R. and Athos, A. (1982) *The Art of Japanese Management*, Harmondsworth, Penguin.

Peters, T. (1988) *Thinking on Chaos*, London, Macmillan.

Peters, T. and Waterman, R. (1982) *In Search of Excellence*, New York, Harper & Row.

Regional Reward Surveys (1985) *Executive Performance and Rewards*, London, Regional Reward Surveys.

Salaman, G. (1981) *Class and the Corporation*, London, Fontana.

Scase, R. and Goffee, R. (1987) *The Real World of the Small Business Owner* (2nd edn), London, Croom Helm.

—— (1989) *Reluctant Managers: Their Work and Life Styles*, London, Unwin Hyman.

Sofer, C. (1970) *Men in Mid-career: A Study of British Managers and Technical Specialists*, Cambridge: Cambridge University Press.

Wickens, P. (1987) *The Road to Nissan*, Basingstoke, Macmillan.

Young, M. and Willmott, P. (1973) *The Symmetrical Family: A Study of Work and Leisure in the London Region*, London, Routledge & Kegan Paul.

4

EDUCATION AND POST-FORDISM: A NEW CORRESPONDENCE?

Mike Hickox and Robert Moore

Our intention in this chapter is to focus upon the notion of 'post-fordism' and to explore its implications for education. In doing this, we are not accepting 'post-fordism' and the analysis that lies behind it at face value. Rather, we are approaching the idea as a current instance of a familiar tendency to attempt to make sense of events in education through an analysis of its relationship to the economy. Perhaps the most influential earlier examples of this are those of human capital theory and correspondence theory.[1] While not accepting post-fordism as a general analysis of an emerging new form of capitalism, we do, however, see it as glossing certain substantive changes within areas of production which might have significant educational implications. We will use our discussion of post-fordism as a way of exploring these implications and also, at a more general level, of focusing upon the problems of using general models of production as ways of making sense of education.[2]

Although post-fordism is particularly associated with a tendency in current marxist theory, the general form in which it depicts the changes occurring within the British economy are echoed in other areas, for instance the Training Agency (TA) (previously the Manpower Services Commission (MSC)). Hence the group which Ken Jones has called 'the conservative modernisers' (Jones 1989) present a similar picture of the developing requirements of the modern industrial economy. Within education in Britain, this position is associated with the Technical and Vocational Education Initiative (TVEI) (Dale *et al.* 1990) and is called upon to promote and justify a particular model of vocationalism. Interestingly, it is one which shares many features of liberal-progressivism in its emphasis upon process and experiential learning as opposed to either academic education or the traditional transmission of non-transferable craft skills. Whereas marxists employing the correspondence principle might be inclined to utilize post-fordism as a way of *explaining* educational change, the modernizers invoke it as a way of *legitimating* the changes they advocate.

Unlike 'the modernisers', the marxist proponents of post-fordism have paid little direct attention to education and, at the same time, post-fordism has yet to appear to any significant degree within the marxist sociology of education. However, given the position and influence of 'correspondence theory' over the past decade or more, it is clear that the concept of post-fordism could have clear implications for how marxists and others could come to conceptualize the emerging form of educational change.

It is possible to offer a simplified scenario whereby one form of correspondence, as outlined by Bowles and Gintis (1976), based on the manufacturing practices of the fordist era, gives way to another, more functionally adapted to the needs of post-fordist society. Thus one might argue that whereas the fordist production line demanded a robotic compliant worker, reproduced through a 'traditional' authoritarian pedagogy, the new post-fordist production line, with its stress on flexibility, decentralization and worker autonomy, will necessarily imply the adoption of a progressive form of education (although one shorn of its socially critical aspects) which lays the emphasis on pupil autonomy. This will be reinforced in post-fordism by the increasing significance of the critical, highly selective *consumer* as much as the flexible worker! Just as the mental/manual division was central to both the organization of work and the stratification of education in the fordist period, so it is inevitable that this distinction becomes blurred under post-fordism.

Certainly there are many elements of 'the new vocationalism' which might be used to fit such a theory. Thus the stress on pupil autonomy, process learning, the construction by students of their own learning packages (which form a central element of the TA's (TVEI) educational philosophy) might be interpreted, at least in part, as an attempt to produce the flexible, autonomous worker who 'learns to learn'. This might be interpreted as representing the emergence of a new form of education more appropriate to the needs of a post-fordist age. Certainly, advocates of 'the new vocationalism' tend to justify it in these terms. By the same token, one could argue that those who support a more 'respectful' traditional subject-based curriculum, of the kind proposed by neo-Conservative New Right educators in the 'Black Paper' tradition, are essentially still rooted within the preconceptions of the fordist era.

Without completely dissociating ourselves from analyses of this type, we would want to argue that the situation is considerably more complicated than such a simplistic model would imply. Thus we shall suggest that the post-fordist rhetoric of contemporary new vocationalists has relatively little relationship to any fundamental changes within the UK economy and that there is little evidence of any correspondence between education and the economy in the fordist period. Rather, we would claim that post-fordism may witness the beginnings of a type of limited correspondence *for the first time* in capitalist development.

As stated above, we are not committed to the view that post-fordism represents a completely new form of capitalist society, as proposed by recent contributors to *Marxism Today* (Murray 1988). Elsewhere in this volume Kumar provides a systematic critique of this concept. We shall use it as a useful device covering a number of loosely associated developments occurring within the economic structures of advanced industrial societies which have particular implications for the ways in which the labour process is organized. However, we believe that it is, in fact, difficult to make any distinct temporal divisions between 'fordist' and 'post-fordist' periods of industrialization since, in retrospect, it is obvious that many of the central elements of post-fordism have typified countries such as Sweden and Japan for much of the post-war period. Hence our use of the terms 'fordist/post-fordist' in what follows should be seen as reflecting a nominal rather than absolute periodization of capitalist development.

A further difficulty in establishing the nature of the correspondence between education and the economy in post-fordist society is the fact that currently there are several different models of post-fordism to choose from ranging from the small business driven industrial sector of 'the Third Italy' (favoured by the market right) to the statist quasi-corporatist economies of Germany and Sweden (typically favoured by the left). Nevertheless, it is clear that the advanced industrial economies will increasingly demand a skilled, flexible workforce and that systems of education will play a role either in directly providing them (the Swedish model) or in providing the basis on which later vocational training can be built (the German model).[3] However, there is no reason for supposing that the transition to post-fordism will involve a total transformation of the social structures of the societies concerned. As Paul Hirst (1989) has pointed out, several of the countries which have, in certain respects, moved furthest towards post-fordism (e.g. Japan and Germany) possess highly conservative social structures.

Finally, it is also important to acknowledge the highly diversified and uneven *local* distribution and development of industrial forms and accumulation strategies (Hudson 1988). This is true not only for notions of an emerging post-fordism, but also for fordism itself. This is particularly significant as far as education is concerned where vocationalist programmes or interventions tend to be organized around a model of some 'general' form or trend within the economy. Teachers are provided with a model of 'the needs of industry' (often presented through a celebratory rhetoric) which may bear little relationship to the actual conditions of their local labour market and its traditions. Ashton and Maguire (1986) have suggested that local labour market variations and their associated cultures may well be a more significant variable than class as such in shaping the variations in the work experiences of young people.

We shall set out, in this chapter, to do three things. First, we shall examine the relationship between education and the economy in the 'fordist' period and argue that this differs markedly from that suggested by Bowles and Gintis (1976) and other 'correspondence' theorists. This relationship, we will argue, was characterized by *weak* rather than *strong* linkage between the two systems.

Second, we shall argue that post-fordist developments do, however, suggest that education may be required to address more directly the immediate interests of production (especially as far as working-class education is concerned) *for the first time*.

Finally, looking more specifically at the case of Britain, we shall suggest that, here, 'post-fordism' (especially in the 'modernisers' variant) has operated more at the level of rhetoric than reality and has functioned chiefly to legitimate the activities of the Training Agency and others with a vested interest in the development of a 'new vocationalism' in education. The implication of this being that the New Right educational reforms of the 1980s are not (as correspondence theory might suggest) immediately intelligible in terms of a post-fordist picture of the British economy. In short, neither the British economy nor the Education Reform Act can be convincingly described as post-fordist.

POST-FORDISM

In essence 'post-fordism' can be seen as an attempt to conceptualize the developments occurring within the Western capitalist economies as a result of the economic crises of the 1970s and early 1980s and of increasing Japanese penetration of Western markets. Unlike post-industrial society theories of the 1960s (with which it has many elements in common), post-fordism has been developed as a concept largely within the context of marxist theory where it has been premised on the assumption of the collapse of traditional working-class politics and the search for new forms of resistance to capitalist domination. In this sense, it provides an interesting counterpart to the correspondence model which has dominated marxist approaches to the sociology of education.

We take post-fordism as consisting essentially of the following elements. At a general level there is an on-going shift from an economy based on manufacture to one based on services. At the same time there is a growth of rapidly changing and highly differentiated patterns of consumption involving frequent changes in taste which has important consequences for the organization of production. At one level there is a new emphasis on the role of design in the creation and marketing of products. Within the factory itself these changes are reflected in the development of flexible manufacturing systems involving short production runs which replace the high volume mass production of relatively standardized products which typified the classical fordist assembly line. With these changes comes a new emphasis on quality control and on 'right first time' manufacturing.

The appearance of 'the new production' (Coriot 1980) implies a reversal of many of the trends occurring within the fordist period, i.e. the de-skilling of the work process, the centralization of decision-making, and the separation between conception and execution, all of which were consequential upon the adoption of Taylorist techniques of 'scientific management' (Braverman 1974). Thus post-fordist manufacturing involves the decentralization of decision-making throughout the organization, in contrast with the hierarchical bureaucracies of fordism, together, typically, with a new drive to establish a 'trust culture' breaking down the barriers between management and workers involving the creation of quality circles and task groups. While Friedman (1977) has argued that 'direct control' and 'responsible autonomy' represent alternative management strategies for controlling labour throughout the history of capitalism, there can be little doubt that the post-fordist era sees a clear trend towards management adopting the latter technique. From this point of view, post-fordism can entail the reorganization of working practices (e.g. conditions of service) associated with *fordist* production processes as much as the introduction of new forms of production as such (see Hudson 1988).

It is fair to say that these developments have had little echo within the sociology of education, which, we shall argue, has continued to assume a pattern of industrial relations essentially rooted in the fordist period of industrialization. Thus, before going on to look more closely at post-fordism and education, it is necessary to look briefly at existing sociological theories concerning the relationship between education and the economy.

THE HISTORY OF CORRESPONDENCE

Although earlier, relatively crude versions of the theory have been abandoned, it is true to say that radical and marxist theories of education have been dominated by 'correspondence' theories since the publication of Bowles and Gintis's *Schooling in Capitalist America* (1976). In essence this holds that each level of the education system, through the mechanisms of the 'hidden curriculum', functions to transmit appropriate work habits and attitudes to those destined to enter the 'corresponding' sector of the occupational structure. Thus the 'hidden curriculum' of working-class education stresses rote learning and obedience, whereas that of middle-class education lays an emphasis on autonomy and personal creativity.

Correspondence theories have been extensively employed in the area of working-class education (curiously little attempt has been made to apply it to middle-class schooling). Typically it has been argued that, historically, the extension of education to the working class has been motivated primarily by a desire to maintain capitalist control over the workforce. Education is seen as an instrument by which previous attitudes towards work were replaced by those more congruent with the needs of the emerging factory system. Thus, far from education representing a liberating force, as liberal ideologies of education would suppose, it has, through a hierarchical and authoritarian pedagogy, operated as an instrument of capitalist oppression. This approach has been neatly summarized by one critic of correspondence theory who notes that 'a previous generation of Marxists criticised capitalism for denying education to the working class. Today's neo-Marxists criticise it for extending it to them' (Musgrove 1979: 72).

Correspondence theories of this type have been greatly reinforced by marxist analysis of the labour process, particularly that associated with the work of Braverman (1974). Using the fordist assembly line and Frederick Taylor's theories of 'scientific management' as his reference point, Braverman argues that the history of capitalism involves a systematic on-going deskilling of the workforce. This emphasis has dovetailed neatly with the analysis of the working-class 'hidden curriculum' taken by the Bowles and Gintis school. Similarly, Taylor's concern that there should be a separation between the sites of 'conception' and 'execution' within the factory, dividing a management stratum from the rest of the workforce, has given support to the assumption in correspondence theory that capitalist educational systems are divided along the lines of the 'mental/manual' division of labour.

This concern with the *relations* rather than with the *forces* of production has typically led correspondence theorists to reject human capital explanations of the growth of education in terms of its ability to transmit economically useful skills, these being seen as a smokescreen to conceal its deeper ideological purpose. However, correspondence theory has retained human capital's assumption that education is systematically related to the needs of the capitalist economy; instead of providing 'useful skills', it is seen as transmitting useful work habits and attitudes.

Implicit in correspondence theory is the notion that the extension of progressive, child-centred education to working-class children must necessarily tend to undermine capitalist relations of production since 'inappropriate' middle-class values of autonomy and creativity would be transmitted to those destined for occupations requiring obedience to authority. Undoubtedly this goes some way to explaining the strong links in Britain between proponents of the radical 'new sociology of education' of the early 1970s (with its strong progressive inclinations) and marxist theories. Correspondence theory seemed to offer a convincing explanation for resistance to the spread of progressive education. Thus the 'traditional educator' could be seen as a proxy for the wider interests of Capital. Consequently, it has been easy to depict the rise of the educational New Right in Britain during the 1980s as part of a more general 'Thatcherite project' to restore discipline to the workforce.

Criticisms of correspondence

Correspondence theory has been subjected to a wide variety of criticisms since its first appearance, a full discussion of which lies outside the scope of the present chapter (see Cole 1988). It is significant, perhaps, that these rarely focused on the labour process side of the equation where, as we have seen, correspondence theory assumes a fordist industrial structure with a mass of unskilled/semi-skilled workers subjected to direct supervision by a clearly demarcated and hierarchical management stratum. While this assumption has gone unchallenged, greater attention has been paid to correspondence theory's perceived neglect of issues relating to ethnicity and gender and to its failure to take account of working-class 'resistance' to capitalism within education. As a result, it has been argued, there has been a general failure on the part of correspondence theorists to give proper recognition to the 'relative autonomy' of the education system.

Given correspondence theory's basic explanatory principle, we would argue that a more significant criticism is that there is little evidence supporting the claim that education ever functioned as an important site of working-class socialization into appropriate work attitudes. In the nineteenth century, for instance, there appears to have been relatively little relationship between the industrialization process and the provision of mass schooling (see Musgrove 1979). As Marx himself noted, mid-nineteenth-century factory owners preferred the short-term benefits of cheap child labour to the more uncertain advantages to be gained from subsidizing working-class schooling. By the same token, 'control' theories of working-class education have typically ignored the extent to which, both in the nineteenth century and today, sections of the working class (particularly the skilled/respectable working class) have actively sought education for their children as an avenue of social mobility into the expanding white-collar sector. Finally, it has always been difficult to suppose that today's inner city comprehensives have ever functioned as an important site of working-class socialization. It is much more reasonable to see working-class attitudes to and expectations of work as deriving from sources other than formal education, i.e. the family, the peer group, and the wider working-class subculture.[4]

Education and the working class

The problems of correspondence theory, in this respect, were illuminated by Willis's influential, if much criticized, classic *Learning to Labour* (Willis 1977). As far as the position of white working-class boys is concerned, this now seems dated by the fact that it relates to a period before the impact of mass youth unemployment. Also, by concentrating on 'the Lads' to the exclusion of 'the Lobes', Willis understates working-class involvement in the education system, as Phil Brown (1987) argues. Nevertheless, despite these reservations, there can be little doubt that Willis offers a fundamentally accurate picture of attitudes towards education taken by white working-class boys destined for unskilled/semi-skilled employment in the UK's post-war, fordist industries.

This undoubtedly tends to undermine the fundamental tenets of correspondence theory since Willis clearly demonstrates the contempt felt by 'the Lads' for education and for the whole world of 'mental' labour. Nothing could be further from the Bowles and Gintis model of a passive and obedient working class being drilled into appropriate work habits by an authoritarian system of education. It would be a foolish capitalist who entrusts his fortunes to the contemporary comprehensive school.

Willis's work developed out of a cultural studies tradition which differs quite radically from the macro political economy perspective of Bowles and Gintis. Most significantly, as reflected in his ethnographic method, his approach was particularly sensitive to the (contradictory) internal dynamics of class cultural practices and their symbolic fields. Although feminist critics have attacked his apparant neglect of the gender issue, 'the Lads'' relationship to both education and labour can only be understood through reference to the construction of their masculinity. In this respect, the understanding of ideology in *Learning to Labour* is considerably more complex than that in *Schooling in Capitalist America*, which, in essence, remains within a simplistic socialization/value internalization model. As far as Willis's marxism is concerned, he again differed significantly from Bowles and Gintis in that he grounded his investigation of cultural practice and 'the educational exchange' within an understanding of labour from the point of view of value theory and commodity exchange relations.

The net effect of Willis's analysis was to demonstrate the *ineffectiveness* of schooling as an agency of occupational socialization. Indeed, in a significant sense, the school–work relationship is actually *reversed* in that it is precisely their anticipation of 'graft' and their knowledge of the cultural practices and collective skills of working life which positions 'the Lads' within the school and ensures their distancing from its effects. It is on the basis of what they *already know* about labour that 'the Lads' so effectively 'work' the school system. There is a deep educational pessimism in Willis's book in that it suggests that *nothing* the school could do would change 'the Lads' attitude and position. However, as we stated earlier, Willis's book predated the collapse of the youth labour market in the late 1970s. We will go on to suggest that this event, plus changes glossed by the term 'post-fordism', can be seen as effectively interrupting the intergenerational transmission of class cultural practices and the traditional collective skills of that section of the working class which 'the Lads' might be taken as representing.

Willis's work can be viewed as providing a detailed example of a more general finding within the literature on the relationship between working-class youth, the labour market, and the transition from school to work – namely the primacy of 'informal' processes both in effecting the transition into work (e.g. through social network recruitment) and in occupational socialization. The relative insignificance of schooling is reflected in the low priority given to formal educational criteria in employers' recruitment strategies[5] and in the apparently unimpaired capacity of the educationally least able or successful to adjust to working life (Clarke 1980a, b).

We would conclude that from the available evidence it would appear that working-class education in the post-war fordist period has provided *neither* useful skills (which are learned either on the job or through the apprenticeship system) *nor* appropriate work attitudes. Essentially it has functioned as a holding operation delaying entry to the labour market, a function which became increasingly problematic in the 1970s after the raising of the school-leaving age to 16 (in 1972) and the collapse of the youth labour market at the end of the decade. The basic error of correspondence theory has been to seek for deeper/hidden meanings within education when in fact these do not exist.

Education and the middle class

Turning to middle-class education, we have already noted that this has been strangely neglected by correspondence theorists. Arguably, in the post-war period elite education has increasingly abandoned its claims to transmit 'leadership qualities' through various character-building activities, a process reflected, for example, in the shift in the public school curriculum towards a greater emphasis upon examination success. The result has been a tendency in the post-war period for fractions of the middle class to come together at the cultural level through an increasingly shared educational experience.

The primary function of middle-class education has increasingly become that of furnishing the credentials necessary for entry to jobs in the expanding bureaucracies of both the public and private sectors, resulting in the creation of what Randal Collins (1981) has aptly termed 'The Credential Society'. By and large the process of 'credential inflation' which this has involved has enabled the possessors of 'cultural capital' to retain their differential advantage despite rising levels of working-class credentialization (Halsey *et al.* 1980). However, it is questionable how far the pursuit of the credential within middle-class education has been associated with a pedagogy stressing personal autonomy as correspondence theory assumes.

It is interesting to note how the New Right 'modernisers' version of the argument stresses the *lack* of correspondence between middle-class (liberal-humanist) education and the needs of industry. Following the highly influential 'Wiener thesis', elite education is seen as exhibiting an anti-industrial ethos reflecting the 'capture' of the education system by the bearers of an aristocratic landed ethic fundamentally hostile to the spirit of the industrial age (Wiener 1981). Thus, in keeping with the spirit of a Thatcherite age, the education system can be portrayed as the villain of the piece, depriving the middle class of its natural, entrepreneurial vigour![6]

However, both the correspondence and the modernizer versions fundamentally misunderstand the way in which education has evolved in the industrial period. In the first instance, the fact that industrial concerns were typically small-scale and family based meant that middle-class education received its first imprint from the demands of the expanding state bureaucracy, the first sector to recruit on the basis of educational credentials (Ringer 1969). In the subsequent fordist period, based on mass assembly techniques, the bureaucratic structures of industrial management, mimicking those of the state sector, meant that this form of education was enabled both to survive and prosper. Far from representing a pre-industrial hangover, it rather faithfully reflects the organization of production within the fordist period.

Education and fordism

It is true that during the fordist period education systems are typically stratified along mental/manual lines, but we would suggest that this is not systematically related to the organization of the work process in the way supposed by correspondence theories. The stress on de-skilling and 'direct control' at the manual level has meant that typically industry has, *in reality*, made *few demands* upon the education system beyond the provision of basic literacy. Indeed, employers have traditionally expected that working-class children entering industry would be undisciplined and require direct supervision. More mature attitudes to work would be expected to come later as a consequence of life-cycle changes, i.e. marriage and setting up a household (Blackburn and Mann 1977).

One might argue that the 'resistance' to schooling with which left sociologists of education have made so much play is itself built into the structures of fordist production which characteristically involves a trade-off between the benefits of high volume, low cost production on the one hand, and the cost that this entails in terms of worker resistance and alienation on the other. In this respect it is interesting to note that the two industrial societies which, in the post-war period, have gone farthest down the fordist path, the USA and the UK, have both been typified by strong anti-school, working-class youth subcultures.

In short, the lack of any marked pressures from the industrial sector within the fordist period allowed the education system to develop in a largely autonomous fashion. In turn, this has allowed for the educator dominance of the system, in terms of determining the curriculum, which has been such a marked feature of the fordist era. This has been as true of the highly centralized French system as of its more decentralized British equivalent. Professional educators have been in a position to act as 'gatekeepers' controlling the content of the credentials which they supply. One feature of this continued educator dominance has been the failure of successive attempts to create a more 'vocational' education system (Hickox and Moore 1989). While this has been especially true of the UK, it has also been true of France and Germany, both of which have witnessed a 'generalist shift' in education in the late nineteenth and early twentieth centuries and, indeed, today. It is, as Holt and Reid (1988) observe, ironic that while the MSC (Training Agency) and other influential pressure groups have struggled to drive British education down the vocationalist road in the name of increased economic efficiency, our 'major international competitors' are struggling to move back in the opposite direction.

Within this general context, different versions of the liberal-humanist educational ideology have vied with each other for pre-eminence. Within the British system, for example, the decentralization of education (among other factors) allowed for the development of a child-centred version of this ideology during the 1960s after the Plowden Report (Walkerdine 1989). While, arguably, this has had little impact outside the primary sector, it has maintained a strong challenge to what its proponents see as the alienating characteristics, in terms of both curriculum and pedagogy, of 'traditional' education. In the 1970s, as a result of the Newsom Report on non-academic pupils and the raising of the school leaving age (ROSLA), there developed an emphasis on 'relevance' and 'the world of work' in the secondary schools. However, the concept of 'skill' was essentially anti-industrial in spirit, invoking an earlier William Morris craft-based tradition – an anti-industrialism which, ironically, it shared with its traditional, subject-based competitor (Moore 1987).

POST-FORDISM AND EDUCATION: THE DEMISE OF THE LADS?

What, then, of post-fordism? If the term can be taken, at least minimally, as glossing a certain set of related tendencies within advanced industrial economies rather than their radical transformation, what might their implications be for education? We will suggest that, following from our analysis above, there are at least two substantive areas of interest.

First, post-fordism is characterized by the breakdown of industrial bureaucratic structures. The processes of managerial decentralization are associated with an 'entrepreneurial' rather than a 'bureaucratic' model of management and a correspondingly greater emphasis upon initiative flexibility, and autonomy as opposed to legal/rational routine (see Chapter 3).

We have suggested that middle-class education in the fordist period functioned essentially to provide the credentials necessary for entrance to and promotion within the centralized management bureaucracies of both the private and public sectors, thus allowing educators themselves to maintain control over the definition of education. This educator dominance, together with the autonomy of education, is likely to be challenged in the post-fordist era. One would predict – a process already becoming apparent – a tendency to teach 'management' as a separate skill on the basis of other skills already acquired, together with a greater attempt to transform the content of higher education in a more 'vocational' direction, e.g. the boom in business study courses, etc. Associated with this is the more general trend for graduates (especially in the humanities) to acquire postgraduate, professional qualifications. These trends can be seen as mediating the transition from higher education to work and weakening the hold of academic or educationalist constructions of appropriate socialization.

Second, at the manual level, the switch to short run, low volume production demands a much greater degree of efficiency and reliability amongst the workforce. In particular, this requires a degree of commitment and 'trust' which is incompatible with the previous reliance upon the class transmission of occupational social and technical skills and the associated degrees of worker alienation and resistance. As we have suggested, one of the dysfunctions for capitalism of stratified, fordist systems of education (although one which has gone curiously unnoticed by the defenders of correspondence) is precisely the way in which they allow class consciousness to be reproduced. In other words, *for the first time* the educational system might be required to intervene directly in the occupational socialization of working-class pupils, attempting to inculcate a 'possessive individualist' work ethic (Gleeson 1986; Moore 1987) which will replace loyalty to 'mates' with loyalty to 'the company'. Essentially, this entails the dislocation of the form of class cultural occupational socialization associated with social network recruitment, labour market cultures, and the acquisition of 'collective skills'. Certainly, in this sense, a 'correspondence' might be seen between the 'new vocationalism' and the new forms of working practice and conditions of service which 'post-fordist' companies impose upon the labour force in 'old industrial regions' under conditions of high unemployment (Hudson 1988).

In general, one might suppose that attempts would be made to decrease class consciousness and encouage notions of individual citizenship on the basis of a curriculum and pedagogy which attempts to involve pupils in a far greater commitment to the life of the school, providing an anticipatory socialization for the commitment required in later job performance. Thus one might predict, for example, a much greater emphasis on the importance of 'citizenship' in the school curriculum, as in the Swedish system. Conversely, school failure (i.e. evidence of non-commitment) may increasingly tend to mean membership of an 'underclass' relegated to unemployment or to marginal employment.

One thing is clear, whatever form they take, post-fordist economies will demand a more *committed* workforce; they will have no place for 'the Lads'. The new emphasis on flexibility and quality in manufacturing can no longer tolerate the shopfloor resistance which we have suggested is endemic to fordism.

POST-FORDISM AND EDUCATION IN THE UK: RHETORIC WITHOUT REALITY

While we would argue that there are long-term pressures within post-fordism for a closer integration between education and the occupational structures, we would be highly sceptical of any claim that would equate 'post-fordism' and 'the new vocationalism' in education in the context of the UK during the 1980s. Arguably, here the pressures towards vocationalism have derived much more from pressures *internal* to the education system (in terms of problems arising from credential inflation, of dealing with ROSLA, and 'the Newsom Child', etc.) and from immediate political panic created by rising youth unemployment than by any long-term drive to restructure the economy in a post-fordist direction (Hickox and Moore 1989). Indeed, Dale's (1989) metaphor of the MSC acting as a 'fire-brigade' to deal rapidly with immediate problems is extremely apt.

The net result has been, as other contributers to this volume argue, an improvised and ramshackle system of training, developing piecemeal both within and outside the formal education system, offering relatively low-level skills. Thus Prais (1989) has concluded that in Britain, as compared to the Continent, skills training has been low level, confined to the transmission of relatively simple non-transferable skills with negligible theoretical content. This, in itself, can be seen as an expression of the aggressively anti-academic bias of MSC/Training Agency ideology – a bias legitimated by a post-fordist rhetoric centring on the need to produce flexible, autonomous workers but which, in fact, excludes precisely that dimension of more general, theoretical knowledge which is the distinctive feature of more successful training systems abroad. As Ashton argues (Chapter 8, this volume), the net effect of this situation has been to increase the supply of semi-skilled labour for traditional industrial jobs which are on the decline.

Despite the modernizers' 'post-fordist' style of rhetoric, it is difficult, in fact, to see the results of their efforts (the YTS, TVEI, etc.) as representing a realistic reconstruction of training and education around the requirements of such an economy. Indeed, the MSC/TA's approach to training and its model of vocationalism, derived as they are from an essentially behaviouristic paradigm of skills acquisition, can be seen as deeply rooted in a fordist 'scientific management' tradition.

If questions can be raised about the 'post-fordist' character of the modernizers' own contribution to the educational reforms of the 1980s, even deeper reservations can be made concerning the other tendencies which have contributed to the New Right's programme. In particular, the influence of the neo-Conservatives (reflected, for instance, in the subject-based form of the National Curriculum) is difficult to reconcile with a 'post-fordist' restructuring of education. Indeed, their preoccupation with 'the National Heritage' and traditional values, and their rejection of 'relevance', links them with precisely that 'anti-industrial spirit' which the modernizers hold accountable for Britain's industrial decline. It is significant, in this respect, that the neo-Conservative preoccupation with the role of education in the inculcation of traditional moral values has figured much more centrally in public debates than the modernizers' concern with economic efficiency. The continuing debate around History in the National Curriculum is, perhaps, the prime example of this, but media coverage of issues connected with multicultural, anti-racist, and anti-sexist education played a considerable part in the construction of the agenda of educational reform. Both the National Curriculum and the Education Reform Act can be seen as having much more to do with the reconstruction of Britain's past than preparation of any post-fordist future.

Hence it is difficult to see either the modernizers' own contribution or the more pervasive influence of the neo-Conservatives on the educational reforms of the 1980s as realistically representing a 'post-fordist' reconstruction of the education system. As we suggest above, those features which could lend themselves to such an interpretation can be more plausibly accounted for in terms of problems *intrinsic* to education (essentially to do with educational expansion and credential inflation). It is also worth noting how commentators such as Maclure (1989) have pointed to the long-term (pre-Thatcher) character of the programme which culminated in the ERA as a

DES administrative strategy aimed at increasing central control at the expense of the LEAs and teaching profession. The origins of this strategy, it is suggested, are located within the context of the onset of recession in the mid-1970s.

Certainly, none of this is surprising given the fact that the UK economy in the 1980s has failed to develop in a post-fordist direction except in the one sense that its service sector has increased in significance *vis-à-vis* the industrial base. Thus a recent commentator has argued that most of the productivity gains in British industry in the Thatcher period were the result of shedding grossly inefficient plant rather than the provision of a better trained workforce and management (as will be required in the 1990s) (Leadbeater 1989).

Neither the 'new vocationalism' of the modernizers nor the more general framework of New Right educational reform can be unambiguously seen as reflecting a response to 'the needs of industry' in some new, post-fordist form. As Liz Gordon has observed, any attempt to interpret educational change in this fashion tends to be 'based on the theoretical assumption that the state intervenes on behalf of capital ... and that the state can know what the needs of capital are' (Gordon 1989b). The reservations which she records in her examination of the ACCESS Training Programme in New Zealand can well be extended to the British case. Whether as 'explanation' or 'legitimation' of educational change, appeals to the requirements of production invariably beg the question of how such requirements come to be formulated and translated into a coherent and effective educational programme. Underlying this is a more basic problem, namely that it is generally easier for the state (especially post-ERA) to generalize a form of education than it is to generalize a form of production. Hence the 'permeation' of a particular model of 'the world of work' (e.g. as in TVEI) throughout the education system can result in a pronounced lack of 'correspondence' between education and local labour market conditions (Dale *et al.* 1990).

Explanations which attempt to derive generalized accounts of educational change from models of economic development also tend to ignore the complexities of the competing interests involved in any educational reform programme. The tensions between modernizers, neo-liberals, and neo-Conservatives[8] in the British case illustrate this, as do the diversity of ideological purposes which 'education' comes to serve within political discourse (e.g. as a vehicle for constructs of citizenship and 'the Nation', of sexuality and race, for attacking Local Authority power, etc.).

At a more substantive level, numerous studies have indicated how the rhetoric of new vocationalist programmes in the schools tend to founder upon pupils' actual contacts with the *real* 'world of work' (Pollard *et al.* 1988). In part this reflects the earlier point made with reference to Willis's work, that pupils invariably already possess knowledge from their own experience, but such programmes can also undercut their own rhetoric through factory visits and work experience schemes. The celebratory post-fordist rhetoric is deflated by the fordist reality of so much of British manufacturing.

This illustrates a major problem entailed by any attempt to reconstruct education around a model of emerging 'new needs of the economy', namely the inevitability of its 'uneven development'. The immediate experience of 'the world of work' for so many young people bears little relationship to the modernizer's visions of post-fordism as they are embodied in 'the new vocationalism'. Indeed, it could be suggested that, given the distribution of youth unemployment in the 'old industrial regions', the exposure to a 'post-fordist new vocationalism' has been *inversely* related to the actual pattern of emergence of post-fordism in this country. The implications of this both for courses of this type and, perhaps, for post-fordism in Britain are aptly captured by the response of a group of pupils studied by Chris Shilling.

> On the journey back from the factory visit, I asked the group what they thought of the 'example' of the Japanese workers as illustrated by the manager. They had already been talking about this and, with the others nodding in agreement, three shouted out: 'they must be fuckin' mental – nutters!'
>
> (Shilling 1988: 104)

CONCLUSION

Our purpose has been to examine the implications of 'post-fordism' for understanding educational change. In that post-fordism, and the analysis of contemporary capitalism which it represents, is associated with a current in contemporary marxism, we have related our examination of the concept to 'correspondence theory' – the dominant approach in the marxist sociology of education. Whilst acknowledging an apparent parallel between accounts of the requirements of post-fordist production and 'the new vocationalism', we have taken issue with both 'correspondence' as a principle of explanation and, more substantively, with views of either the British economy or 'the new vocationalism' as convincingly 'post-fordist'. Contrarywise, we have also suggested, with reservations, that post-fordism may well carry with it implications for education which could entail a limited 'correspondence' between education and the direct requirements of production *for the first time*.

Moreover, the problems associated with generalizing a model of production within education are compounded by the complex and often contradictory purposes which 'education' comes to fulfil within the broader public and political discourse. In the British case, the tensions between the cultural authoritarianism of the neo-Conservatives and the quasi-progressivism of the modernizers well illustrate this issue. The intrinsic limitations on education's capacity to contribute directly to economic survival are intensified by the wider, contradictory agenda of problems to which it is required to provide solutions – to preserve the 'National Heritage' and traditional family, in addition to creating the modernized 'worker citizen' and privatized consumer.

NOTES

1 On the 'correspondence theory' see Bowles and Gintis (1976) and for discussion Cole (1988).
2 A particularly interesting critique of approaches in this area is to be found in Liz Gordon's paper *Beyond Relative Autonomy Theories in Education* (1989a).
3 See 'Swedish Schools', *Economist* 12 November 1988.
4 See in particular, here, the work of Margaret Grieco on 'social networks' in the labour market and the role of 'informal' processes in occupational socialisation and recruitment (Grieco 1987).
5 On employer recruitment strategies see in particular Ashton and Maguire (1986) and also Finn (1987).
6 On the implications of 'the Wiener thesis' see Moore and Ozga (1991).
7 See Whitty (1989), Quicke (1989), Hickox and Moore (1989).

REFERENCES

Ashton, D., Maguire, M., and Garland, J. (1983) *Youth in the Labour Market*, Research Paper 34, London, Department of Employment.

Ashton, D. and Maguire, M. (1986) *Young Adults in the Labour Market*, Research Paper 55, London, Department of Employment.

Blackburn, B. and Mann, M. (1977) *The Working Class and the Labour Market*, Basingstoke, Macmillan.

Bowles, S. and Gintis, H. (1976) *Schooling in Capitalist America*, London, Routledge & Kegan Paul.

Braverman, H. (1974) *Labor and Monopoly Capitalism: The Degradation of Work in the Twentieth Century*, New York, Monthly Review Press.

Brown, P. (1987) *Schooling Ordinary Kids*, London, Tavistock.

Clarke, L. (1980a) *The Transition from School to Work*, London, Department of Employment.

—— (1980b) *Occupational Choice*, London, Department of Employment.

Cole, M. (ed.) (1988) *Bowles and Gintis Revisited*, Lewes, Falmer Press.

Collins, R. (1981) *The Credential Society*, New York, Academic Press.

Coriot, B. (1980) 'The restructuring of the production line', *Capital and Class*, Summer.

Dale, R. (1989) *The State and Education Policy*, Milton Keynes, Open University Press.

Dale, R. *et al.* (1990) *The TVEI Story – Policy, Practice and Preparation for the Workforce*, Milton Keynes, Open University Press.

Finn, D. (1987) *Training Without Jobs*, Basingstoke, Macmillan.

Flude, M. and Hammer, M. (eds) (1989) *The Education Reform Act, 1988: Its Origins and Implications*, Lewes, Falmer Press.

Friedman, A.L. (1977) *Industry and Labour*, Basingstoke, Macmillan.

Gleeson, D. (1986) 'Life skills training and the politics of personal effectiveness', *Sociological Review* 34 (2), 381–95.

Gordon, L. (1989a) 'Beyond relative autonomy theories of the state', *British Journal of Sociology of Education*, 10 (4), 435–47.

—— (1989b) 'The ACCESS Training Programme: accumulation, legitimation, social control or a Trojan horse?', *New Zealand Sociology* 4 (2), 190–208.

Grieco, M. (1987) *Keeping it in the Family*, London, Tavistock.

Halsey, A.H., Heath, A. and Ridge, J. (1980) *Origins and Destinations*, Oxford, Clarendon Press.

Hickox, M. and Moore, R. (1989) 'TVEI, vocationalism and the crisis of liberal education', in M. Flude and M. Hammer (eds) *The Education Reform Act, 1988: Its Origins and Implications*, Lewes, Falmer Press.

Hirst, P. (1989) *After Thatcher*, London, Collins.

Holt, M. and Reid, W. (1988) 'Instrumentalism and education: 14–18 rhetoric and the 11–16 curriculum', in A. Pollard, J. Purvis, and G. Walford (eds) *Education, Training and the New Vocationalism*, Milton Keynes, Open University Press.

Hudson, R. (1988) 'Labour market changes and new forms of work in "old" industrial regions', in D. Massey and J. Allen (eds) *Uneven Redevelopment*, London, Hodder & Stoughton.

Jones, K. (1989) *Right Turn: The Conservative Revolution in Education*, London, Hutchinson.

Leadbeater, C. (1989) 'The price and pace of change', *Financial Times*, 7 September.

Maclure, S. (1989) *Education Re-formed: A Guide to the Education Reform Act of 1988*, London, Headway/Hodder & Stoughton.

Moore, R. (1987) 'Education and the ideology of production', *British Journal of Sociology of Education* 8(2).

Moore, R. and Ozga, J. (eds) (1991) *Curriculum Policy*, Oxford, Pergamon Press.

Murray, R. (1988) 'Life after Henry Ford', *Marxism Today*, October.

Musgrove, F. (1979) *School and the Social Order*, Chichester, Wiley.

Pollard, A., Purvis, J., and Walford, G. (eds) (1988) *Education, Training and the New Vocationalism*, Milton Keynes, Open University Press.

Prais, S.J. (1989) 'How Europe sees the new British initiative for standardising vocational qualifications', *National Economic Review*, August.

Quicke, J. (1989) 'The "New Right" and education', in B. Moon, P. Murphy, and J. Raynor (eds) *Policies for the Curriculum*, London, Hodder & Stoughton.

Ringer, F. (1969) *The Decline of the German Mandarins*, Harvard, Harvard University Press.

Shilling, C. (1988) 'The schools Vocational Programme: "Factories and Industry". A deficit project for the transition of youth from school to the labour market', in A. Pollard, J. Purvis, and G. Walford (eds) *Education, Training and the New Vocationalism*, Milton Keynes, Open University Press.

Walkerdine, V. (1989) 'Developmental psychology and the child-centred pedagogy: the insertion of Piaget into early education', in P. Murphy and B. Moon (eds) *Developments in Learning and Assessment*, London, Hodder & Stoughton.

Whitty, G. (1989) 'The New Right and the national curriculum: state control or market forces?' in M. Flude and M. Hammer (eds) *The Education Reform Act, 1988: Its Origins and Implications*, Lewes, Falmer Press, also in R. Moore and J. Ozga (eds) (1991) *Curriculum Policy*, Oxford, Pergamon Press.

Wiener, M. (1981) *English Culture and the Decline of the Industrial Spirit, 1850–1980*, London, Cambridge University Press.

Willis, P. (1977) *Learning to Labour*, Farnborough, Saxon Press.

5

EDUCATING FOR THE 'ENTERPRISE ECONOMY': A CRITICAL REVIEW

Gareth Rees and Teresa Rees

> I used to have a nightmare for the first six years in office that, when I had got the finances right, when I had got the law right, the deregulation etc., that the British sense of enterprise and initiative would have been killed off by socialism. I was really afraid that when I had got it all ready to spring back, it would no longer be there and it would not come back. ... I knew that if enterprise was still there it would come out. My agony was: had it been killed? By prices and incomes policies, by high taxation, by nationalisation, by central planning ...?
>
> But then it came. The face began to smile, the spirits began to lift, the pride returned.
>
> (Prime Minister Margaret Thatcher, from 'The Brian Walden Interview', *Sunday Times*, 8 May 1988)

INTRODUCTION

The creation of an 'enterprise economy' has become a keystone of government pronouncements on the resolution of Britain's economic ills. Central to this has been the development of an 'enterprise culture', designed to change the attitudes of young people towards industry and commerce generally; and, more specifically, to foster the notion that they should take responsibility for creating their own jobs. The 'education for enterprise' movement, in which both the state and employers have become increasingly involved, now provides a mechanism through which these attitude changes are sought. The concept of 'enterprise', however, has not been articulated clearly and constitutes a confused set of ideas and policy objectives. In consequence, we argue, the educational practices based upon these notions are incoherent. In what follows, therefore, we seek to clarify the concept of 'enterprise', separating out interpretations within the framework of New Right ideology, with which it has become almost exclusively associated in Britain, from alternatives which offer potentially useful approaches for both the education system and the development of the economy.

The underlying rationale for policies designed to foster the 'enterprise economy' is to create wealth. The principal method of achieving this has been to allow the 'wealth creators' free rein, unfettered by red tape. The main thrust of state activity in attempting to create an environment in which the 'wealth creators' can grow has been to deregulate, and to provide or sponsor a plethora of advice and support to people wanting to become self-employed or set up small businesses. The 'education for enterprise' movement, however, has tackled the other strand in the package of policies aimed at creating an 'enterprise economy', focusing upon the creation of 'enterprising' attitudes amongst young people, thus providing a *cultural* base for economic growth and change.

Clearly, it is difficult to argue a case against 'enterprise' and the development of enterprising qualities amongst young people, although whether such qualities can be *taught* is an issue frequently debated among educationalists. However, our argument here is that a radical distinction should be maintained between encouraging pupils to 'be enterprising' in all aspects of their lives, and the much more narrow range of activities that goes on in British schools in the name of 'enterprise', with many pupils subjected to a curriculum which is confined to self-employment and small business creation. In these latter cases, certainly, the extent to which pupils will generalize lessons learnt from their experience of 'education for enterprise' must necessarily be limited.

The chapter proceeds by means of a brief review of the role which the 'enterprise economy' has played in government policy. This is followed by an attempt to pin down the notion of 'enterprise' and its relationship to theories of 'entrepreneurship'. We then drawn out the implications of these arguments for educational practice, drawing especially on a case study of the Department of Education and Science (DES)/Department of

Trade and Industry (DTI) Mini-enterprise in Schools Project (MESP), which was set up, in part at least, to encourage young people to consider setting up in business (Jamieson *et al* 1988). Despite the rather dramatic shortcomings of this project, it is argued, nevertheless, that there are pedagogic and other benefits from 'enterprise education' which could be developed to address some of the economic and social needs of the contemporary situation. Indeed, governments which do not espouse a New Right ideology *are* producing contrasting and more effective models of 'enterprise education'. We conclude with some tentative proposals for an 'alternative enterprise economy'.

THE 'ENTERPRISE ECONOMY' IN GOVERNMENT POLICY

A decade ago, the principal focus of the government's economic strategy was the control of inflation, thereby producing the conditions in which the economy could flourish and 'real' jobs be created. More recently, and especially since 1983, the creation of an 'enterprise economy' has emerged as the central element in the government's attempt to strengthen the British economic performance. As the 1986 White Paper, *Building Businesses ... Not Barriers*, put it:

> The prime aim of the Department of Employment is to encourage the development of an enterprise economy. The way to reduce unemployment is through more businesses, more self employment and greater wealth creation, all leading to more jobs.
>
> (Department of Employment 1986: i)

More specifically, it is the fostering of *wealth creation* that has come to be prioritized:

> the aim of our policy is thus to encourage the process of wealth creation by stimulating individual initiative and enterprise and by promoting an understanding of market opportunities combined with the ability to exploit them.
>
> (Department of Trade and Industry 1988a: iii)

Hence, the appropriate function of the state is to 'create the right climate so that markets work better and to encourage enterprise' (Department of Trade and Industry 1988a: ii), thereby generating the kind of economic conditions in which the individual wealth creators are allowed the opportunities to make the most 'sensible economic decisions'. And, by implication at least, this will lead to the fulfilment of more concrete objectives, such as the reduction of unemployment.

At the most general level the creation of this 'enterprise economy' can be seen to involve a number of distinct, albeit closely related, objectives. First, there is a clear intention to strengthen the links between government and industry. Thus, for example, civil servants are being seconded to non-executive directorships in – instructively – larger companies; whilst, more generally, they are being required to seek out the views of the private sector.

Second, the removal of perceived bureaucratic barriers has been identified as a key mechanism in 'releasing enterprise' (Department of Trade and Industry 1988b). Now, for example, each regulatory department of government has an 'Enterprise and Deregulation Unit' to ensure 'a permanent and pervasive increase in the value put on the needs of business in all government departments' (Department of Trade and Industry 1988b). Similarly, the abolition of the Wages Councils and minimum wages protection is aimed at improving the flow into employment, with an income support system purportedly protecting the position of low-wage workers.

Third, and for present purposes crucially, the government aims to effect a wholesale change in attitudes towards industry and commerce, thereby breaking down what has been widely viewed as a characteristically British cultural flaw: antipathy to business enterprise and initiative. Accordingly, for instance, teachers are increasingly being required to gain direct experience of business through secondments and new forms of training; whilst employers are becoming increasingly involved with curriculum development and management at all levels of the educational system. Similarly, pupils and students are being exposed much more directly to the world of industry and commerce.

Within this general framework, particular importance has been attached to the role of small business owners and the self-employed. Certainly, recent years have witnessed the growth of an almost bewildering plethora of state initiatives aimed at fostering their growth, which illustrate very clearly the implementation of the government's wider strategy. Indeed, many of these initiatives were revamped and brought together into a coherent package in the DTI's 'Enterprise Initiative' in 1988 (Department of Trade and Industry 1988a).[1] They include: providing support to encourage small business growth (for example, through the Business Growth Training scheme[2] and the Research and Technology Initiative);[3] offering direct financial assistance to encourage self-employment (through the Enterprise Allowance Scheme);[4] indirect financial assistance (through, for instance, raising the VAT threshold); the provision of premises (as in government factory-building programmes); the relaxation of bureaucratic procedures (as, for example, in the Enterprise Zones); the provision of advice and support services (through, for instance, Enterprise Agencies or the Small Firms Service); and the expansion of 'enterprise education and training' in a variety of educational institutions (as, for example, in MESP, the DTI's Teacher Company Scheme and the Training Agency's Enterprise in Higher Education Initiative).[5] Moreover, these central government initiatives are supplemented by those which have been undertaken by regional development agencies and a large number of local authorities.

There is, then, an important sense in which small business owners and the self-employed are paradigmatic of the 'wealth creators' who lie at the heart of the government's wider strategy. Hence, new small-scale firms are widely believed to constitute an especially dynamic sector of an economy and thus to provide an effective basis for the improvement of competitiveness through the development of innovative products and technologies. In the longer run, they may grow into the corporate giants of the future, providing the cornerstone of a revitalized economy. Equally, it is commonly held that small firms and self-employment constitute the most significant source of new jobs in current economic conditions. Moreover, it has frequently been suggested that the quality of the working environment in smaller firms is superior to that in larger ones, thereby contributing to a greater sense of work satisfaction and fulfilment. Perhaps most important of all, however, small business owners and the self-employed are viewed as encapsulating the attitudes and orientations towards business and commerce which express the 'enterprise culture'. Therefore, it is essential not only that the bureaucratic impediments of state controls be removed, but also that every encouragement be given to the fostering of the initiative and innovation which they express.

Accordingly, government sees a role for itself in creating an appropriate climate for wealth generation not simply by removing tiresome, costly barriers and providing encouraging initiatives and incentives, but in contributing to a shift in attitudes towards industry and commerce. What is being attempted, then, is a wholesale resocialization of the population at large into accepting and indeed prioritizing the goals of business and wealth creation. Moreover, it is the small business sector which provides the crucial model here and is viewed as embodying this 'spirit of enterprise'. Not surprisingly, therefore, this is the exemplar offered to school pupils in 'education for enterprise'. In reality, however, there are numerous confusions involved in this programme, relating both to the conceptual framework which informs it, as well as its practical implications.

CONCEPTUALIZING THE 'ENTERPRISE ECONOMY'

The close identification of the 'enterprise economy' and the culture which supports it with individual small business and self-employment in fact represents a wholly unwarranted elision. The key here is the concept of 'enterprise' itself and how it relates to proximate notions such as 'entrepreneurship'. In much conventional theorizing of economic growth (after Schumpeter, for example), a central role has been accorded to the individual entrepreneur as a source of *innovation* and a bearer of the *risk* thereby involved. More recently, writers about small business have adopted a somewhat broader, but essentially equivalent perspective; for example, Curran and Burrows (1987) have defined 'entrepreneurship' as:

> the innovatory process involved in the creation of a new economic enterprise based on a new product or service which differs from products and services offered by others in content, or in the way its production is organised, or in its marketing.
>
> (p. 165)

And this emphasis upon innovation and risk-bearing is more than a narrowly academic matter, in that it is central to the idea that entrepreneurship provides a source of something that is actually new to an economy and that therefore contributes 'value-added' to the existing form and levels of economic activity.

It is clear, however, that this conceptualization of 'entrepreneurship' actually excludes the overwhelming majority of small businesses and single person enterprises. Most of these simply replicate existing businesses and, indeed, where they start up from scratch may do no more than displace other businesses already in operation (with no *necessary* contribution to either wealth creation or employment growth). In addition, of course, many small business owners inherit or purchase existing enterprises, adding little or nothing that is novel to their operation.

Necessarily, then, for the government at least, the 'enterprise culture' embodies more than simply 'entrepreneurship' defined in these strict terms. It would appear that it also embraces a much more diffuse conceptualization in which the fostering of 'enterprise' is viewed as generating a sea-change in societal attitudes with respect not only to business activity, but also individual responsibilities more widely. In this sense, then, small business and self-employment are at the heart of the *social* transformation which has been undertaken by the government. The argument is put well by Scase and Goffee:

> this same entrepreneurship would contribute to a culture emphasising self-reliance and personal responsibility such that governments could increasingly withdraw from economic management and the provision of a wide range of personal, social and welfare services. For many then the example set by entrepreneurs offers a solution to the institutional, attitudinal and cultural ills of present-day Western societies. Thus, it is necessary to return to the core values of Western capitalism, represented by those people.
> (1980: 11)

Two points should be made here, however. First, the relationships between this broadly-based transformation in attitudes and economic development are not clearly specified. Second, we have no firm evidence as to whether such a *cultural* shift is actually taking place. Moreover, it is difficult to see how such evidence could be obtained, given that it would be necessary to know about attitudinal changes in the population at large (not simply amongst small business owners and the self-employed).

The *British Social Attitudes* surveys, conducted annually by Social and Community Planning Research, are the nearest we have to such a source. A recent edition (Jowell, Witherspoon, and Brook 1988) in fact indicates that since 1983, there has been a growing *alienation* from some of the values that might be assumed to underlie an 'enterprise culture'. For example, there is a widespread view that profits from business disproportionately benefit businessmen, share-holders, and managers at the expense of the workforce, customers, and investment. There is little support for privatization of health and education or for cuts in public expenditure. Indeed, Jowell and Topf (1988) maintain that: 'To the extent that attitudes have moved, they have become less sympathetic to these central tenets of the "Thatcher Revolution". ... the British are improbable revolutionaries, even in support of this kind of revolution' (p. 121).

These arguments are of no little significance, as it would require such a *general* shift in attitudes for the 'enterprise culture' to become self-sustaining. Moreover, they expose some of the frailties of a strategy based upon the promotion of 'enterprising' values and attitudes.

THE DEVELOPMENT OF THE 'ENTERPRISE ECONOMY'

It is also clear that serious *empirical* problems arise with a conceptualization of the 'enterprise economy' based upon small businesses and self-employment. Initially, these involve straightforward statistical difficulties as to what should 'count' as a *small* business and *self*-employment. Hence, for example, it has been widely acknowledged that any arbitrary (in itself problematic) cut-off in terms of size of workforce, turnover, market share, and so forth ignores the very real differences between types of economic activity: a 'small' car assembly plant employs far more people than a 'large' firm of solicitors. Similarly, the growth of various forms of sub-contracting, franchising, and homeworking has considerably blurred the notion of self-employment; quite apart from the fact that the legal incorporation of a firm in itself officially switches individuals from self-employment to employed status (see Hakim 1988 for a fuller discussion).

Given these statistical and conceptual problems, it is difficult to be *categorical* about the actual trends with respect to small business ownership and self-employment in the British economy as a whole. Nevertheless, it is clear that those commentators who have regarded the small firm as a relic of an earlier stage of economic development, which would wither away with the emergence of more modern forms of economic organization, are quite simply mistaken. Hence, for example, not only do smaller businesses (with fewer than 100 employees) continue to constitute the overwhelming bulk of firms in manufacturing (95 per cent of all British manufacturing enterprises in 1980), but they also account for some 20 per cent of employment and output. In other sectors of the economy, small firms are even more important: in retailing, private sector professional and scientific services, and construction, for example, they employ about half of those working in these sectors (see Hakim 1988).

More importantly, there has been a significant growth of small manufacturing firms, by some 25 per cent during the 1960s and 1970s; and this trend has accelerated through the 1980s. However, Britain still has a smaller proportion of small enterprises than its major economic competitors such as Japan or the United States. It is also clear that self-employment (including employers and self-account workers) has risen especially sharply during the 1980s, having declined somewhat through the 1970s. Thus, the *Labour Force Surveys* reveal a 34 per cent increase between 1981 and 1987, for example.

Crucially, however, these growth trends cannot be attributed to a single cause or even set of causes. For some commentators – on both the right and the left – the growth of small business and self-employment is to be interpreted as an essentially positive development, reflecting the emergence of a new phase of capitalist economic activity. Hence the increasing sophistication of (especially computer-related) technologies, as well as the growing differentiation of product markets, has created the space for the growth of 'flexibly specialized' manufacturing firms, whose small size is a distinct advantage (and certainly not a hindrance) in fulfilling the demands of both intermediate and final customers (see for example Piore and Sabel 1984). Similarly, the increasing significance of many producer and consumer services has opened up opportunities for small firms and self-account workers better able to respond to highly differentiated and quickly changing markets.

For others, however, it is the recession of the late 1970s and earlier 1980s which provides the essential context for the growth in small enterprises. In the same way that, for example, the inter-war years in Britain witnessed an upsurge in the formation of new small businesses (see Foreman-Peck 1985), so in the most recent economic down-turn conditions have been conducive to parallel trends. Hence it is frequently argued that an important response to difficult market conditions has been for larger firms to increase their 'flexibility' by a combination of sub-contracting, franchising, and home-working (*inter alia*), all of which have increased the range of opportunities for both small firms and self-employed workers to thrive (Hakim 1987).

In addition, the growth in levels of unemployment associated with the recession has increased the pool of individuals for whom the creation of a small business or own-account working is rendered an attractive option, in the absence of realistic opportunities for re-entry to employment. Rubery (1988), for instance, draws attention to the definitional difficulties implied by the overlap between self-employment, home-working, free-lancing, and small businesses with respect to their relationships to the market. Many self-employed people who have taken this option to avoid unemployment have the same subordinate market position as home-workers have traditionally experienced, although the label 'self-employed' does not necessarily imply this.

Our purpose here is not, of course, to judge the merits of these various accounts. Rather, it is to emphasize the *diversity* of small businesses and self-employment, a diversity that is being intensified during the current phase of growth. It seems likely that the latter is the outcome of some *combination* of the processes which have been sketched, as well, of course, as government policy itself.

ENTREPRENEURS IN THE 'ENTERPRISE ECONOMY'

Precisely because it is the outcome of wider processes of economic development, the diversity of small businesses and self-employment is not a random phenomenon. Rather, it is structured by virtue of the differing characteristics and resources which individuals bring with them when they set up on their own; and by the highly uneven distribution of opportunities for *successful* small enterprises in different local economies.

Individuals setting up in business have often been distinguished (from employees) by their individualistic attitudes and commitment to values of independence, flexibility, choice, and freedom. While there is *some* empirical support for this view, it is far from providing evidence of a coherent 'entrepreneurial spirit', still less an 'entrepreneurial personality' (cf. Hakim 1988). On the contrary, it has been suggested that the affirmation of such values represents for some small business owners a *rationalization* of an extremely difficult work situation, in which long hours and uncertain financial rewards co-exist with a considerable vulnerability in terms of sources of capital, markets, and so forth. Indeed, Bechhofer *et al.* (1974) concluded that the 'entrepreneurial spirit' was wholly absent from their sample of small shopkeepers; and general surveys of the 'work ethic' reveal few or no differences between the employed, unemployed, and self-employed in terms of the significance of work as a means of self-expression or achievement (Hakim 1988).

The available evidence would thus seem to suggest that there is almost as diverse a set of attitudes and beliefs amongst small business owners and the self-employed as in the population as a whole. Whilst this conclusion is clearly at odds with some of the presuppositions of government policy, it should not be wholly surprising, given our earlier arguments about the diversity of small enterprises themselves. Hence, it is simply not apparent why one should expect similar attitudes to be displayed by, say, the founder and owner-manager of an advanced bio-technology firm, the inheritor and owner-manager of a corner shop, and a self-employed welder who has set up on his own account in the absence of satisfactory employment.

Moreover, very little is known about the role which attitudes play in determining the *flow* of people into small business ownership and self-employment, particularly during the growth period of the 1980s. And it is this which arguably is most crucial to attempts by the state to foster appropriately 'enterprising' attitudes amongst young people and others. Recent work by the Department of Employment, for example, revealed that for new entrants to self-employment between 1983 and 1987, the desire to be self-employed was the primary stimulus for the majority of entrants, rather than any specific business idea; and this was closely associated with notions of the benefits of working for oneself, rather than an employer. But equally, between one-fifth and one-third of respondents identified themselves as involuntary or at least reluctant entrants to self-employment, in the absence of realistic opportunities of appropriate employment (Bevan *et al.* 1989). Similarly, respondents in a study of the self-employed in Pontypool (in South Wales) 'chose' self-employment in preference to unemployment, but hoped that the arrangement would be temporary; an opportunity to become an employee again would be quickly seized (Miller *et al* 1988). This reluctance to embrace the ethos of self-employment, with its avowed virtues of autonomy and working for oneself, is scarcely surprising in the low-capital, labour-intensive businesses that Miller and his colleagues studied. Moving into self-employment meant taking on the risks normally shouldered by much larger organizations, more able to weather market fluctuations and other vicissitudes. Moreover this reluctance to become self-employed is partly due to a recognition that the propensity to form a new firm and, perhaps more particularly, the propensity of that firm to grow once established, are closely linked with the resources to which the individual 'entrepreneur' has access. For example, Storey (1982) has argued that previous managerial experience (especially, but not exclusively, in a small firm), previous job experience in the chosen market, as well as more general educational attainment, all provide significant advantages in the establishment of successful small enterprises. Similarly, the availability of capital, whether from the private sector, the state, or family sources, has also been shown to play a major role. Moreover, the family has frequently been identified as a major source of support more generally, potentially providing not simply capital, but also labour, business contacts, and advice.

What these arguments suggest, therefore, is that the nature and extent of labour market opportunities offered by small businesses and self-employment are structured by the characteristics and resources which individuals bring with them. There is little support for the view that an 'entrepreneurial spirit' is a sufficient or even necessary qualification *generally* for entry to the 'enterprise economy'. Rather, whilst certain 'types' of individual may set up on their own or in family businesses because of the absence of satisfactory alternatives, the crucial factors in determining both the quality and the likely future success of a small enterprise are the possession or otherwise of critical resources, which themselves reflect the exigencies of the market. And again, it is the diversity of the activities subsumed within the 'small business sector' which is most striking. Whilst neither is guaranteed success, there is all the difference in the world between, say, a redundant miner using his redundancy payment and the Enterprise Allowance Scheme (see Note 4) to set up as a window-cleaner or taxi-driver and a computer scientist establishing an innovative high-tech firm, financed by private sector venture capital.

Moreover, 'entrepreneurs' bring these differential resources to bear within widely disparate economic contexts. Most obviously, the market opportunities available vary sharply both regionally and from one kind of local economy to another. And, of course, this is reflected in the actual rates of new firm formation. Hence, during the 1980s, the south east of England recorded the greatest net gains (31 per cent), while 'outer Britain' – the north of England, Wales, Scotland, and Northern Ireland – were by no means as successful. Similarly, the 1989 *Labour Force Survey* reveals that, although self-employment in Britain as a whole increased from 9.5 per cent of all employed in 1983 to 12.3 per cent in 1988, there were stark regional variations, with the greatest growth occurring in the south east, East Anglia and Yorkshire and Humberside and the least in the north and Scotland (Department of Trade and Industry 1989).

Given these factors, therefore, how appropriate is it to encourage young people to start up in business through the 'education for enterprise' movement?

EDUCATION FOR ENTERPRISE

The then Labour Prime Minister James Callaghan's speech at Ruskin College, Oxford, in 1976 was a landmark in the tradition of criticizing the education system as the cause of school-leavers' unfavourable attitudes towards industry and purportedly inadequate standards of literacy and numeracy. Schools were accused of fostering anti-business attitudes, and for being at least partly responsible for the rising tide of youth unemployment.

The conclusive evidence for declining standards was never produced; indeed, it seems likely that what was happening was that the requirements of employers were increasing at a faster rate than educational attainment levels (Finn 1982). Nevertheless, the 'Great Debate' that followed the speech served to focus criticism of the 'liberal' comprehensive schools, where the emphasis on ensuring 'equality of opportunity' was viewed as having produced unemployable young people with inappropriate career aspirations.

During the Conservative administrations since 1979, the education system has remained a focal point of political concern. State control over what is taught has been increased with the advent of the National Curriculum, while policies have been introduced to encourage what Brown (1990) has dubbed 'the ideology of parentocracy', where: 'the education a child receives is increasingly dependent upon the *wealth* and *wishes of parents* rather than the *abilities* and *efforts* of pupils' (p. 66). Moreover, the government's concerns about the shortcomings of school-leavers in the 1980s have remained focused upon their lack of enthusiasm for industry and commerce. Somewhat paradoxically, they have also been criticized for their alleged preoccupation with certification as a route to employment and consequent unwillingness to entertain ideas about creating jobs for themselves. Hence, government strategy has sought to alter these attitudes, and to imbue young people with enthusiasm for the 'enterprise economy'.

A major vehicle for bringing about these changes has been the expanding 'education for enterprise' movement. In fact, Young Enterprise, a voluntary organization funded by industry, predates the Thatcher era; it has been in existence for some twenty-five years and acts as a catalyst for sixth-formers wanting to experience 'enterprise education' as an extra-curricular activity. Again, in the 1970s, there was much talk of the development of young people's control over their own lives, or 'empowerment', an objective supported by the left and the right. The spirit of this type of 'enterprise education' is conveyed by the definition offered by IFAPLAN, the Colgne-based social research agency, which has been heavily involved in both of the European Commission's Programmes of Action on the Transition from Education to Adult Life.

> [Enterprise education is a] collective term for educational or training provision aiming at influencing youngsters' attitudes and behaviour in such a way that they show more initiative and play a more active and independent role in mastering their future.
>
> (IFAPLAN 1986: 9)

On this view, therefore, 'enterprise education' has the pedagogic goals of engaging pupils in activities which will release skills and talents that are broader than a narrow emphasis on academic attainment allows.

During the 1980s in Britain, however, the concept has been commandeered by the government and industrial and commercial interests, seeking to foster the notion among young people that they should create their own jobs through self-employment or setting up a small business. The message is that one should no longer rely upon acquiring qualifications as a route to employment. This dependency upon employers should give way to a realization that the onus to create a job falls upon the individual concerned. And accordingly, the role of 'enterprise education' becomes restricted to giving young people the experience of running a 'mini-company'.

Jamieson (1984) has attempted to systematize these diverse approaches to 'enterprise education'. He identifies three key reasons for schools to engage in 'enterprise education', each of which would produce different models of practice. Hence, schools may seek to: (a) educate young people to start up their own business; (b) develop a curriculum which fosters skills, attitudes, and values appropriate to starting, owning, managing, or working in a successful business; or (c) develop enterprising pupils, with the skills, knowledge, and attitudes to create their own futures and solve their own problems. Crompton (1989) argues that these three positions can be described as 'education *for* enterprise', 'education *about* enterprise', and 'education *through* enterprise'. Moreover, he suggests that underpinning these three perspectives are two opposing, but not wholly contradictory, versions of the 'enterprise culture'.

> The first is dominated by the concern to regenerate the economy through educational programmes that promote an understanding of the processes of 'wealth creation',

> fosters positive attitudes to entrepreneurialism and employment, and provides relevant skills. The second takes the broader view that enterprise or the ability to be enterprising will be an essential survival tool for the individual in a rapidly changing society and that this approach will be required to solve a variety of social, environmental, political, and economic problems. This second perspective demands that enterprise is seen as a theme for the whole curriculum and not as a specific component of education for 'working life'.
>
> (Crompton 1990: 17)

In these terms, therefore, although 'enterprise education' in *all* its forms has grown considerably during the 1980s, it is 'education *for* enterprise' which has been particularly prominent. Indeed, a variety of initiatives has been established or expanded which focus 'enterprise education' firmly on the experience of starting and running a business.

One of the most important examples here is the DTI/DES Mini-enterprise in Schools Project (MESP), which has become increasingly widespread and is well on the way to achieving its objective of ensuring that every secondary school in England and Wales undertakes a 'mini-enterprise' (a school-based company managed by pupils and delivering a real product or service to a customer). The National Westminster Bank, the British Steel Corporation, and the Durham Business School provide between them resources, training, and information packs which help schools in setting up the businesses. The Schools Curriculum Industry Partnership (SCIP) has now merged with MESP, and its programme has been expanded to cover most local education authorities. In Wales, the Welsh Development Agency's Youth Initiative Programme (YIP) involves an increasing number of schools in 'enterprise education'. Moreover, 'education for enterprise' is fast becoming an established part of the curriculum. MESP is now part of the GCSE Business Studies curriculum, and it is suggested that over a third of 'mini-enterprises' in England and nearly half in Wales are curriculum-based (Department of Education and Science 1987; Welsh Office 1987). In addition, there is clearly scope for locating 'enterprise education' firmly within the National Curriculum (Crompton 1990).

In pedagogical terms, 'education for enterprise' of the kind offered through MESP has come to mean a number of things. It has a problem-solving focus and accordingly draws on a variety of conventional disciplines, emphasizing pupils' experiential learning. The projects are intended to be student-led and there is active involvement of people from outside the school – 'Adults Other than Teachers' (AOTs). The approach appears particularly successful in engaging the less academically able; it gives them an opportunity to become involved and do well in an alternative merit system. Truants and difficult children, it is argued, also find this form of 'enterprise education' especially rewarding. Given the orientation of the education system towards producing an elite of recruits for higher education, this is a welcome development. Moreover, there is now considerable debate about how experiences in 'mini-companies' can be followed through to ensure the development of opportunities for progression, rather than providing just a one-off experience.

Rather surprisingly, there has been very little stringent, empirical documentation of these various initiatives in schools or pupils' reactions to them. However, although the DTI/DES evaluation of MESP was commissioned surprisingly late in the day, given its experimental nature and what it represented in terms of new funding for the education system, it does provide some firm empirical evidence for the assessment of the project.[6]

Hence, pupils' reactions to MESP were on the whole found to be favourable: they claimed that it taught them about teamwork, developed their confidence, proved to them the importance of effective communication, and they felt that it was a 'better way to learn' than the more traditional teaching methods offered (Williamson 1989a). However, they also reported an 'overwhelming difficulty' in thinking of a competitive product or service. Just as the small business sector is itself far from characterized by innovative, 'enterprising' concerns, so too the 'mini-companies' were on the whole rather limited, with a narrow range of products and services: trading in sweets or marketing stationery, providing baby-sitting, running a sandwich shop or carwashing. Indeed, in some schools, the task of identifying a business idea was rendered unnecessary: each year a new cohort of pupils took over the running of an existing school-based business, such as the tuck shop.

The evaluation also revealed that the businesses were not

necessarily student-led, although this has always been cited as one of the pedagogical advantages of 'education for enterprise'. There was substantial cushioning from real risk through minimal capital outlay, the potential for loans to be written off, the short-term nature of the enterprise and teachers' ultimate control. In addition, traditional gender roles were found to pertain in mixed groups; although there were examples of all-girl enterprises which undoubtedly have the potential for beneficial de-stereotyping and confidence-building.

It is also clear from Williamson's (1989a) study that running a 'mini-enterprise' is a time-consuming business. So much so that 'the demands of MESP work encroached on students' capacity to get on with their course work'. This time-cost jeopardizes participants' performance in certificated examinations and means, therefore, that it is the less academically able children who are targeted for 'enterprise education', with inevitable consequences for their accumulation of qualifications. Indeed, 'education for enterprise' may be challenged, in similar terms to the Technical and Vocational Training Initiative (TVEI), as having the effect of increasing the polarization of formal certificated educational attainment levels of pupils.

More generally, too, there are a number of concerns here. First, the small business model is becoming so established in schools that the potential of alternative forms of economic organization, such as co-operatives or community business, are hardly considered. Second, the focus on the small business and the consequent privileging of the profit motive implies that other organizational forms which combine income generation for participants with wider social goals, such as community development, are not offered to young people as realistic alternatives. The profit motive becomes a taken-for-granted part of their cultural repertoire. And, of course, this is a key element in the state's objectives for the project and 'enterprise education' more widely.

Third, and perhaps most significantly, the focus on providing youngsters with experience of running a school-based company carries with it its own version of 'blaming the victim', reproducing in a different form the underlying rationales of earlier policies to combat youth unemployment (for example, Atkinson *et al.* 1982). Thus, it endorses a New Right *moral* appraisal of individuals who 'choose' unemployment rather than starting their own business. However, encouraging young people to think that anyone can start a business and succeed is to violate the mass of empirical evidence, which we reviewed at some length earlier, demonstrating that there is a whole range of characteristics that successful entrepreneurs *normally* possess and which are not evenly distributed through the population.

As we have seen, then, young people are likely to be seriously disadvantaged in their access to the key social resources of experience, knowledge, and training, as well as to sources of finance. Moreover, those most at risk of unemployment are likely to live in localities and regions which are the least promising for a business start-up. In short, the odds are stacked heavily against their creating a business that would do more than provide a highly precarious living.

The message which is clearly embodied in 'education for enterprise' programmes, however, is that if you cannot find a job, you have been trained to create your own. If you try the latter avenue and fail, it is the result of your own inadequacies. Accordingly, the responsibility for ensuring participation in productive activity shifts away from the state and on to the individual. In this way, therefore, 'enterprise education' programmes can be seen to play a significant role in the rather fundamental changes in societal organization at which the fostering of the 'enterprise economy' is aimed.

'ENTERPRISING EDUCATION' FOR AN 'ENTERPRISING ECONOMY': AN ALTERNATIVE PROGRAMME

The key to the development of a more effective 'enterprise education' is to detach it from the exclusive concern with small business and self-employment which is embodied in the 'education for enterprise' model. Moreover, some of the elements of viable alternative forms of 'enterprise education' are already available in the practice of states whose political agenda contrasts with that of Britain's New Right administrations.

First, the adoption of a criterion of effectiveness based exclusively upon profitability is by no means a necessary feature of successful 'enterprise education'. Hence, for example, Holmes and Hanley (1989), in their account of school-based 'enterprise education' in Australia, report that the assessment of the performance of school businesses is based upon the originality of the activities, as well as the return on invested capital. The latter criterion is clearly easier to assess than ones concerned with, say, community development. They argue, however, that in developing an idea and business plan to meet an unfulfilled demand for a product or service in the local community, the '"need" may not necessarily be profit-oriented, but can be community based'.

Indeed, an overly narrow concern with conventional small business practice has produced in Britain 'enterprises' of very limited educational value: the dubious virtues of producing and marketing 'pet rocks' and delivering kissograms for relatives and neighbours have been commented on elsewhere (Rees 1988). In fact, this emphasis may well lead to a form of educational practice which is *less* able to develop pupils' capacities to innovate. As Holmes and Hanley comment: 'The concern is that by ensuring that students undertake ventures in a restrictive, almost riskless environment, we are not achieving our goal of teaching small business or entrepreneurship' (1989: 27).

Second – and closely related – there is no necessity to restrict the practice of 'enterprise education' to the organizational form of the small business. In Italy, for example, 'enterprise education' forms a significant part of the curriculum in some schools, but in an economy where co-operatives play such an important role, the model of 'enterprise' on offer is a non-hierarchical one. Accordingly, pupils are trained in the skills of working co-operatively. And they experience forms of economic organization with alternative power relations to those embodied in the capital–labour relationship of conventional firms.

All this contrasts rather sharply, of course, with current British practice. It is instructive, for example, that development workers in enterprise agencies which specialize in fostering co-operatives are increasingly aware of the need for training in the *social skills* of group working and taking collective responsibility for progress within the group, skills which are distinct from the development of substantive and business competences. Co-operative development workers in Wales, for instance, reported that the training they were offered was pitched *as if* they were a co-operative group, rather than in the process of *becoming* one (Williamson 1989b). 'The training in business skills was OK. But we also needed things about groups, about development, about problem-solving ...' (quoted in Williamson 1989b: 12). And not surprisingly, these limitations are reflected outside of the training situation too. Hence, in a study of a young people's co-operative which was actually trading, Williamson (1986) identifies three kinds of guidance and instruction which were needed to improve its effectiveness: in trade skills, in business skills, and in working co-operatively (Williamson 1986: 15).

In effect, therefore, 'enterprise education' which is specifically intended to develop co-operatives has to *undo* the impact of an education system which socializes young people into a highly individualized orientation: team work tends to be reserved for the sports field. Moreover, in school-based 'education for enterprise', the scope for developing group skills is largely missed, though some attention is paid to learning to take joint responsibility, with all participants being exhorted to feel responsible for the success of the venture, and the fostering of trust between peers is encouraged, while identifyng everyone's strengths and weaknesses.

However, the dominant model of the small business imitates a conventional division of labour and consequent hierarchy on the board of directors. Hence, 'education for enterprise' becomes a vehicle for a particular ideology of economic practice, and has the potential to stifle any criticism of existing patterns of power relations within organizations. In short, it has the effect of closing off alternatives, rather than opening them up. Ironically enough, its replication of traditional organizational forms *reduces* the scope for innovatory practices and educational experiences, rather than expanding them.

Third, the tendency towards the 'ghettoization' of 'enterprise education' into particular areas of the curriculum, deemed to be appropriate for only certain types of pupil, should be recognized as a *contingent* feature of its implementation in British schools. As the evaluation studies have revealed, even the current 'education for enterprise' programmes have some pedagogical strengths (Jamieson *et al.* 1988; Williamson 1989a). These positive elements include: the development of better problem-solving and communication competences; improved experience of team-working and project management; greater confidence building; exposure to a wider range of adult experience through the use of AOTs; and the fostering of better relationships between staff and pupils. However, these benefits are restricted because only limited groups of pupils tend to have access to the 'enterprise education' which generates them.

Nevertheless, the development of the National Curriculum in terms of 'enterprise education' is likely to build upon what is already regarded as existing 'good practice' in schools (Crompton 1990). However, even in those cases where pupils have a genuine opportunity to learn 'through' enterprise, this will have little impact unless it is integrated in a much more thorough-going way into the pedagogy of the school. As Crompton argues: 'experience of enterprise activities within a school environment that emphasises teacher control, obedience, didactic learning and non-participation by pupils is not going to produce enterprising people' (1990: 22). In this way, therefore, the development of forms of 'enterprise education' which will be effective in releasing the innovatory potential of young people across the board needs to be a part of a wider restructuring of the schools system. Only as part of such a restructuring will the more ambitious objectives of pupil 'empowerment' be realized.

Equally, of course, 'enterprise education' has been claimed as a means of *local, community* 'empowerment' too. James (1990), for example, describes the devastating feeling of powerlessness that can ensue when a major employer in a local area closes down and unemployment trebles in a single day. He argues that 'enterprise education' should be used to teach pupils about their local economy and the inter-relationships between the economic and social systems; to demystify the often deeply embedded notion that 'economic questions can only be solved by people in distant places' (James 1990: 31). What he suggests, therefore, is a very different sort of 'self-help' from that encapsulated in the 'education for enterprise' model. For some local economies suffering the effects of industrial restructuring, he argues, *collective* local initiatives provide the only realistic source of both job creation and the supply of certain goods and services to the area.

This analysis, in turn, raises more far-reaching questions about the relationships between programmes of 'enterprise education' and wider strategies of economic development. It is clear, for example, that the realization of the kind of community 'empowerment' which has been outlined would – at the very least – be much more likely in the context of a regime of economic development policy which was more sympathetic than the market-dominated one which is current in Britain. By the same token, of course, 'education for enterprise' programmes would require a very different policy environment if they were actually to achieve their avowed objectives of fostering small business and self-employment, thereby widening labour market opportunities and reducing unemployment (Rees and Rees 1989).

In seeking to support the latter, it is clear that more attention needs to be paid in economic development policies to the generation of innovative ideas, in addition to the standard package of advice and training on VAT and accounts conventionally offered to the budding entrepreneur. Targeting the potential entrepreneurs whose social characteristics disadvantage them in seeking to raise capital and start enterprises, and providing tailor-made support programmes, has certainly yielded dividends in parts of Australia. Women, families blighted by long-term unemployment, and communities in depressed localities have all benefited from specialized training provision. Ethical investment funds have provided low-interest venture capital for groups or communities; whilst even state funds have been made available for finance houses in Western Australia to invest in people they would not normally back because of their lack of 'bricks and mortar' collateral. These and other measures have proved highly effective in unlocking talent among the least likely entrepreneurs, and in the most difficult regions, such as Esperance in Western Australia (Rees 1989).

CONCLUDING COMMENTS

All of this, of course, is light years away from the kinds of economic development policies which are currently being pursued in Britain. As our earlier discussion demonstrated, whatever the intentions, the reality of the Thatcherite 'enterprise economy' embodies only the most partial extension of economic opportunities to social groups which are disadvantaged in the labour market. For the most part, then, those who have become an *enduring* part of this 'enterprise economy' have done so by virtue of their prior access to the appropriate social and economic resources.

In this light, therefore, what is offered as 'enterprise education' in Britain's schools is quite simply inappropriate to the needs of the vast majority of pupils. In the main, no amount of school-based 'enterprise' is going to compensate for the massively uneven distribution of the necessary resources. And indeed, it would be surprising if this were not widely recognized by the pupils themselves (Williamson 1989a).

So radical is this disjuncture, it is difficult to escape the conclusion that the primary function of such 'education for enterprise' programmes is to reinforce a particular account of the functioning of the economy: an ideology which places prime causal and, indeed, moral responsibility upon the individual, rather than the community or the state. And in all of this, perhaps the most poignant irony is that, as examples from other parts of the world show, alternative approaches are not only possible, but rather more effective in fostering both wealth and job creation.

NOTES

1 The DTI Enterprise Initiative is a package of services to industry and commerce which includes the Consultancy Initiative, Regional Selective Assistance, Regional Enterprise Grant, collaborative research programmes, the enterprise and education initiative, the 'managing into the '90s' programme, and the export initiative. It replaced or revised previous schemes such as the Business Improvement Services schemes, the Advanced Manufacturing Technology Consultancy Scheme, the business and technical advisory services, the Regional Development Grant, and others (Department of Trade and Industry 1988a).

2 Business Growth Training is designed to help improve business performance and long-term profitability through a package of training services.

3 The Research and Technology Initiative is intended to facilitate the flow of information and support for collaborative research between industrial and commercial firms, the higher education sector, research and technology organizations, and government research laboratories.

4 The Enterprise Allowance Scheme was announced in 1981 and is a £40 a week allowance paid to unemployed people who want to set up in business on their own, but might be deterred from so doing because they would otherwise lose benefit entitlement. Applicants must have been registered unemployed for at least 8 weeks and have £1,000 to invest in the business.

5 Under the Teacher Company Scheme, the DTI provides financial assistance to universities and polytechnics to place graduates in firms planning major operational change. The Training Agency runs an

Enterprise in Higher Education Initiative designed to foster education/industry links and to encourage entrepreneurialism among students.

6 The evaluation was carried out by a joint team from the School of Education at the University of Bath and the Social Research Unit of University College, Cardiff (now the University of Wales College of Cardiff). The study was commissioned by the Mini-enterprise in Schools Project, based at the University of Warwick, and funded by the DTI/DES (Jamieson *et al* 1988).

REFERENCES

Atkinson, P., Rees, T., Shone, D., and Williamson, H. (1982) 'Social and life skills: the latest case of compensatory education', in T. Rees and P. Atkinson (eds) *Youth Unemployment and State Intervention*, London, Routledge & Kegan Paul.

Bechhofer, F., Elliott, B., Rushforth, M., and Bland, R. (1974) 'The petits bourgeois in the class structure: the case of the small shopkeepers', in F. Parkin (ed.) *The Social Analysis of the Class Structure*, London, Tavistock.

Bevan, J., Clark, G., Banerji, N., and Hakim, C. (1989) 'Barriers to business start-up: a study of the flow into and out of self-employment', *Research Paper No. 71*, London, Department of Employment.

Brown, P. (1990) 'The "third wave": education and the ideology of parentocracy', *British Journal of Sociology of Education* 11, 65–85.

Crompton, K. (1990) 'Enterprise and the national curriculum', *Welsh Journal of Education* (special issue on 'Education for Enterprise') 1, 15–27.

Curran, J. and Burrows, R. (1987) 'The social analysis of small business: some emerging themes', in R. Goffee and R. Scase (eds) *Entrepreneurship in Europe: The Social Processes*, Beckenham, Croom Helm.

Department of Education and Science (1987) *A Survey of School/Industry Links in Industry Year 1986*, London, DES.

Department of Employment (1986) *Building Businesses ... Not Barriers*, Cmnd. 9794, London, HMSO.

Department of Trade and Industry (1988a) *DTI – the Department for Enterprise*, Cmnd. 278, London, HMSO.

—— (1988b) *Releasing Enterprise*, Cmnd. 512, London, HMSO.

—— (1989), 'Vat registrations and deregistrations of UK businesses: 1980–88', *British Business*, 25 August, 10–12.

Finn, D. (1982) 'Whose needs? Schooling and the "needs" of industry', in T. Rees and P. Atkinson (eds) *Youth Unemployment and State Intervention*, London, Routledge & Kegan Paul.

Foreman-Peck, J.S. (1985) 'Seedcorn or chaff? New firm formation and the performance of the inter-war economy', *Economic History Review* 38, 402–22.

Hakim, C. (1987), 'Trends in the flexible workforce', *Employment Gazette* 95, 549–60.
—— (1988) 'Self-employment in Britain: a review of recent trends and current issues', *Work, Employment and Society* 2, 421–50.
Holmes, S. and Hanley, P. (1989) 'School-based enterprise in Australia: Where do we go from here?' *British Journal of Education and Work* 2, 17–28.
IFAPLAN (1986) *Education for Enterprise: An Interim Report*, Brussels: IFAPLAN Project Office.
James, W. (1990) 'The enterprise culture: business, social and human goals?', *Welsh Journal of Education* (special Issue on 'Education for Enterprise') 1, 48–53.
Jamieson, I. (1984) 'Schools and enterprise', in A.J. Watts and P. Moran (eds) *Education for Enterprise*, Cambridge, Hobson Press.
Jamieson, I., Hunt, D., Richards, B., and Williamson, H. (1988) *Evaluation of the Mini-enterprise in Schools Project*, Bath, School of Education, University of Bath, and Cardiff, Social Research Unit, University College, Cardiff.
Jowell, R., Witherspoon, S., and Brook, L. (eds) (1988) *British Social Attitudes: the 5th Report*, Aldershot, Gower.
Jowell, R. and Topf, R. (1988) 'Trust in the establishment', in R. Jowell *et al.* (eds) *British Social Attitudes: the 5th Report*, Aldershot, Gower.
Miller, J., Gibbon, R., and Wright, S. (1988) *Business Support and Training Services: Reaching the Micro Business*, Cardiff, People and Work Unit.
Piore, M. and Sabel, C. (1984) *The Second Industrial Divide: Prospects for Prosperity*, New York, Basic Books.
Rees, G. and Rees, T. (1989) 'The "Enterprise Culture" and local economic development: a review', *Report to the Scottish Development Agency*, Cardiff, Social Research Unit, University of Wales, College of Cardiff.
Rees, T. (1988) 'Education for Enterprise: the state and alternative employment for young people', *Journal of Education Policy* 3, 9–22.
—— (1989) 'Women and the enterprise culture: the Australian experience', *British Journal of Education and Work* 3, 57–69.
Rubery, J. (1988) 'Employers and the labour market', in D. Gallie (ed.) *Employment in Britain*, Oxford, Blackwell.
Scase, R. and Goffee, R. (1980) *The Real World of the Small Business Owner*, Beckenham, Croom Helm.
Storey, J. (1982) *Entrepreneurship and the New Firm*, Beckenham, Croom Helm.
Welsh Office (1987) 'Schools industry links', *Welsh Office Statistics Bulletin No. 4*, Cardiff, Welsh Office.
Williamson, H. (1986) *Co-operation, Confusion and Collapse: A Case Study of a Young People's Co-operative*, Cardiff, Social Research Unit, University College, Cardiff.
—— (1989a) 'Mini-enterprise in schools: the pupils' experience', *British Journal of Education and Work* 3, 71–82.
—— (1989b) *The Trainee Enterprise Trainers (TET) Programme: An Evaluation*, Cardiff, Social Research Unit, University College, Cardiff.

6

THE PRIVATIZATION OF EDUCATION

Clyde Chitty

THE CURRENT CLIMATE

> Historians will certainly record the ninth decade of the twentieth century and the accelerating developments of the final months of 1989 as a transitional period in the global political economy. The unexpected collapse of the one-party system in Eastern Europe and the resultant drive for a return to market-driven economies capped a decade which has seen governments worldwide, of all political stripes, embark on substantial privatization programs.

So began the advertisement which appeared in the *Times Educational Supplement* (2 February 1990) for the 1990 International Privatization Congress to be held in Saskatchewan, Canada, in May. No mention was made of education as such, but privatization options were to be considered with regard to government services, health care, housing, transportation, and numerous other areas of social policy.

This advertisement can be said to be illustrative of a concerted campaign by privatizers to present local and national privatizing initiatives as part of a world-wide move away from state responsibility for essential services. According to Oliver Letwin, a key figure in the Downing Street Policy Unit in the period before the 1987 general election,[1] Britain has played a pioneering role in the wholesale abandonment of public ownership, and the Conservative governments of Margaret Thatcher will merit a whole chapter in history on account of their outstanding contribution to 'the global revolution wrought by privatization'. In his view:

> Privatization ... is the point at which the economic and political Thatcher revolutions converge. The idea of selling state assets was born out of a gut feeling in the seventies that businesses would run better if they were free of government's dead hand. There have been other benefits: popular capitalism; cutting the national debt with the proceeds; expanding the City's financial capacity. But few imagined that it would lead to the multi-billion asset sales of British Telecom, British Gas, British Petroleum. ... Yet the most important benefit is still only dimly-perceived: a transformation in the way government thinks and behaves. ... Nationalized industries drag officials and ministers into opposing the customers' interest. Once privatization is complete, the role of ministers in running everything will never be restored. ... Britain is moving back into a position where people in government do not think it is their business to run anything. Four hundred years from now, people will still be talking about Mrs Thatcher. And it will be because of that profound shift in the way government thinks.
>
> (quoted in Hughes 1988)

Another of Mrs Thatcher's former key advisers and a founding member of the right-wing Centre for Policy Studies, Sir Alfred Sherman, has argued in an article in the *Daily Telegraph* (6 August 1987) that the Thatcherite Revolution will be incomplete without the privatization of all schools. Further progress in the 'liberalization' of society was advocated by Sir Geoffrey Howe, the former Foreign Secretary, in a wide-ranging speech to a meeting of Conservatives in the City of London at the beginning of June 1988:

> The new frontier of Conservatism – or, rather, the later stage in that rolling frontier – is about reforming those parts of the state sector which privatization has so far left largely untouched: those activities in society such as health and education which together consume a third of our national income but where market opportunities are still hardly known.
>
> (quoted in *The Independent*, 7 June 1988)

And a delegate to the Young Conservative Conference meeting in Southport in February 1989 received rapturous applause when he told his right-wing audience that it was time both to 'proclaim education a commodity to be bought and sold' and to 'disclaim the Marxian view that education is a right' (quoted in the *Guardian*, 13 February 1989).

It seems clear that a particular view of education is being promulgated with great enthusiasm but, at the same time, certain basic questions about the true nature of education are seldom addressed with any clarity or genuine insight. Does the provision and financing of education in schools require a social commitment or is it essentially a matter of private choice? To what extent can education be totally privatized along lines recommended by the Adam Smith Institute or the Institute of Economic Affairs?[2] Would the long-term consequence of wholesale privatization actually be a discernible improvement in the education on offer to *all* pupils? These questions have acquired extraordinary significance in the light of the hostility to locally-organized systems of state schooling so evident in the 1988 Education Act (see Chitty 1989b). But before we examine them in detail, it is important to be clear about definitions and to look at some of the ways in which, arguably, privatization has already become a guiding principle of the nation's education system.

DEFINITIONS

When applied to education, in both this country and abroad, the term privatization does not necessarily have the same connotations that it carries with regard to the handing over of such public utilities as water and electricity to private ownership and control. In America, for example, the term is used to indicate a measure of independent management and diversity of provision *within* the state system (see Cooper 1987). Admittedly, this is not privatization in the British sense, which usually refers to the total removal of schools from state ownership and control. Yet there is also evidence of the use of the term by both politicians and educationists in this country to indicate a series of half-way houses – measures which fall short of complete privatization but which are nevertheless designed to work towards a system where schools are privately run and also privately owned. In the discussion which follows, the term will be used to embrace various aspects of the financing of educational provision in both state and private schools, as well as other, perhaps more significant, moves towards a situation where education becomes an essentially private concern rather than something appropriate for government responsibility.

TWO ASPECTS OF PRIVATIZATION

Professor Richard Pring has argued in a number of papers (1983; 1986; 1987a and b) that the privatization of education in the 1980s assumed two major forms: the purchasing at *private* expense of educational services which should be *free* within the *public system*; and the purchasing at *public* expense of educational services in *private institutions*. To these could probably be added a third category which would be privatization in the sense of impoverishing the maintained sector to such an extent that anxious parents are more or less obliged to select some form of private education for their children. For Professor Pring, the privatization process can be usefully defined as: 'the eroding (and, perhaps, eventual disbanding) of a commitment to a common educational service based on pupil needs, rather than upon private means, and accessible to all young people on the basis of equal opportunity' (Pring 1983: 1). It has taken place in this country against a background of sustained criticism of the achievements of the state system and as part of the process of subjecting the education service to the same kind of harsh market pressures as those to which any commercial commodity would be subjected. In other words, quality requires choice; and choice requires private enterprise.

The first category would include the various ways in which parents and private firms have been asked to pay for both essential and inessential services within the public sector: special lessons or curriculum areas, resources and books, repairs and maintenance, basic facilities and buildings, even teaching posts.[3] Some might argue that there are a number of extra-curricular activities – for example, visits to the theatre or school trips abroad – for which parents could well be asked to make some sort of contribution. Yet in many cases, parents have been expected not simply to enrich the curriculum for a few but actually to help ensure basic curriculum provision for all. By the middle of the 1980s, the National Confederation of Parent Teacher Associations (NCPTA) estimated that £40m a year was being required of parents for what were regarded as essentials:

books and equipment and lessons. Successive HMI reports have also pointed to the need for parents to contribute large sums of money in order to compensate for a desperate shortage of books and materials. And the Inspectorate has noted, moreover, that such funding is not evenly distributed: schools in the richer shire counties inevitably get more parental money than do those in the inner cities.[4]

Turning to the second category, it seems clear that most independent schools depend on financial support from the taxpayer (see Benn 1990: 4–9). What we find in this case is the government or the local authority promoting the private at the expense of the public sector. Money that could be spent on state schools is diverted by a variety of means, both open and devious, to the independent sector. As Professor Pring has commented (1987a: 296–7): 'it is a shifting of resources, an alteration of the overall structure of education, a policy development that cannot be defended as an enrichment of the curriculum'. It is, of course, defended in terms of making good use of public money to secure the educational welfare of that small but growing minority of pupils able to benefit from the qualitatively superior education of the private sector. Twenty years ago it was estimated (Glennerster and Wilson 1970) that, on average, 20 per cent of the income of independent schools came from those who did not enjoy their benefits. Since then, the subsidies have escalated in cost and proliferated in kind; but, for obvious reasons, it is not always easy to arrive at the exact sums of money involved.

We find, therefore, that grand totals for both direct and indirect subsidies vary according to the specific items that are included in the lists. Some confine themselves to place-buying and charity tax losses; others take account of more intangible factors such as state expenditure on the training of teachers who then subsequently teach in the private sector. A conservative estimate published in 1983 produced a minimum yearly subsidy bill of £200m (Pring 1983: 15); a maximum list from 1980 a national yearly bill of £654m (Rogers 1980). It has been calculated (Benn 1990: 68) that this latter sum would today come to at least £1.3bn a year, but it would still not be the final figure on account of new forms of subsidy resulting from policies initiated by the Thatcher government.

Of special significance here is the Assisted Places Scheme

(APS) introduced by Education Secretary Mark Carlisle in 1980. Indeed, Carlisle apparently believes that the Scheme was one of the two major achievements of his period at the DES (1979–81) (see Knight 1990: 140).[5] It was very much the brainchild of Stuart Sexton,[6] Carlisle's political adviser and now Director of the Education Unit of the Institute of Economic Affairs. Opposed by many Conservatives and unpopular with civil servants at the DES, it nevertheless passed on to the Statute Book because it was the fulfilment of a manifesto commitment. It now subsidizes some 34,000 pupils in 279 private schools in England and Wales – an average of 113 per school;[7] while in Scotland, it involves 41 schools with an average of 65 in each.[8] The cost was already £50m a year in 1989/90.[9]

In addition to the escalating cost of the Assisted Places Scheme, the amount set aside by local authorities to pay for places in private day and boarding schools is also a significant outlay and (excluding the subsidies to special schools) now provides for over 4,700 pupils from two-thirds of the LEAs in England and Wales[10] at a cost of around £19,520,000 a year.[11] Most of these buyers are Conservative-controlled authorities, although not exclusively so (the Inner London Education Authority bought 78 places in 1988). The biggest spenders in 1989/90 were Trafford (buying 1,491 places), Cheshire (916), Wirral (613), and Lincolnshire (610).[12]

All of these subsidies are supposed to enable gifted youngsters from impoverished working-class homes to climb the 'ladder of opportunity' and thereby 'escape' from their humble origins. The Assisted Places Scheme is sometimes defended as a substitution for the old scholarship ladder where, as John Vaizey once put it (Vaizey 1966: 115), 'the aim was to identify the one clever child in a big group and rescue it'. Yet recent research shows that the Scheme has not attracted significant numbers of pupils from poor or deprived areas of the country. Subsidized pupils differ little in social and economic background from full-feepaying, public school entrants; and 'low-income' certainly does not equate with 'working-class'. Moreover, a significant proportion of the recipients of Assisted Places have already attended private schools at the preparatory stage (Edwards, Fitz, and Whitty 1989).

THE EFFECTS OF PRIVATIZATION

Throughout the 1980s, and particularly since 1987, the Thatcher government showed a marked preference for more privatized, competitive, and market-oriented forms of welfare and education provision. And to return to the point with which we began, the loss of confidence in public enterprises was not confined to the UK. As Edwards, Fitz, and Whitty have argued:

> In the past few years ... a loss of confidence in public enterprises in general, and in state education in particular, has led people ... to question the assumption that education is best conceived as a compulsory and universal service both financed and provided by governments. In many countries, the reductions in government spending on education in response to recession have been accompanied by a marked withdrawal of political support from the public sector. Overt displays of lack of confidence may be no more than pragmatic adjustments to declining public belief in the wealth-creating and opportunity-creating effects of schooling. Often, however, they have been expressions of political preference for greater consumer choice or for a transfer of more of the cost of services to their users, or an assertion of belief in the particular capacity of the private sector to maintain academic standards and social values judged to be in danger outside it.
>
> (Edwards, Fitz, and Whitty 1985: 29)

At present, around 7 per cent of the secondary age-group in England and Wales receive their education in the private sector and, for many parents, this is where 'real' academic education is to be found. Direct and indirect support for private schools can be seen as indicative of a lack of confidence in the quality of state education; and the Assisted Places Scheme has, in fact, been described as 'an offensive public declaration by a government that the national system of education is incapable of providing for our most able children'.[13]

Professor Pring has outlined some of the ways in which private subsidies and privatization are harmful to the majority of our children educated in the state sector: loss of resources, the undermining of comprehensive education, the removal of 'influential' people from involvement with state education, the curtailment of choice, the lowering of morale and efficiency in the maintained sector, and a widening of social and economic divisions in society (Pring 1983: 2–3). The right-wing obsession with private education is concerned more with privilege than with individual choice. For example: a disproportionate number of places in certain universities (principally Oxford, Cambridge, and Exeter) still go to applicants from the private sector. And of particular importance among all the factors commonly listed is the issue of democratic accountability since so many important decisions affecting children and society are now being taken outside the normal democratically agreed safeguards that usually operate. Private buying usually costs more per pupil than providing a state place, and yet LEAs are no longer required to notify such expenditure in returns.

Nevertheless, despite the present government's massive commitment to the cause of the independent sector and the large sums of money involved in propping it up, none of the developments so far described goes nearly far enough to satisfy the Prime Minister's more doctrinaire supporters on the Far Right. For them, the complete privatization of education will be achieved only by the introduction of the education voucher.

THE CAMPAIGN FOR THE VOUCHER

The voucher has been described by Arthur Seldon, formerly Editorial Director of the Institute of Economic Affairs, as:

> a highly flexible instrument, with many variations, that would replace the financing of schools through taxes under political control and bureaucratic supervision by payments direct from parents thus equipped with a new ability (for the 95 per cent with middle and lower incomes) to compare schools and move between them.
>
> (Seldon 1986: 1)

And, questioned after a speech to the Institute of Directors in March 1982, former Education Secretary Sir Keith (now Lord) Joseph spoke of the campaign for the voucher in terms almost of a moral crusade:

> The voucher, in effect, is a cash facility for all parents, only usable in schools instead of money. It would come from the

> taxpayer, and, were the campaign to be successful, it would give all parents, however poor, a choice of schools regardless of how much these schools cost, be they in the private sector or the maintained, that is, the public sector. The idea of the voucher is a noble idea. It is the idea of freeing parents from all money considerations in choosing a school for their children. ... A voucher would provide an equal moral treatment for all parents. It would not, of course, provide an equal background for all children, because the home is very important in the education of a child, and homes differ from each other in the combination of love, discipline and encouragement that is given to the child.
>
> (Joseph 1982: 5)

According to its admirers, the voucher would create choice and competition while, at the same time, establishing the principle of consumer sovereignty in education. Since people with top incomes could already send their children to the very best schools, either by paying the fees charged by private schools or by meeting the higher housing costs of districts with the 'superior' state schools, it was only just that the government should make arrangements to extend free choice to everyone. The voucher scheme can assume many forms, but the first systems proposed in this country were based on the simple principle that all parents should be issued with a free basic coupon with a value determined by the average cost of schools in the local area. This would entitle them to a minimum standard place at the local school of their choice, but those who were able to do so would be entitled to supplement the basic voucher with their own money and shop around for a place at a more expensive school. This would seem to imply a system of two-tier provision: the 'minimum price' school place for the majority and the 'more expensive' school place for those seeking something superior.

It looked at one time as though right-wing dreams promoting 'parent-power' through the voucher might be realized during Sir Keith Joseph's five-year stint at the DES (1981–6). The newly appointed Education Secretary received spontaneous applause at the 1981 Conservative Party Conference when he declared:

> I personally have been intellectually attracted to the idea of seeing whether eventually, *eventually*, a voucher might be a way of increasing parental choice even further. ... I know that there are very great difficulties in making a voucher deliver – in a way that would commend itself to us – more choice than the 1980 Act will, in fact, deliver. It is now up to the advocates of such a possibility to study the difficulties – and there are *real* difficulties – and then see whether they can develop proposals which will really cope with them.

As things turned out, the optimism of the Conservative faithful was misplaced, since Sir Keith was unable to deliver the longed-for voucher. In fact, this is the one major occasion in the 1980s when the civil servants of the DES would appear to have *defeated* the politicians. They were able to emphasize the very real practical difficulties which would arise from the many and complex changes required to the legal and institutional framework of the education system. Such was the quality of their argument that by the end of 1983 the voucher idea had apparently been dropped. Speaking at the 1983 Conservative Party Conference, Sir Keith announced: 'the voucher, at least in the foreseeable future, is dead'; and he repeated this in a written statement to the House of Commons in June 1984.

The Thatcher government was clearly not ready in 1983–4 to risk alienating a large number of its traditional supporters. The unexpected abandonment of the education voucher (temporary or otherwise) could be seen as something of a victory for the conservative forces at the heart of the political establishment. Looking back at the government's second term at the beginning of 1986, the *Daily Telegraph* argued that:

> measures dear to the Prime Minister which fell by the wayside include education vouchers, student loans, repeal of rent control. ... Though her aspirations reflect popular feeling, they run counter to those of the political classes ... the establishment, by now accustomed to rule whomever *demos* elects.
>
> (*Daily Telegraph*, 13 January 1986)

What is not really clear is the extent to which Sir Keith himself came to see that it was basically illogical and absurd to try to introduce a market in state education (see Wilby 1987).

The campaigners for the voucher refused to accept defeat, and in 1986 the Institute of Economic Affairs published *The Riddle of the Voucher* which included suggestions for half-way houses and stepping-stones – changes in the way education was managed which fell short of the introduction of a fully-fledged voucher system but which would pave the way for such a move later on. It could be argued that these right-wing campaigners have achieved a sort of belated victory with the passing of the 1988 Education Act.

This Act seeks to erect (or reinforce) a hierarchical system of schooling subject both to market forces and to greater control from the centre. And much attention has been focused on the creation of a new tier of schooling comprising City Technology Colleges and Grant-maintained Schools. The new CTCs are 11–18 schools financed partly by private capital, independent of local authority control, and designed originally to provide a new choice of school in inner-city areas. Grant-maintained Schools are those schools which have chosen to opt out of the locally maintained education system and receive their finance direct from central government. Neither scheme has, in fact, met with unqualified success; and the government has been forced to resort to all manner of financial incentives to secure the creation of this new sub-system (see Chitty 1989a: 37–40; Simon 1990: 74–8).

Yet from the point of view of privatizing the system, the most important provision in the 1988 legislation is probably that for financial delegation, the chief object of which is to make local authorities distribute funds to their primary and secondary schools by means of a weighted, *per capita* formula. Governing bodies are then made responsible for controlling the budgets delegated to them. This development, viewed in conjunction with the provision for open enrolment, has been seen by Stuart Maclure (1988: 42–3) as a subtle means of adapting the education system in such a way as to make a future transition to vouchers possible without undue disruption. The school ceases to be 'maintained' as an institution independently of the choices which parents exercise. Under the new schemes for financial delegation, the *per capita* payments are still paid to the school; but the circumstances have been engineered in which it would be a relatively simple matter to give the money directly to the parents instead – in the form of vouchers or warrants – thereby completing the transfer of effective power from the institutions and the local authority to the parents themselves.

A RECURRING DEBATE

Privatizers claim a respectable ancestry for their ideas by tracing them back to the writings of Adam Smith (1723–90) and Tom Paine (1737–1809). More recently, the idea of providing 'exits' from state schools by distributing earmarked purchasing power in place of the provision of nil-priced schooling was advocated by Professor Milton Friedman in 1955 (Friedman 1955). And in 1964, Professors Alan Peacock and Jack Wiseman were the first economists in Britain to argue that schools need not necessarily be financed by the state and that parents should be enabled by vouchers, grants or loans to shop around in a free market (Peacock and Wiseman 1964).

Arguing from a quite different perspective, Raymond Williams suggested in *The Long Revolution* (1961) that, once all the privileges and barriers of an inherited kind had been abolished in our society, we would still have to choose between two competing and irreconcilable philosophies of the organization of education:

> It is a question of whether we can grasp the real nature of our society, or whether we persist in social and educational patterns based on a limited ruling class, a middle professional class, a large operative class, cemented by forces that cannot be challenged and will not be changed. The privileges and barriers, of an inherited kind, will in any case come down. It is only a question of whether we replace them by the free play of the market, or by a public education designed to express and create the values of an educated democracy and a common culture.
>
> (Williams 1961: 176)

Yet, despite Williams's insight, it can be argued that it was not until the mid-1970s that the views of the privatizers began to be taken seriously when it was at last obvious that a number of influential Conservatives were determined to reverse what Sir Keith Joseph described in a speech to the Oxford Union in December 1975 as 'the left-wing ratchet' (Joseph 1976: 21). For Joseph, 'the blind, unplanned, uncoordinated wisdom of the market' was 'over-whelmingly superior to the well-researched, rational, systematic, well-meaning, cooperative, science-based, forward-looking, statistically respectable plans of governments, bureaucracies and international organizations' (Joseph 1976: 57). The Centre for Policy Studies set up by Margaret Thatcher and Sir Keith Joseph in 1974 was intended to challenge some of the key assumptions of the Welfare State. And it was also at this time that the Institute of Economic Affairs found itself being regarded within the Conservative Party as a generator of attractive ideas (see Griggs 1989: 101).

PRIVATIZATION: THE HIDDEN AGENDA

We appear to have been describing a debate from which the privatizers have emerged totally victorious. Yet as far as education is concerned, there are many questions raised by any voucher scheme – and indeed by the whole idea of a school system subject to market forces – which right-wing proponents do not choose to answer.

It is not clear, for example, whether any right of selection still rests with the school itself or whether, in fact, the top grammar and independent schools will be forced to accept all those pupils whose parents can afford to send them there. Will popular and successful schools be allowed to get inordinately large; while those which do not find favour die? The Hillgate Group pamphlet, *Whose Schools? A Radical Manifesto*, which put forward many of the ideas later contained in the 1987 Conservative election manifesto, manages to support policies which are mutually contradictory. On the same page we are told that parents should be free to send their children to any school of their choice, while, at the same time, 'schools should have the right to control their own admissions' (Hillgate Group 1986: 14). To the objection that 'good schools will attract so many applicants that they will no longer be able to contain all the pupils who seek admission', the pamphlet replies that 'there is no reason why schools should not have a right to place an upper limit on their number of admissions' (p. 19). How will the selection process operate? The pamphlet has a beguilingly simple answer: 'schools should publish and adhere to an admissions policy which is applied objectively, and without bias, to those qualified to apply' (p. 14). This begs so many crucial questions it is almost meaningless as a statement of policy. Or rather the meaning is all too clear, and that is that certain schools will be free to discriminate in favour of those already advantaged within our society. The social or economic implications of the inequalities which will result from such a system have already been outlined in the chapter by Brown and Lauder. For what we have here is a system of parental choice acting as a cover for the return of selection. When one tears away the rhetoric and the pretence, there is nothing remotely democratic or egalitarian about the voucher scheme envisaged by the New Right. As Morris has observed, it is, in reality, a thinly-disguised plot to ensure that 'the wealthier can obtain a superior education at the expense of the disadvantaged and the taxpayer' (Morris 1976: 19).

CONCLUSION

There is then no indication that privatization and the infusion of market values will do anything to raise the standard of education in this country – nor indeed is that their true purpose. The free market philosophy underpinning the 1988 Act has everything to do with competition and unequal treatment and very little to do with a genuine extension of educational opportunities. As Stewart Ranson has noted:

> The market is formally neutral but substantively interested. Individuals come together in competitive exchange to acquire possession of scarce goods and services. Within the market-place all are free and equal, only differentiated by their capacity to calculate their self-interest. Yet, of course, the market masks its social bias. It elides, but reproduces, the inequalities which consumers bring to the market-place. Under the guise of neutrality, the institution of the market actively confirms and reinforces the pre-existing social order of wealth and privilege. The market is a crude mechanism of social selection. It can provide a more effective social engineering than anything we have previously witnessed in the post-war period.
>
> (Ranson 1988: 15)

At a time when only a third of our youngsters stay on in full-time education after the age of 16 and only 15 per cent of the age-group enjoy the benefits of a higher education, we need policies which will heighten rather than dampen educational aspirations. No country can afford to be complacent about such dismally low rates of participation in post-compulsory education and training – a situation which could only deteriorate if the state ceases to concern itself with matters of social justice and equality of provision.

Educational reform in the 1960s received a fair degree of public support because it appeared, for a time at least, that changes to the system could achieve both social and economic goals. The divided system of secondary education, set up in most parts of the country as a response to the 1944 Education Act, was seen to be both socially disruptive and at the same time an anachronism in an age which demanded an educated workforce and put a premium on skills and specialization. As Hunter has observed:

> Together in the mid-1960s Crosland and Boyle presided over the benign consensus which was the basis of the organizational implementation of the comprehensive system. In a period of growing GNP it was possible to support the two potentially opposing objectives: that secondary schooling should work towards creating greater social justice and equality within society *and* be an investment in creating a more efficient workforce.
>
> (Hunter 1984: 274)

We now need to emphasize all over again, in the admittedly changed economic circumstances of the 1990s, that a just and prosperous society is one which both promotes equality (in a very real sense) and seeks to utilize the talents of all its members. For too long we have been obsessed with providing a 'quality' education for the privileged few. Future success depends on the creation of a single unified system of 11–16 comprehensive schools under local democratic control without the existence of private or selective enclaves to dissipate our energies. This should be followed, as Andy Green has argued (Green 1990: 78–81), by a new structure of comprehensive post-16 centres – the tertiary college is an obvious model to emulate – providing a focus for all post-school education and training and seeking to bring levels of access and participation up to those enjoyed by our major competitors in Europe and beyond. The emphasis throughout should be on the right to learn, with allowances for full-time 16–19 students in obvious need of financial support, as in Sweden, and entitlements to paid day release for young employees. Individual fulfilment and the country's economic prosperity are not mutually exclusive; they are inextricably linked.

ACKNOWLEDGEMENT

I would like to thank Phil Brown, Andy Green, Tamara Jakubowska, and Hywel Thomas for their critical comments on an earlier draft of this paper.

NOTES

1 Having been Special Adviser to Sir Keith Joseph at the DES in the period 1982–3, Oliver Letwin held the education and training portfolio in the Downing Street Policy Unit from June 1983 until January 1986 (see Knight 1990: 181).

2 The British version of the Adam Smith Institute was established in 1981; the Institute of Economic Affairs dates from 1955, but its Education Unit (with Stuart Sexton as Director) was not set up until October 1986.

3 For example, parents at an Essex comprehensive school have been asked to pay a levy of £50 to prevent teachers being made redundant. This has arisen because of a deficit of £100,000 faced by the school under the new LMS scheme which gives heads and governors control of their own budgets. According to the headteacher of the school: 'It comes down to saying to parents either we accept a drop in standards or we see an end to the 1944 Education Act which provided a free secondary education for all. We decided to adopt the latter course' (reported in *The Independent*, 9 June 1990).

4 For example: the 1986 HMI Report reported that over one-third of schools in the shire counties received contributions in excess of £6 per pupil; while this was so in only about one-fifth of schools in the metropolitan districts and London authorities (Department of Education and Science 1986: 46).

5 The other achievement, according to Carlisle, was his recognition of the Professional Association of Teachers (PAT) on the Burnham Committee.

6 It was at a meeting of the Conservative National Advisory Committee on Education (CNACE) on 15 September 1979 at the Central Hall, Westminster, that Sexton first presented his formulation of the Assisted Places Scheme (Knight 1990: 148).

7 House of Commons, Question No. 218, 15 February 1990. This total

includes estimated assisted numbers from the 52 new schools added in September 1989 – using the same averages as in existing schools.

8 House of Commons, Question W38, 13 December 1988. Scotland's numbers apply to the year 1987/8.

9 These figures, together with those in the following paragraph, come from Caroline Benn's 1990 *Forum* article.

10 House of Commons, Question No. 219, 15 February 1990.

11 LEA spending as a whole for private schooling, including special schools, has recently risen to nearly £150,000,000 a year (CIPFA, Education Statistics 1987–8).

12 Cheshire and Trafford were also buying heavily in the late 1970s (see the *Times Educational Supplement*, 18 February 1977).

13 This comment was made by the Labour Peer Lord Alexander during the initial House of Lords debate on the working of the Assisted Places Scheme (quoted in the *Times Educational Supplement*, 19 September 1982).

REFERENCES

Benn, C. (1990) 'The public price of private education and privatization', *Forum* 32 (3), 68–73.

Chitty, C. (1989a) 'City Technology Colleges: a strategy for elitism', *Forum* 31 (2), 37–40.

—— (1989b) *Towards a New Education System: The Victory of the New Right?*, Lewes, Falmer Press.

Cooper, B. (1987) 'Privatization – American Style', in S. Sexton (ed.) *The Funding and Management of Education*, Institute of Economic Affairs Education Unit, 13–18.

Department of Education and Science (1986) *Report by Her Majesty's Inspectors on the Effects of Local Authority Expenditure Policies on Education Provision in England – 1985*, London, DES.

Edwards, T., Fitz, F., and Whitty, G. (1985) 'Private schools and public funding: a comparison of recent policies in England and Australia', *Comparative Education* 21 (1), 29–45.

—— (1989) *The State and Private Education: An Evaluation of the Assisted Places Scheme*, Lewes, Falmer Press.

Friedman, M. (1955) 'The role of government in education', in R. Solo (ed.) *Economics and the Public Interest*, New Brunswick, NJ, Rutgers University Press.

Glennerster, H. and Wilson, G. (1970) *Paying for Private Schools*, LSE Studies in Education, Allen Lane.

Green, A. (1990) 'Education and training: a study in neglect', *Forum* 32 (3), 78–81.

Griggs, C. (1989) 'The New Right and English secondary education', in R. Lowe (ed.) *The Changing Secondary School*, Lewes, Falmer Press.

Hillgate Group (1986) *Whose Schools? A Radical Manifesto*, London, The Hillgate Group.

Hughes, C. (1988) 'Privatizer on parade: a profile of Oliver Letwin', *The Independent*, 6 June.

Hunter, C. (1984) 'The political devaluation of comprehensives: what of the future?', in S.J. Ball, (ed.) *Comprehensive Schooling: A Reader*, Lewes, Falmer Press.

Joseph, K. (1976) *Stranded on the Middle Ground? Reflections on Circumstances and Policies*, London, Centre for Policy Studies.

Joseph, K. (1982) Speech to the Institute of Directors; printed in full in a Supplement to *The Director*, May, 3–5.

Knight, C. (1990) *The Making of Tory Education Policy in Post-war Britain, 1950–1986*, Lewes, Falmer Press.

Maclure, S. (1988) *Education Re-formed: A Guide to the Education Reform Act 1988*, Sevenoaks, Hodder & Stoughton.

Morris, N. (1976) 'The economics of the voucher system', *Forum* 19 (1), 16–19.

Peacock, A. and Wiseman, J. (1964) *Education for Democrats*, Hobart Paper (Old Series) No. 25, London, Institute of Economic Affairs.

Pring, R. (1983) *Privatization in Education*, London, RICE (Right to a Comprehensive Education), February.

—— (1986) 'Privatization of education', in R. Rogers (ed.) *Education and Social Class*, Lewes, Falmer Press.

—— (1987a) 'Privatization in education', *Journal of Education Policy* 2 (4), 289–99.

—— (1987b) 'Free ... to those who contribute', *The Times Educational Supplement*, 23 October.

Ranson, S. (1988) 'From 1944 to 1988: education citizenship and democracy', *Local Government Studies* 14 (1), 1–19.

Rogers, R. (1980) 'The myth of independent schools', *New Statesman*, 4 January.

Seldon, A. (1986) *The Riddle of the Voucher: An Inquiry into the Obstacles to Introducing Choice and Competition in State Schools*, Hobart Paperback No. 21, London, Institute of Economic Affairs.

Simon, B. (1990) 'Thatcher's third tier, or bribery and corruption', *Forum* 32 (3), 74–8.

Vaizey, J. (1966) *Education for Tomorrow* (2nd edn), Harmondsworth, Penguin.

Wilby, P. (1987) 'Close up: Kenneth Baker', *Marxism Today*, April.

Williams, R. (1961) *The Long Revolution*, Harmondsworth, Penguin.

7

EDUCATIONAL ASSESSMENT AND EDUCATIONAL STANDARDS: TOWARDS AN ALTERNATIVE VIEW OF QUALITY

Harry Torrance

INTRODUCTION

The main aim of this chapter is to review the assumed link between educational assessment and educational standards which underpins the government's proposals for a programme of national assessment. The government's basic position seems to be that improving educational standards is a key factor in improving the UK's economic performance, and that assessment can influence standards by the process of both setting targets and then measuring whether or not they have been achieved.

The relationship of educational standards to economic performance is a complex one and discussions are all too often coloured by belief and assertion rather than informed by evidence. A full analysis would attend to what we mean by 'standards', what forms of current and future economic organization and output are considered desirable, how educational standards and economic performance actually interact, and how to effect changes in teaching and learning if the evidence suggests this is necessary. Such an analysis is beyond the scope of one paper and my purpose is a good deal more limited, though all of the above topics will be touched on to a greater or lesser degree – particularly the first and the last.

The government clearly believes that educational performance is directly related to economic performance and that standards of education must be raised in order that the UK economy can become more productive and remain competitive in an increasingly fierce world marketplace. The chosen instrument for raising standards is the implementation of a National Curriculum and an attendant programme of National Assessment.

This paper shares the same basic assumption that the relationship between schooling and economic performance is indeed an important one, though one may wish to take on board issues other than straightforward economic competitiveness. How to develop environmental awareness, an informed citizenry, a mature democratic process, and so forth, must also be of relevance here. The paper also assumes that demographic trends pointing to a significant downturn in the numbers of young people coming on to the labour market make the relationship between education and the economy all the more important still. As Nancy Cole (1990) has put it in a recent review of similar issues in the US:

> Young people are a decreasing portion of the total population and, consequently, we will need a larger portion of them to be well prepared educationally to meet the future needs of the nation. Because they will face increasingly complex adult roles as citizens and workers, there is an even greater need than in the past for students to attain advanced educational goals.
>
> (Cole 1990: 2)

However the paper questions the limited definition of educational standards (and their decline) which the government seems to hold. Likewise the paper questions the desirability and feasibility of central intervention in and direction of as diverse and open-ended a phenomenon as educational 'quality', and suggests an alternative, more flexible approach might be rather more effective.

WHAT DO WE MEAN BY STANDARDS?

A crucial issue is of course the one of definition – standards of what, for what? – which in turn must be related to the purpose of education. Traditionally the cry of 'standards' has been associated with a view of scholarly, academic, subject-based achievement, and this can certainly be detected in the government's commitment to a subject-based National Curriculum with a 'core' of English, Maths, and Science, and a 'foundation' of Technology, History, Geography, a Modern Language, Art, Music, PE, and, in Wales, Welsh. Yet it is also clear if one looks at the subject working party reports (and indeed GCSE criteria which were similarly produced in the mid-1980s) that the definition of what counts as Maths, Science, English, etc. is itself changing, with much more emphasis than hitherto being placed on the understanding, application, and communication of knowledge, not just its recall in narrow examination situations. Hypothesizing, investigating, analysing, planning, and communicating (in oral as well as written forms) are the activities around which these subjects are increasingly organized.

Such developments owe a good deal to the many subject-based curriculum developments which took place in the 1970s as well as the more flexible and integrated programmes of work associated with the Technical and Vocational Education Initiative (TVEI) of the 1980s. They can be seen to be grounded in the contemporary debate about the vocational relevance of the curriculum, though in turn also relate to a much longer debate about theory and practice in education and whether a popular, practical (as opposed to academic) approach to teaching and learning could be developed. Additionally, publications such as the Hargreaves Report (ILEA 1984) have proved influential in broadening and popularizing the debate about the role of assessment in learning and expanding definitions of achievement to include personal and social qualities – arguing the case, in effect, from the pupil's perspective (rather than the 'needs of society') and suggesting the need for more relevant and shorter-term learning goals, the need to recognize achievements which may lie outside the traditionally academic, and so forth.

So definitions of 'standards' are changing, and necessarily so. We are becoming more ambitious in what we are trying to achieve. The problem with expanding definitions of standards and achievement in this way is, of course, that they are exceedingly difficult to then measure and report in succinct fashion. Trying to pin down 'quality' in terms of 'benchmarks', in terms of a hierarchically ordered series of behavioural objectives, as seemed to be the government's original intentions (Murphy 1987, 1988) and as exemplified in the Task Group on Assessment and Testing's Report recommendation that attainment should be reported subject by subject on a 10 point scale (TGAT 1987), could only lead to the creation of curriculum specifications of Byzantine complexity. As Margaret Brown, a key member of the Mathematics Working Party, put it: 'the dilemma remains of how to formulate a moderate number of national attainment targets, specific enough to describe individual achievement and sensitive enough to record individual progress . . . [which do not] multiply like vermin' (Brown 1988: 19).

The government seemed to have made a basic conceptual error in identifying the setting of benchmarks (the attempt to define *minimum* basic levels of achievement for all pupils) as a mechanism which at one and the same time could raise standards. 'Benchmarks' are unlikely succinctly to encapsulate the most positive things with which we associate education and neither, of course, are they easily changed once they have been set in place. They could lead to curriculum stagnation rather than the dynamic, flexible system which circumstances would seem to demand. These points will be taken up again later in the paper; suffice to say for the moment that defining educational standards is by no means a straightforward task even in general terms (the sorts of things that ought to be included – academic achievement, practical skills, personal qualities, social understanding, etc.), let alone the specifics of syllabuses and teaching methods.

WERE STANDARDS FALLING ANYWAY?

Given the foregoing discussion, and a recognition that standards are changing, deciding whether or not they are falling is obviously an enterprise fraught with difficulties, and the data which we have at our disposal are limited to fairly traditional measures. Such indications as they give us, however, do not support a view of unambiguously falling standards and, if anything, the reverse is the case.

Interestingly enough, concern over standards in schools has often been manifest at times of economic crisis, as Wood and Power (1984) note in their international review of National Assessment programmes, though a moment's reflection undermines the logic of such a correlation – if we are worried about contemporary economic performance, isn't it the educational standards of ten or twenty years ago that should be the focus of concern? Likewise moral panics over standards have often been just that – concern over morality and behaviour in times of social change as much as over academic performance *per se*. Thus standards became a major focus of concern in this country as the terms of trade moved against Britain towards the end of the nineteenth century and following defeat in the Boer War; likewise in the US as large numbers of immigrants from non-traditional sources (i.e. southern and eastern, rather than northern, Europe) entered the country after the turn of the twentieth century. Concern was expressed at the 'quality' of the population and articulated in terms of declining levels of ability – merging the separate issues of attainment and moral behaviour into the single notion of 'intelligence' (see Torrance 1981, for a fuller discussion).

Governments are now rather less inclined to despair at the intelligence of their populations, or to focus on the concomitant problem of selecting the 'most able' to be educated as future leaders of the nation. 'Standards' are still very much on the agenda however, though now construed in terms of overall educational output – the skills and knowledge which all school-leavers ought to possess – rather than ability. Certainly the British government's unprecedented intervention into curriculum and assessment has been justified in terms of falling (or at least inadequate) educational standards:

> progress has been variable, uncertain and often slow. Improvements have been made, some standards of attainment have risen. But some improvement is not enough. We must raise standards consistently, and at least as quickly as they are rising in competitor countries.
>
> (DES 1987: 2–3)

In fact the evidence is rather more equivocal. For example David Raffe's extensive review of the causes of youth unemployment does not support arguments about lack of skills or qualifications (Raffe 1987). Occasionally disputes surface in the press over reading or mathematics surveys which seem to suggest that standards of achievement are falling (*The Times Educational Supplement* 29 June 1990; *The Independent on Sunday*, 1 July 1990). Similarly, international surveys are often interpreted to suggest that Britain lags behind other countries (IEA 1988; Walker 1976). But equally, successive surveys by the Assessment of Performance Unit (APU) did not find such evidence and in any case the methodological problems inherent in trying to ensure that such studies are actually comparing like with like, over time, are legion (Nuttall 1986; McLean 1990). Moreover the most obvious (if crude) indicators of educational output – public examination results – show that standards are rising: a larger proportion of pupils are entering examinations and gaining graded certificates than ever before (Wright 1977; Gray *et al.* 1983; DES 1986). Critics might argue that the quantity of certificates issued says nothing about the standard of performance required to gain a certificate, and certainly with the move from GCE and CSE to GCSE we are no longer comparing like-with-like, if we ever were in the past. Yet even here, a recent HMI survey has reported that:

> GCSE has proved to be a successful system of examination. ... There have been considerable improvements in the quality of teaching and learning. ... The proportion of fourth and fifth year lessons judged to be satisfactory or better has grown steadily ... it now stands at about four lessons out of five.
>
> (HMI 1988: 3–4)

So, the case over falling standards is by no means proven, and could probably be rejected, but it is hardly adequate to let matters rest there. The quality of educational provision and the accountability of the education service are, and will remain, on the political and economic agenda for some time to come: how standards can be *improved* remains a key issue. Nor is it simply a matter of redefining standards, though it is important to broaden what is included in our definition along the lines outlined in the previous section. Thus Ball's argument, drawing on the Swedish experience, that one can either focus on academic achievement or more general social goals, and that there are bound to be trade-offs between the two (Ball 1988), is clearly inadequate. First of all, it simply accepts the data of lower academic performance in Swedish schools as given, without any of the methodological caveats noted above. Second, and more importantly, it does not consider redefining standards in terms of the *integration* of academic and social goals. It accepts an either/or zero-sum situation, rather than thinking through what a more holistic and appropriate form of educational experience for *future* economic and social performance might look like. I will return to this issue towards the end of the article.

CAN ASSESSMENT RAISE STANDARDS?

> ... at the heart of the assessment process there will be nationally prescribed tests done by all pupils.
>
> (DES 1987: 11)

Examinations have tended to develop in a fairly *ad hoc* fashion in England and Wales, and indeed elsewhere, in response to long-term social as well as educational trends. Thus issues of selection and professional qualification came to impinge increasingly on the school system with key questions of examination design revolving around fairness (to the individual candidate) and predictive validity (for the receiving institution or employer). It is only relatively recently that governments have looked to examinations and assessment processes to provide formal and systematic feedback on the educational system as a whole (though they have always been looked to informally) and to intervene in the design of assessment systems with this aim in mind.

National surveys of levels of achievement were set up in the late 1960s and 1970s in countries such as the US and, briefly, Australia, as well as the UK (the APU). These sampled the achievements of small numbers of pupils in two or three curriculum areas (usually including Language and Mathematics) and at two or three different ages. At the time when the accountability of publicly funded school systems was beginning to become a political issue, the ostensible purpose of these surveys was to find out what children did know and could do, though often the rhetoric of this slipped into that of defining what children *ought* to know and be able to do (see Wood and Power 1984 for a fuller account). As noted previously, the methodological difficulties of defining and measuring standards in this way were challenging enough, but even supposing these difficulties could be overcome, the question is still begged as to how such assessment might actually make a difference to raising standards generally, i.e. by what mechanisms it would or indeed could impact on the learning experiences of all children in all schools. Studies of more blanket approaches to testing, such as local authority monitoring of reading standards, or state-wide minimum competency testing in the US, have raised similar issues, and suggest that such testing really amounts to little more than symbolic reassurance that 'something is being done': responding to the political problem of being seen to be concerned rather than the educational problem of how actually to make a difference (Gipps *et al.* 1983; Airasian 1988).

A further development of this assessment-based approach to raising standards, and one which was designed to respond to the issue of how to make a direct impact on teaching and learning, was (and indeed is, since we are to all intents and purposes beginning to operate with a variant of it now) Measurement-Driven Instruction (MDI). As the nomenclature implies, the term and the associated practice originated in the US. Its development was prompted by criticisms of minimum-competency testing in particular. Minimum-competency testing programmes had been set up with the claimed intention of ensuring certain basic levels of achievement for all pupils. If such programmes were used to provide confidential data to alert the responsible authorities about schools which may require further attention and support then it is possible that they could have a beneficial effect. However, linked to the retention of students, the publication of results, and even financial sanctions on schools and teachers, teachers very soon 'taught to the test' in such a way that curriculum and teaching methods narrowed and minimum competency fast became the maximum targets that schools aimed for. The massaging of results (by further lowering standards so that more pupils passed) and even outright cheating have also been reported (see Alkin 1979; Darling-Hammond and Wise 1985; Corbett and Wilson 1988; Ellwein and Glass 1989; Shepard 1989). In other words test scores and pass rates could well rise while their effect is to make educational standards fall (for a more thorough review of the American evidence see Koretz 1988).

The major lesson which advocates of MDI learned from such disasters was that testing – particularly 'high stakes' testing, i.e. testing linked to significant consequences such as student retention or promotion, and teacher employment – could have a direct effect on instructional processes; the issue was to make that effect positive, rather than negative: 'If properly conceived and implemented, measurement-driven instruction currently constitutes the most cost-effective way of improving the quality of public education in the United States' (Popham 1987: 679). This is a big 'if' of course. For example Popham argues that a well-conceived and well-implemented system must involve combining the clarity of criterion-referenced tests with a manageable number of instructional targets. This is easier said than done, as we have already noted with Margaret Brown's reflections on her experience with the National Curriculum Mathematics Working Group; likewise with the key problem of writing tests which promote rather than inhibit good educational practice: 'The content of high-stakes educational tests should be subjected to intense scrutiny by all concerned clienteles, so that the tests measure truly worthwhile content' (Popham 1987: 680).

Reflecting on such ideas in a 'state of the art' review of assessment which introduced a special edition of *Educational Researcher*, the main publication of the American Educational Research Association, Raymond Nickerson suggested that:

> the development of a truly adequate approach to educational assessment – an approach that not only will measure accurately what has been learned but will also provide useful diagnostic information for future instruction and that will help drive the system as a whole, toward increasing effectiveness in the nurturing of understanding and thinking – will require a considerable research effort over a relatively long time.
>
> (Nickerson 1989: 6)

The patience required of such an approach, and attention to evidence rather than ideological assertion, has not been a hallmark of UK government claims over the National Curriculum and National Assessment yet, interestingly enough, much of what is beginning to emerge from the professional debate in the UK clearly attends to many of the issues raised in the foregoing discussion. Thus the developing national system is being designed to have a direct impact on all pupils in all classrooms – it is not simply being assumed that the ritual of testing will make a difference – and the lengthy assessment 'tasks' (not tests) which the Assessment Consortia are designing and piloting can be said to be attempting to respond to the issue of measuring 'truly worthwhile content'. The intention to 'drive the system' by producing (or trying to produce) good assessment tasks can now be seen as a major objective of the professionals involved in assessment as well as the politicians:

> each SAT [Standard Assessment Task] will contain many varied activities ... [which] will lead to a wide range of written, oral, graphical and practical responses by pupils working alone and in groups. The development agencies will guide training for ... these tasks; provide opportunities for teachers to learn more about the interpretation of statements of attainment ... by means of exemplifications.
> (SEAC 1989 para 6)

> SATs should go beyond present practice. As examples of targets and levels in action they will have an important function in communicating the National Curriculum to teachers. They must disseminate better practice.
> (STAIR 1989: 22)

Questions must remain, however, as to whether this is either feasible or desirable. As we have seen, the extent to which quality in outcome and instructional process can be wholly prespecified is extremely debatable, and if such intentions lead to the overload seen in the 1990 pilot then they are clearly self-defeating (*The Times Educational Supplement* 25 May 1990; *The Independent* 9 June 1990, Torrance 1991). Part of the problem could be said to derive from the inadequacy of assessment theory and practice, part from the inadequacies of the centralized and hierarchical model of change which is being employed.

CONCEPTIONS OF QUALITY AND THE DEVELOPMENT OF PRACTICE

The debate in the US has developed further still with theoretical contrasts being drawn between an essentially behaviourist approach to the specification and measurement of 'basic skills' and a more interactive/cognitive approach to 'higher order skills' such as understanding and problem-solving (Cole 1990); from an emphasis on: 'prediction and control to an emphasis on meaning and understanding. In assessment, specifically, we are seeing a shift from mathematical and statistical models to educational and psychological models' (Dwyer 1990: 23). In these terms, the purpose of assessment in relation to improving quality is less to specify, measure, and certify, and more to diagnose, guide, and support (see also Tyler ments have also surfaced in the UK. Thus Woo on Vygotsky's theory of the 'zone of next likewise suggested the need for a much more and interactive approach to assessment:

> the *zone of next development* ... is the gap present level of development and the pot development. It indicates the level of a task that a child is ready to undertake on the basis of what he can already do, *as long as he receives the best possible help from an adult*. ... Here then we have the idea that the teacher/tester and student *collaborate* actively to produce a best performance.
>
> (Wood 1987: 242, original emphasis)

Practical developments have lagged behind such debates however, and although a more sophisticated attempt is being made to relate assessment to curriculum development and to actual classroom processes, this assessment is still being interpreted in essentially behaviourist terms. Assessment tasks are being used to 'exemplify' the kinds of tasks which should be a feature of teaching methods under the National Curriculum and the teacher is still being asked to stand back and 'assess' pupils rather than 'collaborate actively to produce a best performance'; the focus is on 'delivery' of the National Curriculum via assessment procedures, rather than improving the quality of teaching and learning *per se* (see Torrance 1989 for further discussion of this point).

Central to such an approach is the assumption that quality can indeed be defined and delivered in this fashion. But this is a peculiar assumption for politicians and planners to make: a centrally determined curriculum policed by regular testing hardly accords with the rhetoric of an enterprise culture. Nor is it an assumption that is necessarily still being made in the US, despite the influence of the Measurement-Driven Instruction movement. In a lengthy review of the evidence of standard-setting on educational quality, Andrew Porter points out that: 'Even if we had agreement on the intended outcomes of schooling and on the characteristics of good teaching, the massive problem of implementation would remain' (Porter 1989: 344). He goes on to suggest that 'to have real and lasting effects, standards setting must be persuasive' (p. 348) and quotes the egie Forum on Education and the Economy in its report *A ion Prepared* as arguing for the development of teachers as autonomous professionals': 'the key to success lies in creating a profession equal to the task. A profession of well-educated teachers prepared to assume new powers and responsibilities to redesign schools for the future' (p. 344).

Such views are becoming increasingly discussed in the US. The Carnegie Forum report was given prominence in a recent *Wall Street Journal* special report on education (a 36-page supplement to the main newspaper) which presented the view that:

> US schools ... are still geared to give most students just enough rudimentary knowledge to handle the equivalent of routine factory work, even though that work is disappearing. Neither have they changed their basic organisational model which resembles the factory itself: pupils were products, teachers were the production workers who turned them out, and a large and often inflexible bureaucracy told the teachers what and how to teach. ...
>
> Big Business, its future dependent on a well-educated work force, is appalled at the continuing crisis and is increasingly impatient with mere tinkering. Executives who have learned a thing or two about restructuring to meet world competition now insist that this is what the schools need too. David T. Kearns chief executive of Xerox Corps., is one of them ... he argues that the system needs to emulate not the factory of old but the leanest and meanest of the new high-tech corporations. Among other things, this means flattening the organisation chart by removing rafts of mid-level bureaucrats, and by pushing much more authority and decision-making power down to the classroom level.
>
> (*Wall Street Journal*: 1989, R3)

Allowing for considerable journalistic rhetoric, and the fact that what is good for Xerox Corps is not necessarily good for schools, the most interesting thing about this extract, and indeed the whole report, is its emphasis on decentralization and the need to create a commitment to quality (and the mechanisms to realize this) within individual institutions and classrooms.

TOWARDS AN ALTERNATIVE VIEW OF QUALITY

There would appear, then, to be three inter-related issues which an alternative view of 'standards' and the improvement of quality in education must take on board: a broader definition of quality than is currently being operationalized by the National Curriculum; a more interactive and dynamic approach to the role of assessment in promoting quality; and a more flexible approach to the problem of implementation. Indeed, the *development* of quality might be a better way of phrasing the problem of implementation and of construing the relationship between these three issues.

As we have seen, the subjects of the National Curriculum are by no means the traditional academic school subjects of old, and yet the compartmentalization of a curriculum in subject terms, particularly at primary level, is likely to impede the development of some of the very skills and understandings which the subjects individually all claim to include – investigating, planning, problem-solving, analysing, and so on. At the very least, it could lead to wasteful duplication of effort. Problems are not confined within subject boundaries and although innovative schools will no doubt find ways of planning and teaching to attainment targets across subject boundaries – with one integrated task affording 'coverage' of learning objectives in two or three different subjects – this is likely to prove the exception rather than the rule. While the basic content of the National Curriculum is unlikely to change in the short term, how it is conceptualized and organized needs far more attention, with flexible and integrated approaches to curriculum planning being encouraged, identified, and disseminated. Schools involved in such work must be seen and must see themselves as in the forefront of curriculum development, not as subversives which need to keep quiet for fear of attracting opprobrium.

Furthermore, many aspects of cross-curricular work and pupils' personal and social development – health education, political education, equal opportunity issues, and so forth – are being squeezed out of curricular discussions at the present time as schools attempt, as they see it, to fit a quart into a pint pot. Much more attention must be paid to thinning down subject working party reports so that they do indeed indicate only a 'moderate number of ... attainment targets' (Brown 1988) and offer schools broad goals supported by exemplary material, not overly detailed prescription; in turn, real attention rather than lip-service should be paid to cross-curricular issues, some of which may need to be drawn together in time set aside specifically for tutorial support and social education, but many of which ought to be accommodated within the more generally flexible approach to teaching and learning outlined above. Personal and social goals have always been pursued by schools, in tandem with academic goals, but often covertly or even unintentionally through the 'hidden curriculum'. The challenge now is to plan for their integration in such a way that they support each other, rather than this being left to chance, or their being seen in opposition to one another.

Returning to the issue of the relationship between assessment and learning, a key mechanism for operationalizing a more integrated approach to curriculum planning and reviewing pupil progress is that of Records of Achievement – a development which the government supported in the mid to late 1980s but which has more recently been presented as little more than a way of reporting attainment levels. The development of Records of Achievement has been influenced by many different arguments and there is not space here to review them all (see Broadfoot *et al.* 1988) but essentially they involve teachers in being more explicit about the learning intentions which they have for a particular course or module of work, discussing these with pupils as they review pupil progress and the specific strengths and weaknesses which pupils display, and reporting more descriptively and informatively on what pupils know, understand, and can do. Although originally thought of as a way of reporting on pupils' achievements other than the academic, and in turn drawing criticism as being a possible mechanism of personal surveillance (Hargreaves 1989), their development in schools has been grounded as much in the promoting and implementing of teacher–pupil dialogue within and across individual subject areas as in the process of developing pastoral education. The main point to be borne in mind with regard to the arguments advanced in this paper is that Records of Achievement represent a much more dynamic approach to the relationship between assessment processes and learning and offer the opportunity for pupils to take much more responsibility for their own progress. While the articulation of learning intentions, module contents, and so forth are a significant feature of Records of Achievement, the main fulcrum of such an approach to assessment is the individual pupil, not the prescribed curriculum. The basic premise is that of starting from where the learner 'is' and constantly referring to his or her experience and progress, a premise which seems particularly apposite as we move into a period of demographic downturn when the key issue for educators, including those working on assessment, must be the promotion of learning for all, rather than the certification and selection of a few.

Finally there is the issue of implementing change in schools and developing the quality of the teaching profession itself. Part of the government's thinking with regard to the National Curriculum and Assessment has clearly been to attack teachers as a self-interested professional group ('producers') and strengthen the hand of the 'consumers' (taken to mean parents, rather than pupils or, interestingly enough, future employers). As a strategy for improving quality it is at best unproven, at worst disastrous, as can be seen from frequent discussions of low morale in the profession. We have already seen a quite different approach beginning to take shape in the US. Nor is this simply claim and rhetoric. In Rochester, New York, for example the *Wall Street Journal* reports that:

> high quality teachers can earn up to $70,000, an unheard of sum, and are given power over curriculum, teaching methods and educational goals few of their colleagues elsewhere could dream of attaining . . . .
>
> Their new contract obligates them to put in longer hours, particularly for planning. It provides peer monitoring . . . .
>
> Most important, the central school bureaucracy is yielding power over curriculum, method and standards for student performances to a new kind of animal: individual school planning teams, which include not only the principal but parent and teacher representatives.
>
> (*Wall Street Journal*: 1989, R4–R5)

Reviewing similar evidence, Andrew Porter concluded:

> Simply telling teachers what to do is not likely to have the desired results. Neither is leaving teachers alone to pursue their own predilections. But . . . it might be possible to shift external standard setting away from reliance on rewards and sanctions (power) and toward reliance on authority. . . .

> One approach to building authoritative standards would be to involve teachers seriously in the business of setting standards. . . . Through the process of teacher participation . . . the standards would take on authority.
>
> (1989: 354)

Of course we must be cautious; such reports and reviews are indicators of possible directions in which to develop, not models to unquestioningly adopt. And simply getting teachers to tell other teachers what to do is unlikely to extinguish controversy or differential interpretations of curricular prescriptions (Torrance 1985, 1986); the process of teacher involvement and professional development must also be attended to so that the act of involvement generates understanding and commitment, and change is not left as a still unpredictable consequence of the implementation of the products of such involvement, however much more authority such products may carry. There are many echoes here of the teacher-as-researcher movement which Lawrence Stenhouse argued for so persuasively over fifteen years ago (Stenhouse 1975). But simply making claims for professional autonomy is not enough. Teachers need to generate an understanding of and a commitment to quality, and be held accountable for their endeavours in both the professional and public realms. Within the broad parameters mentioned above this must involve an integrated approach to the planning of teaching programmes, assessment processes, and reporting procedures at departmental (or curriculum area in the case of primary schools) and whole school level. Thus units or modules of work would be collaboratively produced, reviewed by staff outside of the immediate group which produced them, and would be publicly available for scrutiny by other interested parties such as governors. Moderation meetings across groups of schools to compare teaching methods and the standards of work produced (i.e. actual evidence of pupil achievement, not decontextualized grades) would also be an important feature of a system attempting to combine the development of quality with accountability.

These alternative proposals are brief and tentative, grounded in the knowledge that the National Curriculum is unlikely to be substantially modified in the short term but that more flexibility in implementation is essential, both to render it manageable and to maintain the core activities of professional development (conceptualizing, planning, descriptive reporting) on which future developments of quality in teaching will depend. The long-term need is clearly for a substantial decentralizing of curriculum planning, so that small, manageable teams of teachers within a school or locality can respond rapidly to changing needs and circumstances. Likewise, assessment must be construed in terms of the promotion of learning. The emphasis must be on reviewing targets, strengths, weaknesses, and progress, and the provision of a wide range of information to assist pupils and other parties, including selectors and future trainers/education personnel. The reduction of the varied and complex outcomes of education to single level indices (3 in English, 2 in Maths, etc.) is ludicrous. Overall the key idea underpinning this paper is that quality can be developed but it cannot be prescribed in the way that the government appears to be attempting. The conditions under which quality develops can be elucidated but ultimately, if our definition of quality includes flexibility, creativity, and the capacity to deal with the unexpected – for teachers and pupils alike – then these characteristics must be allowed for in the overall system which we design and within which teachers and pupils are expected to work.

REFERENCES

Airasian, P.W. (1988) 'Symbolic validation: the case of state-mandated, high stakes testing', *Educational Evaluation and Policy Analysis* 10 (4), 301–13.

Alkin, M.J. (1979) 'Educational accountability in the United States', *Educational Analysis* 1 (1), 5–21.

Ball, S.J. (1988) 'Costing democracy: schooling, equality and democracy in Sweden', in H. Lauder and P. Brown (eds) *Education: In Search of a Future*, Lewes, Falmer Press.

Broadfoot, P., James, M., McMeeking, S., Nuttall, D., and Stierer, B. (1988) *Records of Achievement: Report of the National Evaluation of Pilot Schemes*, London, HMSO.

Brown, M. (1988) 'Issues in formulating and organising attainment targets in relation to their assessment', in H. Torrance (ed.) *National Assessment and Testing: A Research Response*, British Educational Research Association.

Cole, N.S. (1990) 'Conceptions of educational achievement', *Educational Researcher* 19 (3), 2–7.

Corbett, H.D. and Wilson, B. (1988) 'Raising the stakes in statewide mandatory minimum competency testing', *Journal of Education Policy* 3 (5), 27–39.

Darling-Hammond, L. and Wise, A.E. (1985) 'Beyond standardisation: state standards and school improvement', *The Elementary School Journal* 85 (3), 315–36.

Department of Education and Science (DES) (1986) *English School Leavers: 1983–4*, London, HMSO.

—— (1987) *The National Curriculum 5–16: A Consultation Document*, London, DES.

Dwyer, C.A. (1990) 'Trends in the assessment of teaching and learning: educational and methodological perspectives', in P. Broadfoot, R. Murphy, and H. Torrance (eds) *Changing Educational Assessment: International Trends and Perspectives*, London, Routledge.

Ellwein, M.C. and Glass, G.V. (1989) 'Ending social promotion in Waterford: appearance and reality', in L.A. Shepard and M.L. Smith (eds) *Flunking Grades: Research and Policies on Retention*, Lewes, Falmer Press.

Gipps, C., Steadman, S., Blackstone, T., and Stierer, B. (1983) *Testing Children: Standardised Testing in Schools and LEAs*, London, Heinemann.

Gray, J., McPherson, A., and Raffe, D. (1983) *Reconstructions of Secondary Education*, London, Routledge.

Hargreaves, A. (1989) *Curriculum and Assessment Reform*, Milton Keynes, Open University Press.

HMI (1988) *The Introduction of the General Certificate of Secondary Education in Schools 1986–88*, London, DES.

International Association for the Evaluation of Educational Achievement (IEA) (1988) *Science Achievement in Seventeen Countries*, Oxford, Pergamon Press.

Inner London Education Authority (ILEA) (1984) *Improving Secondary Schools (The Hargreaves Report)*, London, ILEA.

The Independent (1990) 'Tests on seven-year-olds to be scaled down after trials', 9 June, 6.

The Independent on Sunday (1990) 'Reading standards not declining say officials', 1 July, 2.

Koretz, D. (1988) 'Arriving in Lake Wobegon: are standardised tests exaggerating achievement and distorting instruction?', *American Educator*, Summer, 8–15.

McLean, L. (1990) 'Possibilities and limitations in cross national comparisons of educational achievement', in P. Broadfoot., R. Murphy, and H. Torrance (eds), *Changing Educational Assessment: International Perspectives and Trends*. London, Routledge.

Murphy, R. (1987) 'Assessing a National Curriculum', *Journal of Education Policy* 2 (4), 317–23.

—— (1988) 'Great Educational Reform Bill proposals for testing: a critique', *Local Government Studies* 14 (1), 39–45.

Nickerson, R.S. (1989) 'New directions in educational assessment', *Educational Researcher* 18 (9), 3–7.

Nuttall, D.L. (1986) 'Problems in the measurement of change', in D.L. Nuttall (ed.) *Assessing Educational Achievement*, Lewes, Falmer Press.

Popham, W.J. (1987) 'The merits of measurement-driven instruction', *Phi Delta Kappan*, May, 679–82.

Porter, A.C. (1989) 'External standards and good teaching: the pros and cons of telling teachers what to do', *Educational Evaluation and Policy Analysis* 11 (4), 343–56.

Raffe, D. (1987) 'Youth unemployment in the United Kingdom 1979–1984', in P. Brown and D.N. Ashton (eds) *Education, Unemployment and Labour Markets*, Lewes, Falmer Press.

School Examinations and Assessment Council (SEAC) (1989) *National Curriculum: Assessment Arrangements. SEAC's advice to the Secretary of State, dated 12 December 1989*, London, SEAC.

Shepard, L. (1989) 'Inflated test score gains: is it old norms or teaching the test?' paper presented to the American Educational Research Association annual meeting, San Francisco, 29 March.

Standard Tests and Assessments Implementation Research (STAIR) (1989) *Proposal for Funding to SEAC*, Manchester, University of Manchester Department of Education.

Stenhouse, L. (1975) *An Introduction to Curriculum Research and Development*, London, Heinemann.

Task Group on Assessment and Testing (TGAT) (1987) *A Report*, London, DES.

The Times Educational Supplement (1990) 'An exhausting trip for the pilots', 25 May, A12.

—— (1990) 'Psychologists alarmed by fall in reading scores', 29 June, 1.

Torrance, H. (1981) 'The origins and development of mental testing in England and the United States', *British Journal of Sociology of Education* 2 (1), 45–59.

—— (1985) 'Current prospects for school-based examining', *Educational Review* 37 (1), 39–51.

—— (1986) 'Expanding school-based assessment: problems and future possibilities', *Research Papers in Education* 1 (1), 48–59.

—— (1989) 'Theory, practice and politics in the development of assessment' *Cambridge Journal of Education* 19 (2), 183–91.

—— (1991) 'Evaluating SATs – the 1990 pilot', *Cambridge Journal of Education*, 21 (2), 129–40.

Tyler, R. (1986) 'Changing concepts of educational evaluation', *International Journal of Educational Research* 10 (1), monograph.

Walker, D.A. (1976) *The IEA Six-subject Survey: An Empirical Study of Education in Twenty-one Countries*, New York, Wiley Halstead Press.

Wall Street Journal (1989) *The Wall Street Journal Reports: Education*, 31 March.

Wood, R. (1987) *Measurement and Assessment in Education and Psychology*, Lewes, Falmer Press.

Wood, R. and Power, C. (1984) 'Have national asessments made us any wiser about "Standards"?' *Comparative Education* 20 (3), 307–21.

Wright, N. (1977) *Progress in Education*, London, Croom Helm.

8

THE RESTRUCTURING OF THE LABOUR MARKET AND YOUTH TRAINING

David N. Ashton

THE YOUTH TRAINING CRISIS

In some respects the current crisis in the relationship between the educational system and the youth labour market is the most profound yet. What it amounts to is a fundamental disjunction in the relationship between the educational system and the traditional forms of training available to young people. However, this is itself only a reflection of a more profound shift in the relationship between an educational system whose main function has been the reproduction of social classes and the demands of an economy which is now requiring fundamentally different skills to those demanded only two decades ago.

To understand the nature of the present crisis it is essential to establish the traditional relationship between the educational system and the labour market in Britain. The simple reason for this is that in the last two decades the types of skills required for contemporary industry have undergone a radical transformation yet the institutional structures we have inherited for the transmission of skills are still geared to the requirements of an economy that has long since passed away.

THE DEVELOPMENT OF THE BRITISH EDUCATIONAL SYSTEM

The defining characteristic of the British system of education is that historically it has been geared towards the socialization of each new generation for their future position in the class structure and domestic division of labour. Occupational socialization in the form of transmission of technical skills has always played a very subordinate role within the educational system except where they were required for some of the traditional professions (Marquand 1989). The clearest articulation of this relationship was found in the system which existed in the first half of the nineteenth century. Thus, the Schools Inquiry Commission which reported in 1868 distinguished three grades or types of secondary school. The first were the (public) schools filled by the sons of the gentry and the major professions whose functions were described as 'the formation of a learned or literary, and a professional or cultural class'. The second were the schools attended by the sons of the lesser professions and manufacturers whose function was to provide them with a preparation for some form of commercial or industrial life, although the industrial and commercial training was left to the apprenticeship. The third group were the schools which provided a basic education for the sons of tradesmen and superior artisans. Below these were the church elementary schools which provided basic literacy and religious instruction for the working class. In addition, the working classes did have their own schools, the Dame schools. These provided a very basic instruction in literacy paid for by parents and at a time convenient to them.

Another aspect of the British educational system, although not a defining one, was the differential treatment of males and females. While the education of males was designed to fit them for their place in the class structure, the education of females was primarily designed to prepare them for their role as wives and mothers. The form of that preparation was, of course, strongly influenced by class and status considerations (Purvis 1983). Thus, daughters from the middle class were trained in details of etiquette, the management of the household, and the handling of domestic servants; daughters from the working class were trained to be 'good mothers' with the emphasis on the acquisition of practical skills, skills which also prepared many of them for a position in domestic service.

The introduction of mass state education in the latter part of the nineteenth century provided only limited modifications to this system. The private (public) schools with their traditional curriculum based on the classics and some modern science were left untouched to provide the 'model' for state schools for the next century. The attempts by the more affluent sections of the working and lower middle classes to introduce technical schools with a more vocationally relevant curriculum were squashed by the government as the primacy of the grammar school, with its curriculum modelled on the public schools, was established as the main form of state supported secondary education for the middle class (Eaglesham 1967). As for the working class, their own Dame schools which were outside the control of the state were to be put out of business as the children of the working class were forced into elementary schools under the control of the churches (Gardner 1984). These were schools which guaranteed not just an instruction in basic literacy, but also rigorous moral and religious instruction. The working classes were to be educated not so much for the needs of industry but to accept their place within the existing social order.

In its essentials this was the system that lasted well into the twentieth century. Even the introduction of universal secondary education after the Second World War did little to alter the basic structure. The private (public) schools remained intact and untouched at the apex of the system, the grammar schools were expanded to accept the upwardly mobile sons and daughters of the working class, but maintained their traditional curriculum and focus on producing an educated administrative elite for business. A half-hearted attempt was made to introduce technical schools but the main expansion was in the new secondary modern schools to provide a secondary education for the children of the working class. However, the curriculum was still to be a watered down version of the academic curriculum of the grammar schools. There was no longer a major difference in the curriculum offered to males and females but rather the subjects became gendered, with members of each sex being encouraged to take subjects thought appropriate for the performance of their future roles (Deem 1978, 1980). The educational system continued to provide a preparation for the young person's future position in the class structure and domestic division of labour rather than to make an explicit attempt to transmit skills relevant to the requirements of a modern economy.[1]

TRAINING IN BRITAIN

Despite the fact that technical and vocational education was largely disregarded, Britain was an industrial nation by the middle of the nineteenth century, and so certain aspects of the requirements of industry could not be totally ignored. Thus, the curriculum and training provided by the public schools did transmit leadership skills and the intellectual problem-solving skills required by the ruling groups. The grammar schools provided males with the intellectual skills required for entry to a small administrative and commercial elite while their future wives were instructed in the skills of household management. As for the working class, in addition to learning basic literacy males were provided with lessons in discipline and the acceptance of authority, and females with lessons in domestic skills. Female labour force participation rates were low as they were generally only expected to work in paid employment until married.[2] In this context the main agency of occupational socialization remained the apprenticeship system. So long as the educational system could provide the basic training in literacy, numeracy, and social skills, then the knowledge required for the males to earn their living could be acquired through the apprenticeship system.

Inherited from the guild system, the flexibility of the apprenticeship system was such that it could be used for the training of almost any trade. Thus, following on from education, apprenticeships were used for the training of groups ranging from sailmakers to cabinet makers to professional engineers. Indeed, a form of the system was even used to help the early manufacturers recruit child labour for the cotton mills. Such a system was, of course, internally differentiated and access to the different types of apprenticeships depended on such factors as the status of the child's parents, the type of education they had received, and the ability of the parents to pay the indenture fee. Even within the working class the fees for indentures ranged from £7 for the sailmaker to £50 for the cabinet maker, reflecting differences in the learning times and the earnings of the various trades (Ashton, Green, and Hoskins 1989). Women were largely excluded from apprenticeships and confined to unskilled or semi-skilled manual work and domestic service.

The existence of an apprenticeship system meant that as industry developed, the knowledge required to work efficiently within it could be transmitted independently of the educational system. Hence the rigid division within Britain between education and training and the differences in status attached to those who work in the two systems. However, not all forms of occupational knowledge were confined to the apprenticeship system, for from an early stage those occupations which sought the status of professions endeavoured to enhance the status of their knowledge by calling it education and locating its transmission within the educational system. Thus, the more prestigious and powerful professions such as medicine and later engineering were able to dispense with the apprenticeship system and incorporate their training within the context of the universities. This left industry and the less prestigious professions to continue to rely on the apprenticeship system.

The major exceptions were those industries which relied heavily on unskilled labour and for which a period of extended training was not necessary for those who entered. In fact this state of affairs was characteristic of a large part of British manufacturing industry which, throughout the twentieth century, continued to rely on the supply of a large proportion of unskilled youths to provide labour for the footwear, knitwear, textiles, coal, steel, and engineering industries. The apprenticeship system was adequate for the training of the elite of skilled workers, but the majority of the workers in these industries (both male and female) remained unskilled or semi-skilled and were left to pick up whatever skills they required on the job. Thus, for the majority of working-class youngsters, employers were not concerned about whether they had been in the educational system for nine years or eleven years. All they required of the educational system was that it provided basic literacy and young people who could accept the discipline of the factory. Moreover, given that the British economy had established a broad industrial base as a result of the fact that it was the first to industrialize, the basic structure of the economy and its associated demand for labour and skills underwent only a slow process of change during the late nineteenth and early twentieth century. Hence it was possible to maintain, on the one hand, an educational system whose main function was the preparation of young people for their future position in the class structure or domestic division of labour and, on the other, a separate system of industrial training through the apprenticeship system.

CHANGE IN THE RELATIONSHIP BETWEEN EDUCATION AND THE LABOUR MARKET

After the Second World War the system came under threat from three separate sources of change. A combination of ideological changes in the form of a growing belief in egalitarianism together with the increasing electoral power of the working class led to an end to the system of separate schools for the different social classes. Instead, secondary education was made available to all, introducing what Brown (1990) refers to as the 'second wave' in the socio-historical development of the educational system. However, continuity with the past was maintained, at least initially, by retaining the grammar schools and only providing access to them through a selective examination at age 11. This ensured that only the 'brightest' working-class pupils entered them; the remainder were to be educated in secondary modern schools. A growing awareness of the rigidities and waste engendered by such an elitist system led to the introduction of a single system of comprehensive schools in this 'second wave'. The goal of a single system of comprehensive schools was only partially achieved in the 1960s and 1970s as the 'public' schools were left in the private sector. The curriculum was left relatively unscathed and young people from the working class were still provided with a watered-down version of the traditional grammar school curriculum, and an examination system geared towards the selection of young people for university education. In addition, provision was still based on the assumption of 'natural' differences between the sexes which were reflected in a pattern of subject choice which assumed that girls and boys would ultimately perform very different adult roles (Brown 1990).

The second change which took place was in industry. As the economy started to modernize and became exposed to more intense international competition, major changes evolved, culminating in the structural transformations of the late 1970s and the 1980s. In the 1950s and 1960s the change which took place in the industrial base was still relatively slow. The service sector started to expand much more quickly than the manufacturing sector and new technologies started to affect manufacturing industry. One consequence of this modernization of manufacturing was the gradual decline in the amount of unskilled labour required. A further consequence was an increase in the demand for more highly qualified labour and the increasing reliance of employers on 'academic' qualifications in the selection of their labour force. Even before the introduction of comprehensive education, the type of school attended was starting to mean less than the number of school-leaver qualifications possessed when it came to determining what type of job a young person got. The introduction of comprehensive schools completed this process.

The third change was a dramatic increase in the participation of females (especially married women) in the labour force. Until the Second World War it was still the practice among 'model' employers such as Cadbury Bros at Bourneville to employ young females in factory work, but only until such time as they married. Once married they were obliged to leave because of the belief that the married woman's place was in the home. The shortage of labour during the war put an end to that practice and marked a permanent shift in the use of (married) female labour and hence in female participation rates. However, by 1961 females still accounted for only 26 per cent of employees, but by 1986 this had risen to 46 per cent, with the main increase taking place in the 25–34 and 35–44 age range (Maguire 1990). The new employment growth areas such as business services, financial services, education, health, and community services were relying in an almost unprecedented manner on the labour of females who, as we have seen, were traditionally regarded as peripheral to the labour force and hence requiring little preparation for it.

It is against a background of these slow but cumulative changes that we turn to an examination of the more radical changes that took place in the late 1970s and the decade of the 1980s.

THE RADICAL CHANGES OF THE LAST TWO DECADES

On the surface, the most obvious change was the growth of mass unemployment in the early 1980s. However, as we suggested above, this cyclical change in the demand for labour disguised a number of other radical changes which were transforming the demand for labour (Ashton, Maguire, and Spilsbury 1990). Here we identify four main elements which transformed the underlying demand for youth labour and the kind of skills employers required. The first of these was an acceleration in the pace at which capital in the labour intensive industries was relocated to the low wage-cost economies. As mentioned above, Britain had been losing jobs in traditional industries after the Second World War but this trend was intensified especially under the impact of the recession. What is important from the point of view of the demand for youth labour was that these industries were traditionally some of the major employers of unskilled and semi-skilled youth labour.

A second major change was the extension of many product markets from national to global markets. Firms which had held a monopolistic or dominant position in British product markets, for example, in the motorcycle, metal fabrication, car, and machine tool industries, found that their control over the domestic market was threatened by foreign competition. In the case of industries such as motorcycle manufacture the result was the virtual elimination of British firms. In others, such as automobiles, British manufacturers' share of the market fell dramatically. In addition, the early 1980s saw attempts by British firms to export, hampered by the high value of the pound which made their goods uncompetitive. The combination of these forces, together with the impact of the world recession in the period 1980–2, resulted in a substantial programme of plant closures that amounted to a loss of 20 per cent of manufacturing output (Wells 1989). This inevitably produced massive job losses in the manufacturing sector. Thus, between 1979–84 one-third of the jobs in engineering were lost. Moreover, in spite of the economic recovery since then, which saw manufacturing output in 1987 return to the level of 1979, employment in British manufacturing industry continued to fall and by 1987 was still 27 per cent below that of 1979. By contrast in Japan over the same period, manufacturing output rose by 62 per cent and employment in manufacturing by 7 per cent (Rowthorn 1989).

A third change which affected the manufacturing sector was the impact of new technology. The combination of advances in micro-computer technology with improvements in the design of conventional technology created the Computer Numerically Controlled machines and flexible manufacturing systems which generated improvements in productivity which went way beyond anything achieved with conventional technologies. The new technology produced a quantum change in the relationship between employment and output with a devastating effect on the numbers of skilled workers required in parts of the manufacturing sector. The other consequence of these changes was the continued growth in the demand for professional, scientific, and technical workers as the industries became increasingly knowledge-based.

However, while jobs were being lost at an unprecedented rate in the manufacturing sector in the period 1979–84, they were growing (except for a short period at the height of the recession) in the service sector. Indeed, over the period 1979–87, the growth of jobs in the service sector was sufficient to offset the loss of jobs in manufacturing. In qualitative terms the situation was different as most of the jobs lost were full-time jobs, while most new jobs were part-time.

Like the manufacturing sector, the service sector was subject to a number of processes of change. The growth of demand for financial and business services during this period was increasing further the demand for more highly qualified people. A second change was the increasing industrial concentration taking place in the retail, leisure, hotel, and catering industries which had previously employed large numbers of unskilled youths. As these industries became dominated by larger, nationally based corporations which displaced the smaller locally based family firms, this crucially affected the demand for labour. The large national concerns had achieved a competitive advantage in the market place, partly through rationalizing the use of labour. Instead of employing large numbers of full-time (young) workers they ran their establishments with a small core of highly trained professional workers and supplemented these with large numbers of part-time adult female workers to meet fluctuations in the demand for their services (Ashton and Maguire 1986; Ashton, Maguire, and Spilsbury 1990). The result was that the demand for full-time school-leavers was drastically reduced as they were replaced by part-time adult females. This was a trend that was only partially offset by the offer to employers of free youth labour through the Youth Training Scheme.

The impact of these changes was partially disguised by the effects of the recession which brought with it the virtual collapse of the demand for youth labour. Nevertheless, using a quasi-shift share analysis the Labour Market Studies Group was able to establish that the adverse industrial shifts described above

Table 8.1 Changes in youths' (16–19) share of employment within industries 1979–84 (numbers are 000s)

Number due to change in all-age employment (cyclical change)		*Number due to structure change*		*Number due to change in proportions of youths to adults*		*Actual Change*	
Males	*Females*	*Males*	*Females*	*Males*	*Females*	*Males*	*Females*
−76.79	17.4	−42.9	−18.02	18.99	−37.03	−100.35	−37.5

Source: Ashton, Maguire, and Spilsbury 1990: 36

had made a significant contribution to the reduction in the demand for male youth labour which took place over the period 1979–84.

Their results in Table 8.1 show that, overall, young males lost just over 100,000 jobs over this period and, while cyclical change in the demand for all workers accounted for 76,000 jobs, industrial change created an additional loss of 43,000 jobs (19,000 jobs were created by the displacement of adult males by young males). For females, cyclical change created over 17,000 jobs, structural change created a loss of 18,000 but the main loss of 37,000 jobs came from the displacement of young females by adult females. In addition, analysis of the Labour Force Survey data for this period revealed that the demand for professional, managerial, and technical people grew by over 16 per cent. However, the proportion of 16–19-year-olds relative to the proportion of all employed persons in those occupations fell consistently in each occupation and for both sexes. In some cases, for example in Professional and Related occupations in Science, the ratio fell from 0.75 to 0.38 for males and from 0.78 to 0.63 for females.[3] This progressive exclusion of young people from these more highly skilled occupations was due to the process of qualification inflation (Ashton, Maguire, and Spilsbury 1990).

The combined effect of these changes was to produce a massive reduction in the demand for the labour of 16-year-old school-leavers. Whereas in 1978, 85 per cent of school-leavers entered employment, by 1985 this figure had fallen to 30 per cent. The transformation of the British economy from a strong manufacturing base to a 'post-industrial' service base had brought with it a collapse in the demand for the labour of unqualified youths.

The other consequence was a change in the type of labour required. Once again this trend stemmed from a number of different sources. As we have seen, one source was the growth of professional and scientific occupations, another was the more highly sophisticated production systems that were being introduced. A further source was the restructuring of firms' internal organizations in response to intensified competition. This has been variously termed the trend towards the 'flexible firm' (NEDO 1986) or the salaried model of the internal labour market (Osterman 1988), and has led to an increasing demand for general problem-solving skills which reflect an ability to learn and adapt and work in less highly structured work situations (Marquand 1989; Ashton, Maguire, and Spilsbury 1990).[4] Fewer and fewer employers are now looking for docile labour.

During this same period an equally radical change was taking place in the availability of forms of training for young people. The growth of female labour force participation and the increasing reliance of employers on female labour created a demand for the training of young women, particularly in such fields as clerical, secretarial, hotel, and catering work. Employers were reluctant to provide the institutional support (e.g. to create an apprenticeship system) or meet the costs of this training, which were increasingly absorbed by the state. Thus this period witnessed the rapid growth of vocational provision in these areas within Colleges of Further Education.

While new forms of state financed training were expanding, the traditional form of training for young males, the apprenticeship, was contracting. In 1965 the number of young people in apprenticeships stood at 155,000. By 1985 it had fallen to 73,000 and by 1988 it was down to just under 58,000 (Ashton, Green, and Hoskins 1989). Similar falls took place in what are officially defined as 'other trainees'. In short, by the end of the 1980s, one of the main institutions on which British industry relied for the training of the next generation of workers had virtually collapsed (see Vickerstaff, Chapter 11, this volume).

THE RESPONSE OF THE THATCHER GOVERNMENT

In the educational sphere, the response of the Thatcher administration was to act on the critiques of the comprehensive system which had surfaced in the course of the Great Debate initiated by the Labour Party during the Callaghan administration. The educational system was seen as failing to meet the needs of industry and youth unemployment was blamed on the schools for failing to provide young people with the skills required by employers. The response was first to introduce a new form of curriculum for working-class pupils in the form of TVEI, to encourage the growth of private schools, and later to establish separate specialist new technology colleges, and finally to encourage other schools to opt out of local authority control.[5] The effect has been to revert to the traditional policy of having different types of school for those destined for different positions within the class and status systems. This is not to deny the advances made in the organization of TVEI, although these have been offset somewhat by the introduction of a national curriculum based on the old 'academic' model. Overall however, the response of the Thatcher government has been to regress to and restore aspects of the traditional British approach to the provision of state education. Of course, this new system is not the same as earlier forms, indeed Brown (1990) has argued that in a nascent form it represents a 'third wave' in the socio-historical development of the education system. It is distinctive in that it combines elements of free market provision with a more selective form of state education, but its social consequences are the same as the earlier forms.

In the field of training, the response of the government was more pragmatic. The virtual collapse of the youth labour market in the early 1980s led to the introduction of the Youth Training Scheme (YTS). In many respects this was a compromise between the objectives of the Manpower Services Commission, which aimed for a national system of training provision, and the requirements of the government for a scheme that would take youths off the streets as quickly and as cheaply as possible (Turbin 1988). Following the riots in a number of cities in 1981 this latter objective became paramount.

In practice the Youth Training Scheme, which provides for up to two years work experience and training, is not one scheme but a series of schemes which feed into different segments of the youth labour market (Lee *et al.* 1990). This is not surprising given that the scheme is 'market driven' and, as such, merely reproduces the pattern of segmentation found in the wider labour market.

Effectively it provides what Cockburn (1987) refers to as a system of two-track training, one for males, another for females. However, these tracks are further divided by skill level. For males the more prestigious schemes lead into some of the few remaining apprenticeships, for females they lead to clerical and secretarial work. For those who are obliged to enter the less prestigious schemes, males move either into semi-skilled or unskilled manual or service sector work while females are highly concentrated in the less skilled service sector jobs. One of the main contributions of YTS for them has been to keep the doors open to such jobs in the face of competition from married women (Ashton, Maguire, and Spilsbury 1990). Yet in spite of this, for some young people, especially those in the depressed areas, the end result is no job at all but a move into unemployment. Because of its focus on the preparation of young people for semi-skilled and unskilled jobs in the lower segments, YTS continues to train young people for jobs in a shrinking labour market.

The increase in the demand for labour in the late 1980s was reflected in a cyclical upturn in the demand for youth labour although, given the regional inequalities in the distribution of jobs, this has not resulted in a corresponding improvement in the position of young people throughout the country. In the south east the increased demand, coinciding with the fall in the numbers of 16–19-year-olds, has produced an increase in the chances of employment. It has also decreased the proportion entering YTS as employers bid for available youths. In parts of the north and other depressed areas, neither the fall in the numbers coming on to the market nor the economic recovery have been sufficient to 'cure' the problem of unemployment. There, YTS continues merely to hold young people until they leave for spells of unemployment.

The main problems of youth training in Britain can now be clearly specified. The traditional industries which recruited large numbers of unqualified youths have declined, as have the industries which relied on skilled manual labour. Technological change and the growth of new knowledge-based industry has created a demand for a much greater proportion of more highly educated workers than was necessary under the old system. The result is that for a number of years employers have consistently reported shortages of highly qualified labour. We are thus left with an underlying situation characterized by an oversupply of unqualified labour and an undersupply of more highly qualified labour.

ALTERNATIVE POLICIES

The experience of other countries suggests a range of alternative policies which could be adopted, not all of which are mutually exclusive. However, it has to be remembered that the legacy of our past will create distinctive problems that have to be overcome.

Option 1

One strategy would be to abandon the existing remnants of the apprenticeship system and seek to enhance the general level of school education for all young people until the age of 18. That would provide the means for enhancing the problem-solving skills which are essential for the development of modern knowledge-based industry. It would then be left to the firms to provide more company-specific training.

If this policy were pursued it would be important to discard once and for all the idea of separate schools for those destined for different positions in the system of stratification. Such a system has conveyed to working-class youth in the past that, no matter how well they did in the field of education/learning, they were destined for jobs in the lower levels of the labour market. In addition, the existence of public schools has played an important part in closing access to some of the top jobs to young people from the middle and working classes. To prevent this, the resources of the state could be used to discourage private schools and to abolish the distinctions that are becoming more prevalent between different types of semi-private schools (e.g. those which opt out and the city colleges which are in a position to be selective in their intake). This means greatly increasing the resources of comprehensives and thus removing the advantages attached to different types of school which are becoming increasingly important under the present government's policies. It would also mean basing the curriculum on the idea of a broad based set of skills for life which are essential for all members of a democratic society.

The form of school which would be particularly well suited to this endeavour is the Community College, precisely because it has its roots in the whole community, providing education and learning experiences for both younger and older members in the same context. Such colleges also perform an important function in conveying the message that education is not a once and for all experience but is a continuous process lasting throughout a lifetime.

The experience of other countries suggests that it is possible to use both academic and vocational curricula as the means for transmitting problem-solving skills. The French have achieved this result through the use of a vocational curriculum, as have the Japanese through an academic one. However, given the problems which working-class youth in Britain have encountered with the traditional academic curriculum, it would be advisable to move in the direction of a curriculum which transmitted more work-based and community-based skills. Such a curriculum would provide young people with more than just the technical skills for jobs. It would also equip young people to participate more effectively in the community decision-making process, in the management of households, and in the skills necessary for the upbringing of children.

If we are to increase the participation rate of working-class youth we will also need to counteract the negative attitudes which the old system of education engendered in them. In view of their past experience of an irrelevant, watered-down academic curriculum it will be necessary to convince members of the working class that what is on offer represents a new departure. It will not be enough to make changes in the organization of schools and then expect working-class youth to flood in. In this respect we need a new concept of education/learning (similar to that spelled out above) which stresses its role in the development of the human potential which exists in all members of society irrespective of gender, race, or class.

There is a further modification which is essential to increase participation within the educational system and that is to stop certifying educational achievement at 16. This only reinforces the message that education has now officially ended. It would be necessary to abolish the existing GCSE and A-levels and introduce a new single examination, based on the curriculum described above, which would mark the attainment of a given standard by all young people. This standard would normally be achieved by age 18, and would provide a message to all youths that educational development normally continues beyond 18. In addition, there would be one Board certifying the competences of all young people at the age of 18, irrespective of whether these competences had been achieved in formal education or in the workplace. This would have the advantage of eradicating the distinction between academic education, vocational education, and training.

Another set of changes crucial to achieving the above objectives would be to discourage employers from recruiting young people for full-time jobs at age 16. At the moment, both the offer of a job (perhaps an apprenticeship) or even a YTS place at 16 provides a monetary incentive for young people to leave education. This incentive is even more appealing when the alternative is a meaningless academic curriculum. Strong steps need to be taken to encourage employers to switch their recruitment to 18-year-olds. A direct route to this would be to make full-time education compulsory to age 18. A more indirect approach would be to compel employers to support 16–18-year-olds in part-time further education for two days a week.

Option 2 – transferable skills training

This set of policies would keep the school leaving age at age 16 and then provide a comprehensive set of training programmes for all school-leavers. This system, similar to the German apprenticeship, would require the collaboration of employers, unions, and state in the establishment of an institutional framework capable of overseeing training in every trade. The system would focus, as it does in Germany, on the provision of transferable skills. The training would last for a minimum of two years and involve an element of part-time further education which could be provided either by the employer or on a day-release basis. However, the majority of apprenticeships/traineeships would be three years in length and would lead to a nationally recognized qualification equivalent in status to the examinations entered by 18-year-olds who remain in education.

The system would replace YTS altogether as the focus would be on the delivery of intermediate-level skills, rather than the type of low-level skills which predominate in YTS. This form of apprenticeship training would not be seen as a means of disguising/solving the unemployment problem. The separation of training measures from unemployment measures is essential if we are to avoid the denigration of training which has occurred as result of the present government's attempt to 'sell' low-quality training as a solution to unemployment when the unemployed were only too well aware that the training was often training in name only.[6] This separation would also facilitate the collaboration of the trade union movement in any attempt to build up a genuine national system of training.

The training provided would need to be open to all adults and not exclusively available to youths. This is necessary not just on the grounds of equity, but also to avoid rigidities in the labour market, whereby training at 16 would lock a person into that trade or occupation for the future. Access for adults could be ensured through an agreed training wage which was related to progress through the traineeship as measured by success in examinations. There would be no age restriction on entry.

Finally, because this system has a degree of autonomy in relation to employers, it would be more successful in combating gender inequality in training opportunities. Freed from the immediate constraints of employers' selection criteria, steps could be taken to break down gender stereotypes.

The system would be administered by a national skills training agency similar in function to the former MSC. This would consist of a board headed by employers, union, and state representatives and the schemes would be administered by semi-autonomous boards at the local level. These boards would also be run by representatives of employers, workers, and educationalists. Information about local skill needs would be fed into the deliberations of the local boards from local employers and community groups through mechanisms such as employers' surveys. Steps would also have to be taken to ensure that women were adequately represented on these local boards. The boards would be free to purchase the appropriate training from educational institutions, private trainers, or employers. The national and local boards would have a regulatory function and would not deliver the training themselves. One final point is that, given the legacy of the educational system and the conservatism of educators steeped in the academic curriculum, it would be important that the local boards rather than the educationalists administer such an apprenticeship system. Furthermore, such boards are likely to be far more responsive to market changes than educationalists have been in the past.

Finance would be provided by a levy on employers' payrolls, plus income from the government and the EC. The effect would be to socialize the cost of training, and the employers would then have to spend relatively little on firm-specific training if the experience of the German employers is valid for Britain. Moreover, if the first option were implemented, then employers could expect to pay far more for their company-specific training, as in France.

Option 3

One major disadvantage of option 2 is that research has revealed a number of industries where transferable skills are not necessary and, indeed, where employers argue that attempts to deliver them in the workplace hinder their own training objectives, which are to deliver more firm-specific training (Ashton, Maguire, and Spilsbury 1990). These are usually firms operating in rapidly changing markets. In view of this, under option 3, some young people could opt at 16 for apprenticeships in those industries which have a clear requirement for transferable occupational skills. For example, these have been shown to operate in the case of skilled work in the engineering and construction industry, although they also operate in clerical work, in the hotel and catering trades (chefs), and in the new computer trades such as programming. Such apprenticeships would be financed by a levy on employers' payrolls in those industries and by income from the government and the EC. They would also be controlled by a board, as in option 2, and would automatically have part-time further education and the opportunity to take a nationally recognized examination as part of their training. The boards would also provide the autonomy necessary to combat sex discrimination at the point of entry to training programmes.

However, under this option, those young people entering other jobs within the above industries which did not require transferable skills, or entering specified industries not covered by apprenticeships but offering firm-specific training, would have a statutory right to continue their education part-time through day release and to take a nationally recognized qualification at age 18 or 19, with their employer covering the cost. That certificate would mark the end of the young person's formal education and acknowledge their achievement of a nationally recognized minimal level of competence.

Because the training of young people in firm-specific skills is achieved through employer-controlled schemes, additional measures would need to be taken to move towards gender equality in provision. As employers are increasingly dependent on female labour, there will inevitably be pressure on them to open up training opportunities to females. However, these need to be complemented by other measures. Research is revealing that one of the crucial factors both in preventing employers investing in the training of females (Ashton, Maguire, and Spilsbury 1990) and in ensuring females' commitment to continuity in their work careers (where such careers are available) are the obligations surrounding their dual role and especially their responsibility for child care (Armstrong and Armstrong 1987). Hence one of the most effective ways to combat this problem is through enhanced provision of nursery education. Such a programme of provision would, of course, have an impact not just in the field of firm-specific training, but throughout the labour market.

CONCLUSION

What we have argued is that because the legacy of the British system of education has led it to focus on the preparation of young people for their position in the stratification system, this has left the task of training young people for jobs to the apprenticeship system. Such a system 'worked' for an economy which required large numbers of semi-skilled and unskilled workers, a smaller group of craftworkers, and an elite of managers and administrators. As the economy has been transformed the demand for skills has changed. The new service economy now requires the majority of workers to have mastered problem-solving skills. Yet what we have is an educational system which continues to produce large numbers of relatively unqualified young people with a negative or indifferent attitude towards education.

In addition, the apprenticeship system which had been relied on to provide industrial training has collapsed. What has been put in its place is a scheme designed to train young people for semi-skilled and unskilled jobs which are rapidly disappearing. In the meantime employers continue to complain of skill shortages across a number of areas.

To rectify this problem we have proposed a number of alternatives. As shown by the experience of other countries, which have already tackled these problems and adjusted to the demands of the service economy, there are a number of possible solutions. Elements of these solutions can be readily applied in the British context, although their introduction would require modifications to cope with the distinctive British legacy in this area. However, all of the alternatives we propose require a radical change in the present educational system, in order to increase the participation of working-class youth.

One of the problems faced by any attempt to introduce reforms is that of combating the entrenched interests which emanate from existing sets of beliefs and institutions. In this respect societies such as Germany and Japan were in a position after the Second World War to start afresh and develop new institutional structures appropriate to the needs of an advanced industrial society. Britain, by contrast, still has powerful institutional structures devised in an earlier era. As we have seen, some of these are acting as a brake on the society's education and training performance, others offer the promise of a base for further development. The task of effective policy intervention and reform is thus to build on existing structures while removing outmoded institutions and replacing them where necessary with more effective provision. For these reasons we advocate a combination of options 1 and 3.

The problem with trying to implement option 2 is that it would require radical restructuring of industrial training and would be time-consuming and expensive to implement. It would require new institutional structures to be established for every industry, which would take time and meet with active opposition from employers in those areas where the dominant demand is for firm-specific as opposed to transferable skills.

Option 1, by contrast, being primarily concerned with education, is an area directly under the control of the state and more radical measures can be introduced. It is also an area where urgent action is required if we are to improve the general level of problem-solving abilities and the ability to learn, which is the foundation on which both transferable and firm-specific skills are built. To option 1 we would advocate adding a modified form of option 3 with entrance to apprenticeships or firm-specific training at age 18. The advantage of option 3 is that it builds on existing experience in providing transferable skills in certain occupations, but improves upon it. However, rather than confronting the interests of some of the larger employers by imposing a uniform scheme, it recognizes that different firms and industries may have different training needs. In doing this it uses the resources of the state to shape and improve upon the practices of employers in those industries requiring firm-specific skills. Yet in doing so, it is modifying their practices in the direction of broader political ideals of equity and social justice.

ACKNOWLEDGEMENT

This paper draws on the work of the Labour Market Studies Group at the University of Leicester. The author is also indebted to the participants of the Kent workshop for comments on an earlier draft, especially Phil Brown and Hugh Lauder, and to Maureen Ashton for comments on the policy section.

NOTES

1 The concept of skill is, of course, problematic and space precludes a discussion of the issues involved here. Elsewhere we have distinguished between three different types of skill: manual dexterity, applied skills, and conceptual skills. Of these, it is the latter that are increasingly demanded by the modern economy (see Ashton, Maguire, and Sung 1991; also Marquand 1989).

2 There were always some exceptions to this, for example, industries such as hosiery, clothing, and footwear have traditionally relied on female labour, of which married women formed a substantial component.

3 These figures refer to the Relative Concentration Ratio. A value of one indicates that the order employs the same proportion of the demographic group as it does of all persons in general: a value of less than one indicates under-representation. Full details of these results can be found in Ashton, Maguire, and Spilsbury (1990).

4 There is an extensive debate over just how far these trends have progressed, see Pollert (1988), Rubery (1989), and Woods (1989).

5 This refers to legal provision which enabled the Governors of Schools to apply to the Secretary of State for Education for

permission to take the control of funding for their school away from the Local Authority and instead receive a direct grant from the Department of Education and Science. This action takes the school out of the comprehensive system and provides a greater degree of control by the school authorities over its intake of pupils.

6 For this reason unemployment measures have not been discussed. The question of appropriate forms of unemployment measures is discussed in Ashton, Maguire, and Spilsbury (1990), Ch. 9.

REFERENCES

Armstrong, P. and Armstrong, H. (1987) 'The conflicting demands of work and home', in K.L. Anderson *et al.* (eds) *Family Matters: Sociology and Contemporary Canadian Families*, Toronto, Methuen.

Ashton, D.N., Green, F., and Hoskins, M. (1989) 'The training system of British capitalism: changes and prospects', in F. Green (ed.) *The Restructuring of the UK Economy*, Hemel Hempstead, Harvester Wheatsheaf.

Ashton, D.N. and Lowe, G.S. (1990) 'School to work transitions in Britain and Canada: a comparative perspective', in D.N. Ashton and G.S. Lowe (eds) *Making Their Way: Education, Training and the Labour Market*, Buckingham, Open University Press.

Ashton, D.N. and Maguire, M.J. (1986) *Young Adults in the Labour Market*, London, Department of Employment Research Paper No. 55.

Ashton, D.N., Maguire, M.J., and Spilsbury, M. (1990) *Restructuring the Labour Market: The Implications for Youth*, London, Macmillan.

Ashton, D.N., Maguire, M.J., and Sung, J. (1991) 'Institutional structures and the provision of intermediate level skills: lessons from Canada and Hong Kong', in P. Ryan (ed.) *International Comparisons of Vocational Education and Training*, Lewes, Falmer Press.

Brown, P. (1990) 'The third wave': education and the ideology of parentocracy', *British Journal of Sociology of Education*, 2 (1), 65–85.

Cockburn, C. (1987) *Two-track Training: Sex Inequalities and the YTS*, London, Macmillan.

Deem, R. (1978) *Women and Schooling*, London, Routledge & Kegan Paul.

—— (1980) (ed.) *Schooling for Women's Work*, London, Routledge & Kegan Paul.

Dore, R.P. and Sako, M. (1989) *How the Japanese Learn to Work*, London, Routledge & Kegan Paul.

Eaglesham, E.J.R. (1967) *The Foundation of Twentieth-century Education in England*, London, Routledge & Kegan Paul.

Gardner, P. (1984) *The Lost Elementary Schools of Victorian England*, London, Croom Helm.

Lee, D., Marsden, D., Rickman, P., and Duncombe, J. (1990) *Scheming for Youth: A Study of YTS in the Enterprise Culture*, Aldershot, Gower.

Maguire, M. (1990) 'British labour market trends', in D.N. Ashton and

G.S. Lowe (eds) *Making their Way: Education, Training and the Labour Market*, Buckingham, Open University Press.

Marquand, J. (1989) *Autonomy and Change: The Sources of Economic Growth*, Hemel Hempstead, Harvester Wheatsheaf.

NEDO (1986) *Changing Work Patterns*, London, National Economic Development Office.

OECD (1987) *Structural Adjustment and Economic Performance*, Paris, OECD.

Osterman, P. (1988) *Employment Futures: Re-organization, Dislocation and Public Policy*, New York, Oxford University Press.

Pollert, A. (1988) 'The "flexible firm": fixation or fact?', *Work, Employment and Society*, 2 (3).

Purvis, J. (1983) 'Towards a history of women's education in nineteenth-century Britain: a sociological analysis', in J. Purvis and M. Hales (eds) *Achievement and Inequality in Education*, Milton Keynes, Open University Press.

Rowthorn, B. (1989) 'The Thatcher Revolution', in F. Green (ed.) *The Restructuring of the UK Economy*, Hemel Hempstead, Harvester Wheatsheaf.

Rubery, J. (1989) 'Employers and the labour market', in D. Gallie (ed.) *Employment in Britain*, Oxford, Basil Blackwell.

Turbin, J. (1988) 'State intervention into the labour market for youth: the implementation of the Youth Training Scheme in three local labour markets', unpublished PhD, University of Leicester.

Wells, J. (1989) 'Uneven development and de-industrialization in the UK since 1979', in F. Green (ed.) *The Restructuring of the UK Economy*, Hemel Hemsptead, Harvester Wheatsheaf.

Woods, S. (ed.) (1989) *The Transformation of Work? Skill, Flexibility and the Labour Process*, London, Unwin Hyman.

9

BEYOND VOCATIONALISM

Shane J. Blackman

INTRODUCTION

The question of how education can best meet the needs of the economy has been consistently addressed since the inception of state education in 1870. Even before this date, Chartists and other radical organizations, along with reformers such as Robert Owen, identified the division between manual training for one social class and liberal education for another as an essential factor in the maintenance of a rigid class-based society (Johnson 1970). By examining the on-going relationship between schools and industry, we have an opportunity to understand some of the changes which have taken place and the conflicts of interest on both sides. Analysis of the historical context of vocational education will bring us nearer to an understanding of the present issues that pervade the debate on English secondary school curriculum in the 1990s.

THE MEDIEVAL CURRICULUM

Current educational reform is presented without an historical context, leaving the policy rationale in a self-evident vacuum; galloping logic, too preoccupied with its modern relevance, ignores the errors of the past only to be condemned to repeat them. Williams states: 'The fact about our present curriculum is that it was essentially created by the nineteenth century, following some eighteenth-century models, and retaining elements of the medieval curriculum near its centre' (1961: 172).

From the Renaissance until the present century, English education has been dominated by the literary tradition.

Challenges to this curriculum were easily dismissed, for example in 1805, when Lord Chancellor Eldon, in a lawsuit concerning the introduction of new subjects at Leeds Grammar school, upheld Samuel Johnson's definition of a grammar school as 'an institution for teaching grammatically the learned languages'.[1] He passed judgement against the teaching of French, German, and mathematics, and anything but Latin and Greek in the school (Archer 1921). Thus, in public and grammar schools the classical linguistic disciplines reigned, themselves of a vocational nature, suitable for the pursuits and leisure of the ruling class.[2] The education of the masses, on the other hand, has been distinctly utilitarian, i.e. apprenticeships or learning from experience. Schools for the poor traditionally devoted themselves to the three Rs, and to religious texts.

THE RISE OF TECHNICAL EDUCATION

In the nineteenth century scientific developments transformed the techniques of industrial production and communication and changed the structure of the economy, which in turn brought pressure for corresponding changes in the structure of state institutions.

However, there was no place for the 'new knowledge' in the curriculum and, according to Williams, it was understood 'not in terms of its essential contribution to liberal studies, but in terms of technical training for a particular class of men' (1961: 163). Science, technology, and technical training were fused and seen not as part of a liberal education but, as Lester Smith explains, 'a capitalist device for exploiting children for the benefit of employers' (1957: 209). Scientific and technological advance have historically been held back by class prejudice, as this 'new knowledge' became intimately linked to the training of the lower social classes. And it is from this premise that we derive the modern conception that learning can be undertaken without reference to practicality.[3]

Paradoxically, the rise of technical education seems to have been brought about by Britain's economic decline from 1851 onwards (Halévy 1929). Shilling (1989) shows that the government's attitude towards vocational schooling in the late 1850s was to keep the cost of schemes low, with the least government involved. In the 1870s the London Livery Companies drew up plans for a national system of technical education and founded the City and Guilds of London Institute. However, there was little financial support from government for the enterprise; technical education flourished only within some types of elementary school and evening classes, financed by local rate-payers, state-aided grants, and charities, under the control of the School Boards.

Under the Liberal governments of the 1880s and 1890s and especially through Education Ministers Mundella and Aclaud, School Boards received encouragement to diversify provision through the use of grants from the Department of Science and Arts.[4] On the basis of local democratic support, School Boards used these monies to implement curriculum change by widening the limited scope of reading, writing, and arithmetic (and needlework for girls) towards higher level work, especially in science. Evans summarizes the impact of the School Boards' advances as:

> the introduction and expansion of higher grade elementary education which afforded a secondary-type schooling (with scientific, technical or commercial bias) for abler working class children who were prepared to stay on beyond the age of twelve. The Sheffield School Board pioneered this development in 1880 and the example was followed by Bradford, Nottingham, Halifax, Manchester, Leeds, Birmingham and London; by the late 1890s there were some seventy higher-grade schools with over 25,000 pupils and many more 'higher tops' in ordinary elementary schools, a development encouraged by the introduction of a new standard VII in 1882. A trickle of students was even able to reach university by this new avenue of advance.
>
> (Evans 1985: 47)

These developments were commended by the Royal Commission on Technical Instruction in 1884, especially in the area of teaching methods and the use of resources.

However in 1887/8, the Royal Commission on the Elementary Education Acts (Cross Commission) identified expansion in this sector as a direct threat to fee-paying grammar schools. Their evidence paints a picture of stagnating and badly organized grammar schools, in contrast to properly staffed elementary schools with good teaching equipment.[5] The Cross Commission split, with the Liberal radicals producing a minority report that assessed higher grade elementary schools as providing the basis for a widespread system of industrial, technical, and commercial education. The Conservatives' majority report emphasized segregation and separation of education for different social classes.

Through popular support the School Boards had widened the curriculum and crucially developed rate- and grant-supported secondary-type schooling, albeit within an elementary setting. It was the latter issue which the Cross Commission found politically and morally unacceptable. It maintained that fee-paying secondary schooling was to be only for the 'wealthier classes' and that the working classes ought to receive only a delimited and elementary education (Roderick and Stephens 1972, esp. p 14). Between 1895 and 1905, the primary political purpose of the Conservative governments in the field of education was the abolition of the elected School Boards.[6]

MORANT AND THE CONSEQUENCES OF THE COCKERTON JUDGEMENT

Robert Morant was a rising professional administrator at Whitehall who, with the Conservative government solidly behind him, engineered the case of Regina v. Cockerton. This skilful manipulation drew attention to the illegality of secondary education taught within elementary schools.

Although Morant is often seen as the villain of the piece, his moves against early specialization in technical and scientific subjects found a sympathetic hearing in many educational quarters.[7] Tropp (1957) reveals that the Headmasters' Association (est. 1890) was itself founded to oppose the higher grade elementary schools. Banks quotes the 1898 *Schoolmaster Journal* as evidence that grammar school Heads wanted to

> give the working class people just enough of the rudiments of education to make them know and keep their status in life, reserve all higher training such as is essential for the securing of all professional and higher class mercantile and commercial and government posts for the children of the better classes.
>
> (Banks 1955: 19)

Following the 1900 Cockerton judgement, which brought about the abolition of the School Boards, Morant used his tenure as Permanent Secretary at the Board of Education between 1902 and 1911 to further enforce the distinction between elementary and secondary schooling. His predilection for the classical curriculum of the grammar school meant subordination for the scientific and technical curriculum previously developed within the higher grade elementary schools.

The political priority of maintaining an education system differentiated by social class meant that access to education for working people became severely restricted. The new impetus for practical, scientific and technical studies was not to be developed in Morant's 1904 Regulations for an academic curriculum (Gosden 1962). Although science had slowly eased itself into first the public and then the grammar school curriculum, this was only as a theoretical subject; the older traditions of literature and linguistics retained their high-status as the 'true' vocations (Peters 1963). The practical response to decades of evidence concerning the decline and neglect of grammar schools was the reassertion of an academic curriculum.

Thus, under the Balfour Act 1902, investment was placed in the 'needy' secondary grammar schools which were to provide better classical education for the middle classes. At the same time, advanced work carried out in elementary schools was not only cut back, but wholly stigmatized by the pervasiveness of the Cockerton judgement. Mass popular demonstrations in London and other cities against the Education Bill of 1902 amounted to nothing as parents' views went unheeded (Simon 1965).

THE 1907 FREE-PLACE SYSTEM REGULATIONS

The scholarship system was not put into practice until the Liberal government required fee-paying secondary grammar schools to make at least 25 per cent of their places available to elementary pupils of proven ability. The Free-place Regulations of 1907 represent a moment of contradiction in the history of educational equality of opportunity.

On the one hand, the free-place system rejects the nineteenth-century philosophy that secondary education is the prerogative of the middle and upper classes (Szreter 1984) and lays down an ideological framework for educational equality. Thereafter, what begins as a narrow bridge for only a few able elementary pupils to pass into the fee-paying sector becomes, by the outbreak of the Second World War, an overcrowded thoroughfare. Banks argues that the rationale for parallel systems of education based on differentiation by social class could not be sustained as 'the free-placers could hold their own with the fee-payers and formed the backbone of the developing Sixth Forms' (1955: 68).

Throughout the 1920s and 1930s reports issued by the Board of Education gradually began to show that free-place pupils were indeed out-performing their fellow fee-paying pupils in the School Certificate. (This is also true of the current Assisted Places Scheme, where recent findings published in the *Times Educational Supplement* (12 January 1990) show that both at GCSE and 'A' level, the Assisted Place pupils are out-performing their classmates.)[8]

On the other hand, the free-place system reinforced the perpetuation of two types of schools for two social classes; parental aspirations for children to succeed in the qualifying examination were ultimately thwarted due to the limited supply of free places. This put pressure on the elementary school to act as a 'staging post' for the entry to grammar school. Innovation in elementary education went into decline, as Dent remarks: 'Elementary schools began systematically to coach and cram their abler pupils for what quickly became in many places a highly competitive examination' (1961: 25). This also applied to the 11+ under the 1944 Education Act, as Jackson observes: 'Primary school teachers consequently organised their classes in such a way that the obviously gifted child could move rapidly into the top class, while the obviously dull child remained in the bottom classes' (1964: 148).

During the inter-war wars the scholarship ladder was criticized in a host of empirical studies, and not least by the Board of Education. The system was deemed inadequate to capture all the ability within the primary school, and there was massive wastage of human potential.[9] Gray and Moshinsky (1938) pointed out that children within elementary schools with high IQs were being excluded from secondary schools, and that in practice their places were still being filled by weaker fee-paying pupils (Blackman 1991).

THE SCHOOL CERTIFICATE

The introduction of the School Certificate in 1917 determined the grammar school curriculum in favour of academic preparation for university, and ensured the neglect of practical and vocational schooling. This examination, as Williams (1961) makes clear, was tied to the traditions of the public school upon which the grammar school was modelled: 'From the 1850s, a system of University local examination, first called "Middle Class Examinations"' (1961: 159) enabled endowed schools to aim at a recognized standard (Roach 1962). Thus, the considerable power embodied and exerted by the University Examination Boards effectively sealed off secondary education from quasi-vocational influences.

During the early part of the century the School Certificate and the Scholarship were recognized as the two major sources of educational division which together sustained discrimination and class privilege (Lindsay 1926); elementary schooling was viewed as a sorting device, grading pupils for specific occupational destinations.[10]

VOCATIONAL SCHOOLING

As we have already seen, government played a protective role towards the grammar school, by ensuring that its provision was not replicated in other places. This cast the elementary school in a quite different, albeit an equally viable, role. Elementary provision took place in Junior Technical, Day Trade, or Central Schools. Commenting upon the purposes of each school in turn, Hadow (1926) states:

> These schools are definitely intended to prepare pupils either for artisan or other industrial occupations or for domestic employment.
>
> (p. 33)

> They were designed to take boys on or near the completion of their elementary school career for a period of one, two or three years, and give a specialised training that would fit them to enter about the age of 16 into workshop or factory life.
>
> (p. 32)

> The chief object of the central school is to prepare girls and boys for immediate employment on leaving school and that the instruction should therefore be such that children will be prepared to go into business houses or workshops on the completion of the course without any intermediate special training.
>
> (p. 31)

The main regulation applying to these free schools was that their provision should not approximate too closely to that in the fee-paying sector. However, local authorities were beginning to find elementary schools difficult to administer; under the Education Act of 1918, pupils could stay longer at school and, due to the shortage of secondary school places, some local authorities were forced to operate selective central schools. These 'higher elementary' schools began to attract criticism from conservatives who saw in them a re-emergence of the challenge to the grammar school associated with School Boards, providing approximate and free secondary education (Eagleshaw 1956). Once again, the Headmasters' Association in 1926 considered this expansion of opportunity undesirable.

TECHNICAL SCHOOLS

The perceived threat in the 1930s to the grammar school monopoly of secondary education came from the Junior Technical Schools, where teachers were not only faced with restrictions concerning what subjects they taught, but also worked under a Board of Education that persistently classified their schools as vocational. Meanwhile, the technical associations wanted neither trade nor grammar schools. Banks (1955) makes clear that their demand was for schools with secondary status and conditions, retaining close links with industry. It was becoming increasingly apparent that some local authorities and technical associations were dissatisfied with the dominance of the academic tradition. Public recognition of this problem was shown in the Spens Report (1938), which put forward plans for a new type of technical secondary school, equal to the grammar school. The rigid dual education system could not respond to the growing needs of employers, nor adapt to the changing conditions of work and could not produce the would-be future

future technologists, innovators, and industrial managers. The grammar school was criticized for the tendency to promote literary and scientific aspects of the academic curriculum, rather than the practical and vocational areas related to industry. Conversely, the Junior Technical Schools were now beginning to seriously challenge the grammar school, with more extended and liberally-based courses being introduced (Cane 1959).

STREAMING FOR THE SCHOLARSHIP

Before streaming emerged in the 1920s, becoming consolidated by the 1930s, pupils were grouped by 'Standards'. A teacher's income depended upon the number of girls and boys they were able to coach through to the next Standard. This was the much criticized system of 'payment by results'. Under the scholarship system, however, schools graded their pupils according to a formal hierarchy of 'streams' where pupils would only do work that was considered appropriate to their stream, either able, average, or backward. This grading began at 'seven plus', with further testing to ensure that the classification remained precise (Jackson 1964). Once created, this administrative machinery took precedence over effective individual assessment. Simon argues: 'The actual practice of classification greatly relieved pressure on the gate of the "scholarship at 11, for B and C children tended to be eliminated from the course while only the picked A contingent pressed ahead"' (1974: 226). The dominance of the scholarship principle had a duel effect: it created a 'second best' atmosphere within serious elementary schools which reacted by becoming strongly vocational, and where 'marking time' became an instrument of social control. Second, the grammar school approach to educating middle-class pupils changed, with even greater emphasis placed on intellectual achievement, especially after revelations concerning the hitherto unknown abilities of the free-placers over the fee-payers.

SELECTION BY DIFFERENTIATION: TYPE, MIND, AND SCHOOL

The Hadow Report encouraged the emergence of selection by differentiation and opposed selection by elimination. Hadow saw in the 'measurement and prediction' work of the educational psychologists a potential rationale for differentiation. He states:

> By the time that the age of 11 or 12 has been reached children have given some indication of differences in interests and abilities to make it possible and desirable to cater for them by means of schools varying types.
>
> (Hadow Report 1926: 74)

Hadow did not fully embrace the machinery of psychological testing, but saw it as a useful mechanism to identify pupil interests and aptitudes. By the 1930s this concept had become subtly transmuted so that streaming by IQ tests was being described in terms of meeting pupils' differing needs. The implications of this change from 'interests' to 'needs' suggests that social classification had taken priority over learing. As Simon makes clear, few questioned this: 'The findings of psychologists seemed the more scientific in that they so precisely reflected current ideas about the social order' (1974: 241). It was assumed that matching of IQ test results to streaming or differentiated courses when a pupil entered school could accurately predict a pupil's progress through both primary and secondary sectors. Thus education could feed into an existing social order; children who failed to enter secondary school did so through an apparently objective selection test (Daniels 1961).

Apart from justifying the inequalities of the existing system, the perceived success of classification and testing ensured that traditional teaching methods and learning programmes were protected from change. Dominated by the University Examination Boards, education innovation had to occur outside the classical grammar school curriculum; although the Spens Report (1938) had pointed out the shortcomings of a narrow, over-specialized secondary curriculum, it did not see any necessity either to change or to make it more widely available. Unlike the Hadow Report, Spens totally accepted the Burt (1959) formulation on the predictive power of intelligence tests (pp. 123–5).

Chamberlain's Conservative government welcomed the tripartite strategy proposed by the Spens Report, but did not favour abolition of fee-paying. During the Second World War the Norwood Report (1943) examined in detail the tripartite framework, which later became the foundation of the 1944

Butler Education Act. The Norwood thesis was that all secondary pupils fall into three psychological categories: academic, technical, and practical. Each group would be best served by an accurate identification of their needs, and by devising distinctive forms of curriculum within three types of school: grammar, technical, and modern.

Post-war secondary education was promised as an 'education for all', though the Act did not mention selection nor the tripartite framework. LEAs were required to provide secondary education to all pupils according to age, aptitude, and ability. In common with Spens, the Norwood Report (1943) did not favour the comprehensive (multilateral) alternative and, due to the discretion built into the Act, the 1950s and 1960s were dominated by the struggle between selective and comprehensive approaches.

What impact did the 1944 Education Act have upon provision of vocational education? On the assumption that modern schools were non-selective, it was considered that a practical curriculum would be most relevant to non-academic pupils; indeed, modern schools were not permitted to enter pupils for external examinations. It was not until 1955 that the Ministry of Education abandoned this policy. Therefore, without the restrictions of external examinations, Dent found a 'spectacularly rapid growth of vocationally-biased courses which took place in secondary modern schools from about 1950s onwards' (1958: 41). Alongside these developments modern schools were officially encouraged to experiment with teaching and learning methods, to enable students of all abilities to fulfil their potential. Progressive ideas flourished, such as pupil-centred approaches (Taylor 1963).[11]

GRAMMAR OR VOCATIONAL SCHOOLING?

Modern schools were caught between two opposing sets of policies and demands. At policy level they had to provide a curriculum which would be biased towards vocational schooling, as spelt out by the Norwood Report (1943), while parents expected that they should opt for a diluted version of the traditional grammar school curriculum. The omnipotence of the grammar school curriculum brought active differentiation into the modern school. From the third year onwards able pupils were prepared for GCE while the average, less able, or less interested pursued specialized vocational courses. Hargreaves (1967) investigated how the streaming system within modern schools moulded the social relations of pupils. He found that A-stream pupils were bright and could succeed, while C-stream pupils defined themselves as failures.

The effect of this arrangement in schools was twofold: staff actively engaged in the process of differentiation, i.e. the function of separating and ranking pupils according to the values of the school became an exercise beyond mere labelling (Lacey 1974). Then, differentiation led to pupils at opposite ends of the streaming system developing subcultures which became increasingly polarized in terms of their attitudes to schooling itself (Willis 1982).[12]

THE NEW 'STAYERS'

A possible solution proposed by the Crowther Report (1959) was a new secondary examination, different from GCE. This was followed closely by the Beloe Report (1960), which provided the rationale for the separation. The Ministry of Education sanctioned the introduction of the new CSE to cater for modern and comprehensive schools. Designed for pupils of average ability, the CSE was characterized by some radical features, such as teacher control, project work, and oral testing. In this way the CSE did not approximate to nor threaten the GCE. The former was launched in 1965 and drew mounting support from ROSLA, due to massive expansion of CSE over GCE entries (Finn 1987).

The 'reluctant stayers' in the fifth year pursued CSEs but the social costs and discipline problems imposed by a diluted academic course began to emerge, especially when pupils discovered that the new qualifications possessed little marketable value.

Teachers were supportive of the raising of the school leaving age (ROSLA), and the professional autonomy created by the CSE (Pring 1989). However, these developments did not in themselves challenge the supremacy of the grammar school curriculum. The Newsom Report (1960) embodied the continuity of a dual education system by assuming that parents accepted the legitimacy of tripartism.[13]

The Schools Council worked hard in supporting the professional skills of teachers on curriculum planning, and especially for the average and below average pupils (Bell and Prescott, 1975). Experiential and experimental, Schools Council work pioneered new developments in assessment and learning which have been extended under vocational education.[14] However, it presented no challenge to academic learning enshrined in the GCE,[15] as Shipman states: 'New developments are only welcomed if they do not disturb the examination streams or reduce the number of subjects that can be taken by (abler) pupils' (1971: 105).

An integrated curriculum became the norm for CSE pupils, whilst transfer to a GCE high status course became 'a bridge too far'. The curriculum operated as an agency of discrimination, especially for Newsom pupils. Burgess (1983) found that both teaching staff and pupils became saturated by the stigma of Newsom.

> Teachers compared the pupils unfavourably – in terms of work and behaviour – with those pupils who followed examination courses. Newsom pupils were seen in negative terms ... these pupils attacked teachers' identities by redefining and manipulating classroom situations. This assault on the teacher role and on conventional ideas of schools and schooling earned these pupils their hatred; a hatred which was released in conversation and in jokes where teachers could control the pupils.
>
> (Burgess 1983: 130)

Burt and Newsom are comparable on the basis of the former's preoccupation with 'backwardness' and the latter's adherence to extensive remedial courses which amount to a form of compensatory education – what Cunningham describes as an example of 'educational apartheid' (1971: 19).

POLITICAL CONTEXT FOR RELAUNCHING VOCATIONAL EDUCATION

The value of 'secondary education for all' came to be questioned throughout the 1970s. For both the right and the left, the springboard for this debate was the apparent failure of social policy to achieve any major redistribution of educational opportunity.[16] Under the shadow of the economic crisis of 1973–5, criticism of state education focused on three key issues: preparation, standards, and behaviour.

Leading the critique against schools were major employers and chief representatives of industrial capital, such as Sir Arthur Bryant, Head of Wedgwood Pottery, Sir John Methuen, Director General of the Confederation of British Industry, and Sir Arnold Weinstock, Managing Director of the General Electric Company (Chitty 1989). Their speeches and reports criticized the educational system for failing to meet the needs of industry. Their pronouncements were sensationally reported in the media, which led to calls to make the school curriculum more vocationally relevant.

Prior to the Second World War, employers revealed no anxieties over the schooling received by the majority of pupils. Indeed, Abbott (1933) found that industry generally viewed vocational education without enthusiasm, preferring to organize the vocational aspects themselves (Carter 1966). Complaints about secondary education from employers were largely targeted at grammar schools, for not producing industrial entrepreneurs and managers. However, during the 1970s industry's attention turned towards the schooling of the whole labour force. This coincides, as Reeder (1981) carefully notes, with the development of a regressive attitude to educational equality coming from organized industry. Furthemore, it is at this point that the right replaced the principle of equal access to state education for all with that of differentiation in the market place. Thus, vocational education becomes merely one of many strategies designed to increase social inequality, and make schools more responsive to market forces (see Chitty, Chapter 6, this volume). The preoccupation of right-wing ideologists with differentiation is premised on the concept of 'necessary inequality' – to provide differential rewards through a competitive market. Educational reform has been based, as Ball makes clear, on: 'an act of faith and an act of ideology. The conservative New Right have been more than keen in the past to castigate left wing local authorities for putting ideology before common sense' (1990: 12).

IS THERE A RADICAL CASE FOR VOCATIONAL EDUCATION?

It is important at this point to specify who should benefit from vocational education. Is it the bottom percentage of pupils who feel disenfranchised from the world of academic subjects – or the able pupils who are currently exhorted to concentrate on science and technology? The development of vocational courses such as TVEI in the early 1980s were initially associated with low status pupils, and exacerbated curriculum division between pupils in school. Gleeson identifies that 'in the wider society prevocational courses have the stigma of being second rate. Their credential value remains invested with employers, who tend to develop their own skills and aptitude tests in the selection of young recruits' (1989: 75). This low status may have been further reinforced by the close link of TVEI with youth training shemes which have a reputation of being for the unemployable. Pring now claims that

> It is ironic that many teachers, who, five years ago, at the inception of TVEI feared the vocationalisation of education through the MSC, have subsequently looked at the body as the protector of liberal education against the illiberal encroachments of the Department of Education and Science.
>
> (Pring 1989: 26)

Ironically, TVEI has become synonymous with modular learning, mixed abiity, profiling, accreditation, guidance, negotiated assessment, school/college collaboration, and a whole host of other developments which have challenged the old dichotomies between vocational and academic education (Blackman 1987). One can conclude that vocationalism has enhanced the professional skills of teachers in curriculum planning, but whether this can ultimately lead to empowerment for teachers and learners as suggested by Hodkinson (1989) is a question for further discussion.

Before such claims can be justified it is worth noting that the sheer diversity of TVEI practices makes comparative analysis difficult (Dale 1989). The current strength of the vocational argument rests upon TVEI's change from a list of technical and vocational subjects to be taught in school into an educational principle, to be pursued throughout the curriculum for all pupils. The effect of TVEI's radical challenge may be measured against its influence upon the GCSE, which many teachers regard as significant.[17] Under TVEI, two major developments have been changes in style of learning and modes of assessment. An emphasis on student autonomy and responsibility has encouraged active learning, allowing students to follow individual programmes. However, the emergence during 1985–6 of a common examination system at 16+, for which teachers had campaigned since the mid-1960s, did not greatly benefit from the advances of the vocational movement (Elliott 1988).

Differentiation operates within the GCSE so that some candidates may not be eligible for higher grades. This is due to the differentiated nature of examination papers and/or questions: from here, pupils are on separate routes within the same subjects and achieve different results. Goldstein and Nuttall (1986) conclude that

> Our present assessment systems embody a hierarchy in which abstract, theoretical achievement is almost always accorded a higher status than the practical and the affective, and this status is intended to reflect what is believed, in the tradition of the 11 plus and 'intelligence', to influence life chances.
>
> (1986: 65)

Differentiation is central to the tradition of dual education provision, both at pre- and post-16 levels, with the specific purpose of restricting opportunity. A significant development came in 1986, with the setting up of the National Council for Vocational Qualifications (NCVQ), whose brief was to bring all vocational qualifications within a framework of four levels (to be operational for most occupations by 1991). NCVQ concentrates on traditional manual skills, such as construction, engineering, and hairdressing, which very much affirms the existing division between manual and non-manual employment.

Manifestly, NCVQ appears to be a great leveller, through the principle of open access, making occupational specialization more readily available to pupils of all abilities: removal of barriers will enable young women and men to embark upon training and then to enter the trade most relevant to them. The latent effect is to present occupational choice as resting upon individual self-socialization, where young people still gain employment in relation to their social class, gender, and ethnic origin. Young people fix their class and gender identity through celebration of occupation and sexual stereotypes in order to conform to role models within their class culture (Blackman 1987). Thus, active continuity between pre- and post-16 vocational routes, effectively precluding transfer to academic subjects, ensures the reproduction of the existing division of labour.

However, we should not underestimate the radical effects that vocational education has had on the academic curriculum. Certain vocational initiatives have made the academic curriculum more accountable and even responsive to the needs of the majority of pupils. From the Schools Council to TVEI, vocationalism has demanded innovation, with the result of both challenging and enhancing the classical tradition. It is at this point that vocational initiatives become devalued, and a distance is reasserted between the two curricula. This separation disenfranchises students from the learning process by creating artificial academic barriers leading to predetermined occupational routes. The fundamental supporting ideology of liberal education is that it offers individual social mobility. However, in practice, liberal education has been confined to and restricted within the grammar school curriculum, and has been demonstrated to induce opposition to learning (Hargreaves 1967; Willis 1982).

Certain features of the TVEI entitlement curriculum resemble Dewey's idea of critical vocational education: 'a negotiated curriculum, allowing for individual differences in pace and style of learning'. This approach, combined with political, economic, and social awareness, offers the potential for flexibility and relevance, whereby pupils not only learn to understand the world around them, but to take an active role in it. Further, the adoption of an 'Open University' framework for unit or credit-accumulation within the curriculum would enable all pupils to be working within the same framework, rather than following a hierarchy of courses. But the fundamental problem remains that no matter how innovative a curriculum is, it counts for little unless differentiation is dismantled. As Dewey recognized, in times of widening access to education, existing inertia is only one of the problems to be overcome – there is also 'the opposition of those who are entrenched in command of the industrial machinery and who realise that such an education system, if made general, would threaten their ability to use others for their own ends' (1915: 319) (Blackman 1991).

CONCLUSION: EXPANSION V. ELITISM

The dominant feature of the English education system over the last one hundred years has been its preoccupation with grading and sorting pupils to fit a bipartite framework, in which distinct social classes pursue selective curricular of unequal currency. This period has also seen significant challenges to the dominance of the grammar school curriculum:

1890s – School Board Higher Elementary Schools
1920s/1930s – Central and Junior Technical Schools
1950s/early 1960s – Modern Schools
1970s – Comprehensive Schools

This chapter has drawn attention to the way in which these initiatives have been recognized by Conservative educationalists and politicians as a viable threat to the monopoly of secondary education traditionally enjoyed by grammar schools.

Historically, these developments have not been cumulative: although each initiative has represented an extension of opportunity, with secondary education moving beyond a narrow social group, this has always been followed by a reassertion of elitism. Following each episode, Conservative governments have introduced education policies which, by working on both an institutional and an ideological level, decrease opportunity and restore a dual system of schooling

The response of Conservative governments to these challenges to the grammar school from the school boards and later from the Comprehensive movement has been to dismantle local democracy (School Boards, LEAs) and to reorganize the institutional structure of education (Eagleshaw 1956; Hickox and Moore 1990). The supportive ideology of intelligence testing and streaming by differentiation suffered a fundamental breakdown following examination successes by pupils who had been predicted to fail. Rather than continuing on a path of educational expansion, the Conservative response has been to re-introduce constraining forms of vocationalism, whose popularity has rested on making schooling appear more relevant to future working life (Davies, Holland, and Minhas 1990). Additionally, 'carrots' of limited opportunity were introduced, such as the Scholarship, 11+, and Assisted Places, which offer individual social mobility, while justifying an edifice of discrimination. It is at the point where educational expansion exposes the failure of elitist educational policies that Conservative governments attempt to protect inequality by reassertion of the academic/ vocational divide.

The relaunch of vocational education by Lord Young in the early 1980s was a political response to a prevailing labour market problem of too many young people chasing too few jobs. However, due to the demographic turn-around, there are signs that young people are now deserting youth training for wage labour. Furthermore, employers facing recruitment problems have begun to offer incentives to employees, such as higher wages and training. Nevertheless the question remains that after decades of developing theoretical models and spending millions of pounds, the Training Agency (MSC) is still no nearer a solution to the problem of training to secure economic efficiency.

The forced introduction of an 'educational market' within secondary schools allows the student the apparent choice, via the market mechanism, of their vocational course preference. However, this must be seen against the overall decrease in equality of opportunity in education (Chitty 1989); whilst students are not actually coerced into the vocational options, its provision within a structure of overall inequality ensures an environment in which they will select it of their own free will. This once again leaves liberal education for an elite, and therefore appearing to need little reform. Segregation within a secondary system puts the maintenance of class interest before employer demands for a broad, balanced, general education. The New Right education policy is an experiment with other peoples' life chances. Here, the social order is determined by the 'natural' discipline of the market. Under this process of reification, vocational education is merely a mechanism for reinforcement of class relations within a new structure of inequality.

NOTES

1 Quoted from Hutchinson and Young (1962: 61).
2 Goodson (1983).

3 See Dewey (1915) for the ancient understanding of the division between vocation and education, especially pp. 308–9.

4 A conflict emerges between the philanthropy of liberalism and the *laissez-faire* approach, where free education subsidized by state grants and rates support from the School Boards begins to offer better schooling than that paid for by the middle class in grammar schools (Roderick and Stephens 1978).

5 Simon (1965), especially pp. 117–86.

6 A parallel exists here with the abolition of the Inner London Education Authority in April 1990 under the third Thatcher administration.

7 Sadler is generally regarded as Morant's leading opponent, but both shared certain common views on vocational schooling, although Sadler's (1905) paper reveals his greater insight into a potentially divisive educational system.

8 See Whitty, Fitz, and Edwards (1989); also Wall (1986).

9 See Lindsay (1926), Lowndes (1937).

10 Szreter (1984) provides a useful account of different influences upon state education during the inter-war period.

11 The notion of intelligence and its measurement are discussed by Brown and Lander (Chapter 1) and Ashton (Chapter 8) in this volume.

12 See also Quine (1974).

13 See Dent (1958).

14 In fact certain educationalists such as Professor R. Pring have been key figures in both decades of school reform.

15 See the collection of varied papers edited by Bell and Prescott (1975).

16 For Britain see Westergaard and Resler (1975) and for the USA see Jencks (1972).

17 In a recent interview a Head Teacher in South West London states:

> The impact of TVEI has been truly significant because of its access to resources, innovations, developments; we would not have got the best out of GCSE that we have and this will probably be the same for the National Curriculum. It is in the teachers' delivery – teachers adapted TVEI and they will adapt the National Curriculum through integrative cross-curricular themes.

REFERENCES

Abbott, A. (1933) *Education for Industry and Commerce in England*, London, Oxford University Press.

Archer, R.L. (1921) *Secondary Education in the Nineteenth Century* London, Oxford University Press.

Ball, S. (1990) 'Markets, morality and equality in education', *Hillcole Group, Paper 5*, London, Tufnell Press.

Banks, O. (1955) *Parity and Prestige in Engish Secondary Education*, London, Routledge & Kegan Paul.

Bell, R. and Prescott, W. (eds) (1975) *The Schools Council: A Second Look*, London, Ward Educational.

Beloe Report (1960) London: HMSO.

Blackman, S.J. (1987) 'The labour market in school: new vocationalism and issues of socially ascribed discrimination', in P. Brown and D.N. Ashton (eds) *Education, Unemployment and Labour Markets*, Lewes, Falmer Press.

—— (1991) The politics of pedagogy: problems of access in higher education, in Chitty, C. (ed.) *Post-16 Education: Studies in Access and Achievement*, London, Kogan Page, 135–44.

Burgess, R.G. (1983) *Experiencing Comprehensive Education*, London, Methuen.

Burt, C. (1959) 'The examination at eleven plus', *British Journal of Educational Studies* 7 (219), 99–118.

Cane, B.S. (1959) 'Scientific technical subjects in the curriculum of English secondary schools at the turn of the century', *British Journal of Educational Studies* 8, 52–64.

Carter, M. (1966) *Into Work*, London, Penguin.

Chitty, C. (1989) *Towards a New Education System: The Victory of the New Right?* Lewes, Falmer Press.

Crowther Report (1959) London: HMSO.

Cunningham, H. (1971) 'The young school leaver', in H. Cunningham and D. Lawton (eds) *ROSLA and After*, Vol. 1, London, BBC.

Dale, R. (1989) *The State and Education Policy*, Milton Keynes, Open University Press.

Daniels, J.C. (1961) 'Effects of streaming in primary schools', *British Journal of Educational Psychology*, 31 (1 and 2), 69–78, 119–27.

Davies, A.M., Holland, J., and Minhas, R. (1990) 'Equal opportunities in the new era', *Hillcole Group, Paper 2*, London, Tufnell Press.

Dent, H.C. (1958) *Secondary Modern Schools*, London, Routledge & Kegan Paul.

—— (1961) *The Educational System of England and Wales*, London, University of London Press.

Dewey, J. (1915) *Democracy and Education*, New York, Macmillan Free Press.

Eagleshaw, E. (1956) *From School Board to Local Authority*, London: Routledge & Kegan Paul.

—— (1960) 'Planning the Education Bill of 1902', *British Journal of Educational Studies* 9 (1), 3–24.

Elliott, J. (1988), 'The state v. education: the challenge for teachers', in H. Simons (ed.) *The National Curriculum*, London, British Educational Research Association.

Evans, K. (1985) *The Developments and Structure of the English School System*, London, Hodder & Stoughton.

Finn, D. (1987) *Training Without Jobs: New Deals and Broken Promises*, London, Macmillan.

Gleeson, D. (1989) *The Paradox of Training: Making Progress out of Crisis*, Milton Keynes, Open University Press.

Goldstein, H. and Nuttall, D. (1986) 'Can graded assessment, records of achievement and modular assessment co-exist with GCSE?', in C. Gipps (ed.) *The GCSE: An Uncommon Examination*, Bedford Way Paper No. 29, University of London Institute of Education.

Goodson, I. (1983) *School Subjects and Curriculum Change: Case Studies in Curriculum History*, London, Croom Helm.

Gosden, P.H.J.H. (1962) 'The Board of Education Act 1899', *British Journal of Educational Studies* 9 (1), 44–60.

Gray, J.L. and Moshinsky, P. (1938) 'Ability and opportunity in English education', in L. Hogben, (ed.) *Political Arithmetic*, London, Allen & Unwin.

Hadow Report (1926) 'The education of the adolescent', London, HMSO.

Halévy, E. (1929) *Imperialism and the Rise of Labour 1895–1905*, London, Ernest Benn.

Hargreaves, D.H. (1967) *Social Relations in a Secondary School*, London, Routledge & Kegan Paul.

Hickox, M. and Moore, R. (1990) 'TVEI, vocationalism and the crisis of liberal education', in M. Flude and M. Hammer (eds) *The Education Reform Act 1988: Its Origins and Implications*, Lewes, Falmer Press.

Hodkinson, P. (1989) 'Crossing the academic/vocational divide: personal effectiveness and autonomy as an integrating theme in post-16 education', *British Journal of Educational Studies* 37 (4), 369–83.

Hutchinson, M. and Young, C. (1962) *Educating the Intelligent*, London, Penguin.

Jackson, B. (1964) *Streaming: An Education System in Miniature*, London, Routledge & Kegan Paul.

Jencks, C. (1972) *Inequality: A Reassessment of the Effects of Family and Schooling in America*, New York, Basic Books.

Johnson, R. (1970) 'Education policy and social control in early Victorian England', *Past and Present* 49, 96–119.

Lacey, C. (1974) 'Destreaming in a pressured academic environment', in J. Eggleston (ed.) *Contemporary Research in the Sociology of Education*, London, Methuen.

Lester Smith, O.W. (1957) *Education*, London, Penguin.

Lindsay, K. (1926) *Social Progress and Educational Wastage*, London, Routledge & Kegan Paul.

Lowndes, G.A.N. (1937) *The Silent Social Revolution*, London, Oxford University Press.

Newsom Report (1960) London: HMSO.

Norwood Report (1943) London: HMSO.

Peters, A.J. (1963) 'The changing idea of technical education', *British Journal of Educational Studies* 11, 142–66.

Pring, R. (1988) 'Education Act 1988: lessons not learnt from TVEI', in H. Simons (ed.) *The National Curriculum*, London, British Educational Research Association.

—— (1989) '50 years on', *British Journal of Educational Studies* 37 (1) 17–29.

Quine, W.G. (1974) 'Polarised cultures in comprehensive schools', *Research in Education* 12, 9–25.

Reeder, D. (1981) 'A recurring debate: education and industry', in R. Dale, G. Esland, R. Ferguson, and M. MacDonald (eds) *Education and the State, vol. 1, Schooling and the National Interest*, Lewes, Falmer Press.

Roach, J. (1962) 'Middle-class education and examinations: some early Victorian problems', *British Journal of Educational Studies* 11, 176–93.

Roderick, G.W. and Stephens, M.D. (1972) *Scientific and Technical Education in Nineteenth-century England*, Newton Abbott, David & Charles.

—— (1978) *Education and Industry in the Nineteenth Century: The English disease?* London, Longmans.

Sadler, M.E. (1905) 'The school in some of its relations to social organisation and to national life', *Sociological Papers* 2, 123–39.

Shilling, C. (1989) *Schooling for Work in Capitalist Britain*, Lewes, Falmer Press.

Shipman, M. (1971) 'Curriculum for inequality', in R. Hooper (ed.) *The Curriculum: Context, Design and Development*, Edinburgh, Oliver & Boyd in association with the Open University Press.

Simon, B. (1965) *Education and the Labour Movement 1870–1920*, London, Lawrence & Wishart.

—— (1974) *The Politics of Educational Reform 1920–1940*, London, Lawrence & Wishart.

Spens Report (1938) London: HMSO.

Szreter, R. (1984) 'Some forerunners of sociology of education in Britain: an account of the literature and influences c. 1900–1950', *Westminster Studies in Education* 7, 13–34.

Taylor, W. (1963) *The Secondary Modern School*, London, Faber & Faber.

Tropp, A. (1957) *The School Teachers*, London, Heinemann.

Wall, D. (1986) 'The Assisted Places Scheme and its operation in London girls' public day schools trust schools', MA Dissertation, Institute of Education, University of London.

Westergaard, J. and Resler, H. (1975). *Class in Capitalist Society: A Study of Contemporary Britain*, London, Heinemann.

Whitty, G.,Fitz, J., and Edwards, T. (1989) 'Assisting whom? Benefits and costs of the Assisted Places Scheme', in A. Hargreaves and D. Reynolds (eds) *Education Policies: Controversies and Critiques*, Lewes, Falmer Press.

Williams, R. (1961) *The Long Revolution*, London, Chatto & Windus.

Willis, P. (1982) 'Male school counterculture in popular culture', V 203, Block 7, Unit 30, Milton Keynes, Open University Press.

10

EDUCATION AFTER BASIC SCHOOLING

Malcolm Maguire, Susan Maguire, and David N. Ashton

In recent years there have been frequent criticisms of the inadequacies of the British system of vocational training, and, as a consequence, the deficiencies of the British labour force, in terms of qualifications and skills. At a time when the pace of technological change is effecting a transformation in the distribution of occupations, with an ever-increasing demand for a more highly educated and trained labour force, there has been a notable lack of coherent policy to make further education more responsive to these demands.

TRENDS IN FURTHER EDUCATION

The establishment of an elitist system of secondary education has restricted the development of education after basic schooling in the UK. For those who failed to be selected for the academic stream which provided the requisite training for entry into higher education, the English system of post-secondary education has traditionally made scant provision. Attempts were made in the early years of the twentieth century to establish a system of technical schools. However, these were soon discarded in favour of a system of grammar school provision. After the Second World War, the 1944 Education Act attempted to establish technical education as part of a system of tripartite provision, but this was only partially implemented. This minimal provision for technical education formed the basis of the present Colleges of Further Education (CFEs).

The main thrust of post-secondary education has always been to provide a training in certain 'academic' subjects as preparation for entry into the professions and commerce or, for the fortunate few, higher education. The requirements for entry into universities and the professions have thus dominated the system of post-secondary education. Vocational education and training were seen to be the responsibility of individuals and their employers. What were to become the CFEs provided vocational training for those who left school at 15 and later 16, as most were encouraged to. Those who entered apprenticeships as craftsmen or technicians were predominantly male, and usually received training on a day-release or night-class basis. Apart from hairdressing, few apprenticeships were open to female school-leavers. In the absence of employer-funded training for females, the state and local authorities, through CFEs, provided training in commerce and clerical and secretarial skills on a full-time basis.

Although this provision was minimal, the system of part-time education fulfilled an important function in providing an alternative route of occupational mobility for those (males) who left school at the minimum school-leaving age (Lee *et al.* 1987). Females were able to obtain the basic skills necessary for entry into the growing number of white-collar jobs. An extra year at college enabled the daughters of aspiring, working-class parents and of middle-class parents to avoid the alternative of factory work.

As recently as 1974 only 10 per cent of 16-year-olds were in CFEs, whereas 27 per cent remained at school. By this time the colleges were providing a second chance for young people to take 'O'-levels as well as offering an alternative context to school for those pursuing 'A'-levels. Many young people preferred what they perceived to be the adult atmosphere of the CFEs to the context of the school, which was associated with childhood.

As a consequence the colleges began to compete directly with the schools through the provision of academic courses for those following the conventional route to the professions and higher education. At the same time their function in providing a vocational route as an alternative to the academic one started to decline. This was caused by the fall in the number of apprenticeships and a shift in employers' recruitment strategies as they started to switch to 'A'-level students and graduates as their source of future managers.

Thus, by the 1980s the CFEs contained an uneasy combination of academic and vocational courses, resulting from the dissatisfaction on the part of many young people with their situation in conventional schools and the demand for vocational education which mushroomed in the 1980s. This increased demand for vocational education was partly attributable to the emergence of mass youth unemployment in the early 1980s. The introduction of the Youth Training Scheme (YTS), with its promise of the opportunity for acquiring a vocational qualification, placed increased demands on the CFEs, while at the same time many young people who were reluctant to enter YTS turned to Further Education as an alternative.

The result of this increased demand was that by 1987 the proportion of 16-year-olds who entered Further Education had risen to 18 per cent, bringing the total in education to 50 per cent of the age group. Thus, the CFEs absorbed almost all of the increase in the demand for education beyond basic schooling which had taken place since 1974. It should also be noted that, within FE, there has been a considerable expansion in the numbers on full-time vocational courses.

What is particularly significant about this increased demand is that many of the young people who chose to enter FE either on a full-time or part-time basis would not have done so in the past. These were the YTS trainees and those who could not find a job. They may not have done well in their CSEs or 'O'-levels (at least not in terms of the traditional standards required for entry into the sixth form), and were looking for a meaningful alternative to O-levels. In addition, some young people opted for full-time vocational courses, such as Business Studies, as an alternative to 'A'-levels, with a proportion of these subsequently gaining access to Higher Education and the professions.

In response to this demand for vocational qualifications the City and Guilds Institutes and Business and Technician Education Council (BTEC) extended their activities by introducing new certificates. In addition the DES introduced the Certificate of Pre-Vocational Education (CPVE), while the extension of the Technical and Vocational Education Initiative (TVEI) into the CFEs provided another set of developments.

In developing courses for this maze of certificates, and accepting young people for them, the CFEs took on another function. They were now providing fairly general vocational education for young people who were uncertain of their destination in a labour market which provided them with relatively few points of entry but a bewildering variety of qualifications.

ROUTES THROUGH THE SYSTEM

The result of the above changes has been to create a variety of possible routes which young people can take into the labour market. In order to clarify the main ones we have presented them in diagrammatic form (Figure 10.1). The Figure highlights the relationship between the young person's intitial general education, formal training, and the status (in terms of salary level, job prospects) of the job entered and is derived from data from our earlier research (Ashton and Maguire, 1986). The Figure illustrates five main pathways which young people typically follow through the system of vocational education and training in Great Britain.

Route 1 is characterized by low achievers from the system of general education who move directly into either a semi-skilled or unskilled job on leaving school at 16. The proportion of young people following this route fell dramatically with the advent of YTS (now YT). In addition, there are large regional variations in the proportions following this 'one step' route, depending on local labour market conditions. The initial results of the Economic and Social Research Council (ESRC) 16–19 Initiative show that in 1985 36 per cent of males and 26 per cent of females followed it in Swindon but only 9 per cent of males and 8 per cent of females in Sheffield (Bynner 1990).

Route 2 also involves a move through the system of general education, but then into YTS where the young person may undertake some further education. Some may have spent a short period in full-time FE prior to entering YTS. Many of those following this route are likely to enter the same type of semi-skilled and unskilled jobs as those following Route 1, although almost 30 per cent enter clerical jobs (*Labour Market Quarterly Report* 1988). Unlike those following Route 1, a proportion will obtain a vocational qualification. However, once again it must be emphasized that there are large regional variations in the success achieved by YTS graduates in obtaining a job.

Route 3 is followed by school-leavers or college-leavers who have some formal educational qualifications and who then succeed in entering jobs which involve sponsored training, such as an apprenticeship, before entering a skilled manual job or its equivalent in the service sector.

Route 4 has expanded recently and involves school-leavers

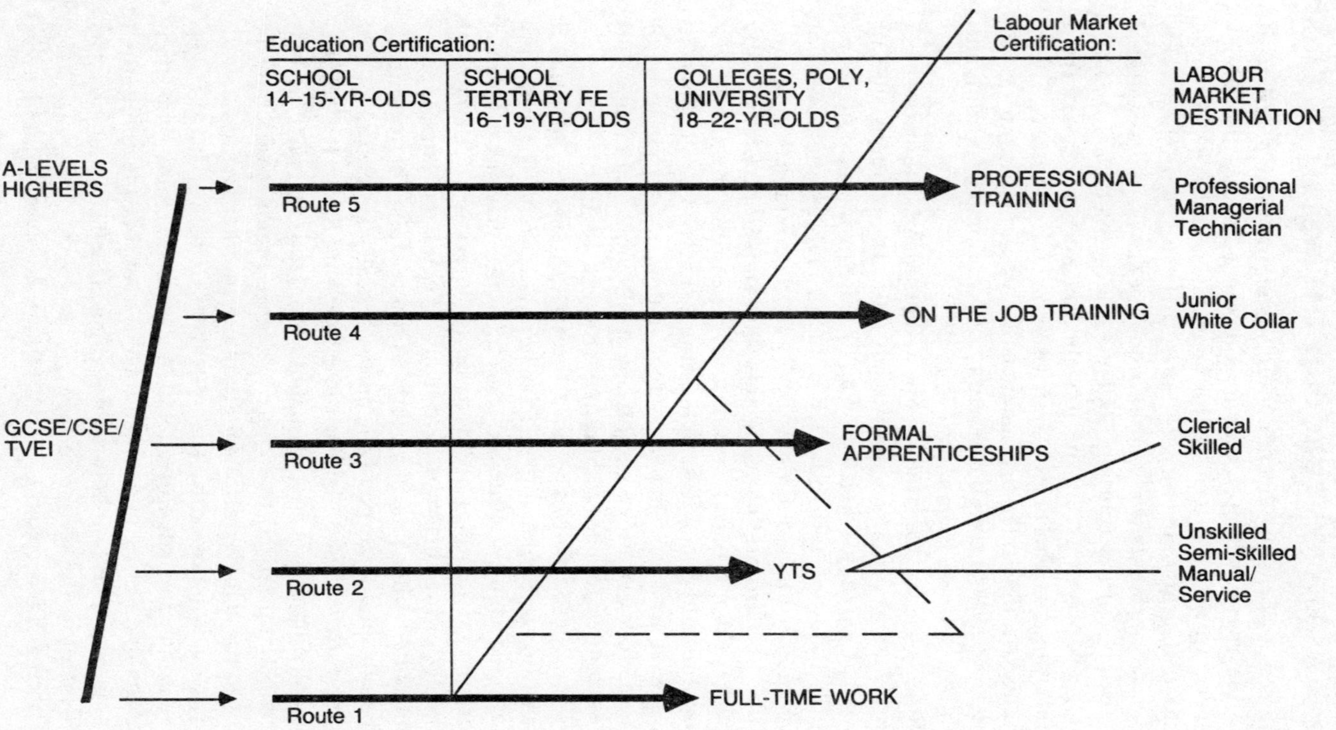

Figure 10.1 Institutional context and certification

moving into CFEs at age 16. There they undertake vocational courses such as BTEC (First/National Diploma courses) or, for a minority, CPVE, before entering junior white-collar and clerical employment (or possibly Higher Education in order to take an HND or degree). Once again this group obtain some form of vocational qualification. In Scotland this route leads through the National Certificate Programme and is followed by a higher proportion of the population.

Route 5 is the traditional academic one involving moves from GCE or GCSE to 'A'-level or Scottish Highers into Higher Education and ultimately entering jobs in the upper reaches of the occupational hierarchy. The proportions following this route have remained relatively stable over the last decade and could even have shrunk (see Raffe 1988).

These ideal-type routes are subject to considerable variations when individuals' work histories are examined. For example, those following Route 1 may experience an 'upward drift' (Ashton, Maguire, and Spilsbury 1990) to higher level jobs on entering the labour market. In addition, a limited number of entrants to Route 4 may be able to use their 'vocational qualifications' to obtain entry into a university or polytechnic.

There are also substantial variations in the gender distributions of those following the different routes. For example, far more females than males follow Route 4, while the opposite is true for Route 3. This is because the gender composition of those following the routes tends to reflect the gender composition of demand in the labour market. However, the link between the flow of young people through these routes and the demand for their labour in the market is not always precise and there is often a mismatch in the relationship between the proportions of young adults leaving these routes and the demands of the economy. This can occur for a number of reasons, such as: a time lag before young people and their advisers respond to changes in demand that are signalled from the labour market; changes in educational policy which restrict provision and hence the proportions who can follow a given route; cyclical and structural changes in the demand for youth labour.

SOURCES OF CHANGE ACTING ON THE SYSTEM

There are a number of changes acting on the system. Here we concern ourselves with the major political and economic ones. With regard to the economic changes, perhaps the most profound has been the underlying shift in the occupational structure. On the one hand there has been a rapid decline in the number of full-time manual jobs in manufacturing, a decline that has affected not just the unskilled and semi-skilled jobs but also the more highly skilled manual jobs (see Ashton, Maguire, and Spilsbury 1990). The result has been a dramatic fall in the number of jobs which offer a formal period of training, as is the case with an apprenticeship. For example, the total number of apprentices and other trainees, which stood at 388,600 in 1965, had fallen to 93,300 by 1988 (Ashton, Green, and Hoskins 1989). However, this has not been matched by a reduction in the flow of young people following Route 3, for such jobs remain highly desirable to those entering the labour market from working-class communities. The signals from the labour market take some time to bring about a change in the perceptions and behaviour of young people.

Partly offsetting the decline of full-time manual jobs there has been a growth of professional, scientific, and administrative jobs in both the manufacturing and service sectors. Thus, in terms of full-time jobs, there has been a growth of jobs demanding a high level of skill and training and a decline in the need for unskilled labour. Significantly, this has not been matched by an increase in the flow of young people into Higher Education.

Changes in the distribution of the various types of full-time jobs have reshaped the occupational structure but have not contributed much to the overall growth of jobs which took place following the depths of the 1979–82 recession. Most of the job growth which has taken place in the economy has been a result of the creation of part-time jobs in the service sector, many of which are unskilled. To date the main source of labour recruited for these jobs has been from outside the educational system, namely married women returning to work. Whether that source of labour will continue to be sufficient to meet the demands remains to be seen. The experience of societies such as Canada and the USA, which have larger service sectors than Britain, suggests that eventually employers may start to look to young people as a potential source of labour for such jobs.

The persistent skill shortages in the higher level occupations have generated pressures to expand the Higher Education route and to broaden access to include more students of working-class origins. In the middle levels, the decline of the traditional apprenticeship, the impact of new technology, and the more intensive foreign competition facing firms are producing demands from companies for more flexibility in the training process and a greater degree of control over it. Despite the persistence of skill shortages, the system still produces a greater number of young people with low-level skills and few qualifications than is commensurate with the development of an advanced industrial economy. This situation is aggravated by the geographical imbalance in the distribution of available jobs. Overall, these changes are creating strong pressures for a general increase in the amount and quality of vocational education and training within the system.

In addition to these economic trends, the provision of education after basic schooling has been affected by a number of important political changes, some of which were touched on above. For those following the first three routes, one of the most significant has been the introduction of TVEI as an attempt to introduce greater vocational relevance into the curriculum. Although TVEI has had a measure of success in that objective (Bell and Howieson 1988), it has neither affected the status of the traditional academic subjects nor reduced the rigid distinction between academic and vocational education which pervades the system. Indeed, the introduction of the National Curriculum is likely further to reinforce this distinction.

Occupations in the middle levels have been affected by major innovations involving the introduction of a whole series of new vocational qualifications. Some, like CPVE, stem directly from the actions of government departments, while others, like the BTEC and City and Guilds certificates, are products of the attempts of examining bodies to meet the demand for qualifications from those who have an indifferent performance in the GCSE but who wish to obtain further vocational qualifications in the hope of enhancing their chances in the labour market. These innovations have had a major impact on the CFEs and those following Route 4.

The main political factor affecting those following Route 5 has been the decision to restrict spending on Higher Education and hence the provision of places. This has resulted in an intensification of competition for access to this route. By doing this, at a time when the demand for the products of Higher Education has been expanding, these political decisions have contributed towards the creation of skill shortages. However, they have also increased the pressure from within Further Education to open up the alternative route which the higher level vocational qualifications can provide to Higher Education.

The combined effect of many of the political changes on the CFEs has been to create considerable confusion about their role. The colleges are now pulled in three different directions. They are expected to respond immediately to the demands of the labour market by providing relevant vocational courses for local employers. They are being called on by students to provide a rigorous academic curriculum in response to the entry requirements of the universities and polytechnics. Finally, they are being required to provide a range of courses for young people who are seeking to improve upon the academic qualifications they obtained while at school.

Within the colleges, the rapid growth of this group of students has created unforeseen demands. Traditionally, young people entering colleges at 16 had already made their vocational 'choices', either to seek entry to Higher Education or to enter clerical work or a trade. Now the colleges have another expanding group of clients following Route 4, many of whom have yet to make a choice or are unclear about what exactly they can expect in the labour market or which doors their 'new' vocational qualifications will open.

This new clientele will have a variety of reasons for entering FE: some will be returning to college because they have failed to find a job with formal training; some will wish to obtain some form of vocational qualification which may help them in the labour market; some will be seeking to pursue the vocational route to Higher Education – some will have inadequate GCSE results to gain entry to traditional 'A'-level courses offered by schools. The problem for these entrants is which of the various options or pathways to pursue, e.g. CPVE, re-take GCSE, BTEC, City and Guilds, and so on. For them, the present system appears, to say the least, confusing.

In summary, we can highlight three main points of stress in the system of Further Education. First, there is the mismatch between the flow of young people out of education and the demands of the labour market. Second, the CFEs are caught in cross pressures, with contradictory demands on their resources, trying to meet the academic requirements of universities and polytechnics and the vocational training needs of local employers. Third, they are facing fresh demands from their new group of clients for better guidance through the maze of current provision.

THE DISTINCTIVE FEATURES OF THE BRITISH SYSTEM

A comparison of education after basic schooling in Britain with that of other industrial societies reveals other distinctive aspects of provision in Britain, especially of that in England and Wales. Perhaps the one most frequently cited is that even with the larger numbers following Route 4 and moving into Further Education, Britain still has a large proportion (approximately 50 per cent) of young people who leave full-time education at 16 to enter the labour market. As we have already noted, persistent skill shortages are signalling the inability of the educational system to produce sufficient highly educated youth to meet the demands of the economy. How is it, then, that other industrial societies have been able to overcome this problem?

In Canada the solution to the problem was created by a combination of factors. First, their educational system combines both academic and vocational education in the mainstream curriculum and so there has never been any need to make separate provision for vocational courses in secondary education. Partly because of this there does not exist the rigid distinction between academic education and training that is found in Britain. Thus, many of the courses which the UK CFEs provide, such as commerce, business studies, and clerical courses, are to be found within the Canadian high school. Moreover, the Canadian system does not certify young people at 16, thereby sending signals to the majority that their formal education is now finished. The combination of a more relevant academic and vocational curriculum, together with high school graduation at grade 12, creates a system which educates the majority (between 70 and 80 per cent) of young adults until they are 18 years of age. There, the training of apprentices and technicians takes place in Institutes of Technology and the training of nursery nurses and similar occupational groups within Community Colleges. However, these usually cater for an age group much older than that which populates British CFEs.

In the 1960s France had a similar problem to Britain, namely that a high proportion of its 15- and 16-year-olds were leaving school with few or no qualifications. The solution adopted was to expand educational provision and introduce new higher status vocational qualifications to be obtained within the context of mainstream education. In some respects the French were fortunate in only having a weakly developed apprenticeship programme. This meant that high status vocational education could be relatively easily incorporated into the mainstream curriculum as there were few well established alternative centres of provision, so encouraging young people to stay on at school. The result has been a substantial increase in the proportion of young people who remain within the education system beyond the age of 16 and who leave with a nationally recognized vocational qualification.

In Japan, where compulsory education ends at 15 (Dore and Sako 1989), the problem of encouraging young people to continue within education has been solved through a combination of general and vocational courses. However, the vocational courses contain what is by British standards a high level of general academic education; for example, approximately half the total hours of teaching on the vocational courses are devoted to general education. Between them these general and vocational courses are followed by 95 per cent of the 15–18 age group, with 67.5 per cent on general courses and 26.1 per cent on vocational courses.

What these examples suggest is that the solution to the problem of the high drop-out rate, or early leaving rate, which characterizes British education can be resolved by academic, vocational, and mixed forms of curriculum. Recent research points to the importance of the educational system exhibiting a degree of congruence with the labour market institutions into which it 'feeds' the products of the educational system. Thus, what is distinctive about all three of the above societies is that the products of their educational system tend to be recruited into firms which have clearly defined internal labour markets characterized by long career ladders. These offer progression within the firm to both blue- and white-collar workers but usually involve the young recruit entering the firm at the bottom of the career hierarchy and then working their way up. By retaining young adults and developing their abilities to learn, the educational system provides them with the problem-solving skills which the more advanced industries require of their labour forces.

An alternative way of establishing the link between the educational system and the labour market has been pioneered in Germany. Their experience shows that a low staying-on rate is not necessarily significant in itself as long as young people move in to other forms of educational or training experiences.

On leaving school at 16 the majority of young people in Germany move into an apprenticeship in which employers, unions, and educationalists combine to organize a three-year course of integrated vocational education and training. This involves an element of part-time further education until at least the age of 18. This system produces workers with occupational skills which can be utilized across a range of firms forming occupational labour markets. From the workers' point of view these transferable skills enable them to move freely between different employers while remaining within the same trade. From the employer's point of view it provides them with a steady supply of highly skilled workers. Thus, German firms are characterized by shorter career ladders than those found in Canada, France, and Japan.

It seems unlikely that the British problem of low staying on rates could be solved easily by adopting, in their entirety, either of the two models which underlie these solutions. For the British system is distinguished from all the above in that the educational institutions are expected to perform both functions at once. Firms in the service sector and in some parts of the manufacturing sector expect the educational system to deliver highly qualified young adults who can then be trained in company-specific skills. These organizations, such as banks, are similar in their internal organization to the French and Japanese companies in that they have relatively long internal career ladders. These firms then deliver the firm-specific skills necessary to move up the ladder. On the other hand we still have the remnants of the apprenticeship system which, like the German system, delivers transferable occupational skills. Firms which still rely on this system are to be found in the engineering and construction industries, although certain firms in the service sector, especially in the hotel and catering trades, also make use of transferable skills. Thus, the British system of secondary and Further Education is faced with delivering on two fronts.

POLICY IMPLICATIONS

The above discussion has identified a number of areas where urgent policy action is required: (i) the mismatch between the outflow of relatively unqualified youth into the labour market and the demand for more highly qualified labour; (ii) the contradictory pressures being placed on the CFEs which are trying to respond to increasing demands for both academic and vocational education with few additional resources; (iii) the problems of students faced with a variety of new vocational qualifications and little or no guidance as to their relative merits and worth in the labour market; (iv) we have noted how the English and Welsh system of post-basic education is trying to prepare young adults for various types of labour market which require different forms of training.

The problem of the mismatch between qualifications possessed by young entrants to the labour market and those demanded by employers is perhaps the most urgent one. To deal with this there is a growing consensus that, in order to catch up with our industrial competitors, we must increase the level of participation in education, of one form or another, by 16- and 17-year-olds. This is imperative if we are to have a labour force equipped with the basic knowledge and problem-solving skills necessary for modern industry.

There are a number of changes which would achieve this objective. One is the use of direct financial incentives, such as the awarding of grants to ease the financial cost of remaining within the education system. Such an initiative operates effectively in New Zealand, where the state provides a financial inducement to people to stay on in school or Further Education. There, all young people over the age of 15, including those at school or FE, get a grant from the state which is equivalent to the youth dole rate. It is means tested and increases with age.

A second set of measures concerns the development of a more relevant curriculum capable of holding the attention and interest of working-class youth. TVEI has already made some steps in that direction, but a great deal more needs to be done if we are to break away from the stranglehold which the traditional academic curriculum has on the English and Welsh educational system. To be effective this means rethinking the National Curriculum and providing parents and pupils with a greater say in the construction of the school curriculum, thereby making it relevant to the lives of working-class youth in an age of information technology.

Perhaps of equal significance to a change in the curriculum is the need to change the form of authority within the school: to get away from the teacher–pupil relationship, with all its connotations of authority and deference, which is so much a part of the contemporary school. Thus, a third set of measures is required, aimed at replicating the atmosphere of the CFEs throughout the post-basic education system. Perhaps the most effective way of doing this is through the location of all post-basic education in Community or Tertiary Colleges. Such colleges would replace existing secondary schools and would provide a wide range of courses of both an academic and vocational character. What is crucial is that such colleges are open to adults and are flexible in both their hours of opening and in the provision of courses so that they cater for the full range of community needs. Thus, older adults as well as young people would work together in courses which prepared them for both academic and vocational qualifications. In addition, attendance could be on a part-time or full-time basis.

The participation of adults in such colleges would go a long way towards ensuring that the traditional teacher–pupil relationship was replaced by a more student-centred learning focus. In addition, the participation of adults in the learning process alongside young adults would effectively destroy the idea that education is something that finishes when one leaves school. It would also integrate the educational institutions more firmly within the local community.

This would, of course, require greater flexibility on the part of teaching staff in terms of the hours taught and in the form in which courses are provided. However, the result would be a learning environment which was far more conducive to the needs of adults and youths in the 1990s.

In some parts of the country the Tertiary Colleges already

approximate to this model. In Canada, the idea of Community Colleges has been widely adopted. The purpose of introducing them there was to increase the provision of intermediate level skills. Thus, the Colleges provide a mixture of academic and vocational courses ranging from initial apprenticeship training to high school and first year university courses. They provide comprehensive post-basic education. Ideally, such institutions should be highly decentralized if they are to deal with the kind of cross pressures which we identified above as one of the sources of stress on the existing CFEs. This is important if we are to move away from a situation in which vocational courses are regarded as inferior and so suffer in the allocation of resources and staff. It is equally important if the provision of vocational and 'training' courses is to be made responsive to the needs of the local labour market, for the kind of curriculum and teaching arrangements appropriate for an academic course may be totally inappropriate for a short training course.

A fourth set of measures crucial to increasing the participation rate of working-class youth is to abolish the practice of certifying the educational achievements of young people at the age of 16. As we have seen, the English and Welsh system of education is distinguished by the fact that the system of certification ensures that the majority of young people are defined as 'failures' at the age of 16. Having failed to obtain the requisite qualifications for access to a post-16 academic 'A'-level curriculum, there is little point for many in staying on and improving their level of achievement. To overcome this means abolishing the present practice of having national examinations at the age of 16 and delaying the process of certification until young people have achieved a minimal level of competence, which for the majority would be in their seventeenth or eighteenth year. Such a system would not necessarily entail extending the age of compulsory education. Instead, it would replace the desire to leave the system, which the present form of certification produces, with an incentive to stay within the system to finish basic education. Those who wished to get out earlier would be free to do so, but the balance of pressures would have been reversed in favour of staying within the system.

An integral part of this strategy would be to place pressure on employers to prevent them enticing young people out of the educational system and into dead-end jobs by offering a relatively high wage at 16. This could be achieved by making anyone employing 16- or 17-year-olds meet the cost of part-time further education. An element of compulsion could be introduced here by making part-time education compulsory until the age of 18 as is the case in Germany.

In reforming the system of educational certification it would be desirable to continue the work of the NCVQ in rationalizing the maze of qualifications now available. This may involve refusing recognition to many of the bodies currently issuing certificates in order that we can create clear signals to young adults, employers, and guidance experts on the level of achievement symbolized by the various certificates and the paths which they open up for young people. Ideally, the various academic and vocational boards would be replaced with a single examination authority so that young people faced a single examination at the age of 18, irrespective of whether they were in an apprenticeship or in college. In the absence of that, a single authority such as the NCVQ could be used to license a series of different examination boards.

Notwithstanding the introduction of measures to increase the participation rate of young people in education, an immediate response is required to the problems created for students by the confusing array of courses currently available for those who enter CFEs. Initially, this would require the colleges to take their new role in this area far more seriously than has hitherto been the case. They should be obliged to come to terms with the fact that they now cater for a range of students, many of whom have still to make decisive career choices. Consequently, these students require far more information on the options which are created by the various qualifications available to those following Route 4. They also require more information and advice on the value of the different courses in the eyes of employers. The acknowledgement of this as a priority will, of course, have to be accompanied by the provision of greater resources to provide the appropriate guidance services.

The remaining problem is how to integrate this form of extended education with the training required to prepare some young people with the transferable skills required for occupational labour markets and others with the more firm-specific skills required for the firms' internal labour market. The answer to this dilemma may well lie in the Canadian experience. For those who wish at the age of 16 or 17 to acquire the transferable skills necessary for a trade, then the training could start within the educational system. There is no reason why vocational courses within the Community Colleges or CFEs should not exempt those who complete them successfully from the first year of their apprenticeship. Alternatively, their training for a trade could be combined with at least two years further part-time education. Yet another alternative is to start the training in occupationally specific transferable skills at the end of formal education, at the age of 18. However, given the history of early initial training for apprentices in Britain, the former options of incorporating aspects of that training into the educational system may be preferable.

Those who do not elect to follow this route but opt to enter companies where they will acquire more firm-specific skills face a different situation. It is important that they first complete their formal education if they are to acquire the level of knowledge and the problem-solving skills necessary for participation in the labour market. Subsequently, on obtaining a nationally recognized certificate which indicated their level of competence, the firm-specific training would start. Part of their final two years of education could contain vocational courses which might prepare them for the general area of work which they might eventually enter, but the firm-specific training would only begin after graduation from the CFE or Community College.

Not all young people would continue in post-basic education until 18, although this would be the objective of these policy changes. A small proportion would drop out for a number of reasons, but the delaying of certification until the age of 18 or thereabouts, the change in the structure of the post-basic provision, and the encouragement to employers to delay recruiting for the 'good' jobs until the age of 18 would encourage enhanced participation in education and minimize the number of those who choose to drop out.

In conclusion, we would reiterate that many of the policy suggestions put forward here are complementary rather than alternative strategies. Given the magnitude of the problems, it is clear that the solution to Britain's inadequate system of post-basic education provision requires action on a number of fronts if the country is not to fall even further behind in the competition between industrial states.

REFERENCES

Ashton, D.N. and Maguire, M.J. (1986) 'Young adults in the labour market', Department of Employment, *Research Paper No. 55*.

Ashton, D.N., Green, F., and Hoskins, M. (1989) 'The training system of British capitalism: changes and prospects', in F. Green (ed.) *The Restructuring of the UK Economy*, Hemel Hempstead, Harvester Wheatsheaf.

Ashton, D.N., Maguire, M.J., and Spilsbury, M. (1990) *Restructuring the Labour Market: The Implications for Youth*, London, Macmillan.

Bell, C. and Howieson, C. (1988) 'The view from the hutch: educational guinea pigs speak about TVEI', in D. Raffe (ed.) *Education and the Youth Labour Market*, Lewes, Falmer Press.

Burnhill, P., Garner, C., and McPherson A., (1988) 'Social change, school attainment and entry to Higher Education 1976–1986', in D. Raffe (ed.) *Education and the Youth Labour Market*, Lewes, Falmer Press.

Bynner, J. (1990) 'Transition to work: results from a longitudinal study of young people in four British labour markets', in D.N. Ashton and G.S. Lowe (eds) *Making Their Way: Education, Training and Labour Markets*, Buckingham, Open University Press.

Dore, R.P. and Sako, M. (1989) *How the Japanese Learn to Work*, London, Routledge & Kegan Paul.

Gleeson, D. (ed.) (1983) *Youth Training and the Search for Work*, London, Routledge & Kegan Paul.

Labour Market Quarterly Report, October 1988, Sheffield, Training Agency.

Lee, D., Marsden, D., Hardey, M., Rickman, P., and Masters, K. (1987) 'Youth training, life chances and orientations to work: a case study of the youth training scheme', in P. Brown and D.N. Ashton (eds) *Education, Unemployment and Labour Markets*, Lewes, Falmer Press.

Raffe, D. (ed.) (1988) *Education and the Youth Labour Market*, Lewes, Falmer Press.

Walker, S. and Barton, L. (eds) (1986) *Youth, Unemployment and Schooling*, Buckingham, Open University Press.

11

TRAINING FOR ECONOMIC SURVIVAL

Sarah Vickerstaff

INTRODUCTION

In Britain 'education' and 'training' have traditionally been seen as separate. Education happens in schools, colleges, and universities, training happens, in the main, at work. Until the late 1970s government responsibilities in these areas were clearly delineated between the Department of Education and Science and the Department of Employment. Thus, the notion of an integrated vocational education and training (hereafter VET) system arrived late on the British scene. However, the recognition that the British system failed to provide an adequate level of training in the workforce as a whole has a very long history. As far back as the 1910s Britain's training system was compared unfavourably with that in Germany, noting that in the British case the vast majority of young people going into employment received no further systematic training or education (Sheldrake and Vickerstaff 1987: 6). A recent CBI Vocational Education and Training Task Force report commented: 'Repeated studies have shown that Britain's workforce is under-educated, under-trained and under-qualified' (CBI 1989a: 12). The same report noted that over half of the workforce in employment in 1987 received no training whatsoever in that year (p. 12).

Thus, the diagnosis of Britain's training problems is not new. It has been observed throughout the century that a poorly trained workforce serves to undercut economic performance at the level of the individual company and for the economy as a whole. Since the early 1960s these problems have been seen to warrant something more than benign indifference. The economic significance of a weak VET system and unfavourable comparisons with Britain's main economic competitors have forced governments to seek solutions to the poor record on training.

This chapter will explore these attempts to improve training efforts by concentrating upon four main areas of concern. First, we will consider whether training really matters, second, we will explore the historical traditions of training in the British context, next we will see why attempts to change the system in the last thirty years have failed to 'cure' the training illness, and, finally, we will assess present policy prescriptions and whether they are likely to provide the long hoped for recovery. In conclusion, we will suggest possible policy alternatives and pose the question of what our society wants and needs from its VET system.

DOES TRAINING MATTER?

One of the differences often noted, but less often explained, is that British companies and indeed individual British workers are less likely to see the value of training than their western European, American, or Japanese counterparts. The ethos of voluntarism in the British system, namely that industry should be allowed to get on with its own business and train or not train according to its own requirements, has remained peculiarly resistant to change. What does now seem to be clear is that these attitudes and habits have become self-perpetuating and increasingly damaging to the economic vigour of the country as a whole.

In the absence of any statutory duty or accepted social responsibility to train, the majority of British companies assess the desirability of training activities on a short-term cost basis, rather than as part of a longer-term human resource development strategy. Research indicates that this kind of short-term planning, which is highly rational from a day-to-day operational perspective, is perpetuated by the relative lack of formal training and education amongst British managers (Leicester 1989: 56–7). British line managers are still likely to have reached managerial levels through primarily work-based experience rather than qualifications and, therefore, are less likely to recognize the benefits of formal training and development. Such managers are also more prone to see the managerial task as a hands-on operational job than an activity of analysis and forward planning.

These problems are also evident in other aspects of British management and industrial structure. As Finegold and Sockice indicate, this kind of short-term planning also helps to explain, in part, the tendency for product development to be slow, resulting in products with low skill content, and of relatively poor quality. Thus, a cycle of poor peformance exists of which attitudes to training is one element (Finegold and Sockice 1988: 27–9).

In the heyday of apprenticeships in the 1950s trade unions also had little to gain from a radical challenge to the prevailing training system. Restricted entry to skilled trades ensured the market value of craft workers, the bedrock of the industrial labour movement; and in conditions of near full employment, a lack of skills was not a barrier to gaining a job for the majority of the working population. The defensive and protectionist stance of the unions with regard to apprenticeships is understandable, if not with hindsight particularly defensible. It is only under the pressure of more recent technological change that many trade unions have started to recognize the potential benefits of a more broadly based training system.

Governments have generally acquiesced in the assumption that training is really industry's business. This is entirely consistent with the wider voluntarism that has characterized British industrial relations for the major part of this century.

Educationalists have tended to be wary of training; the status traditionally accorded to the more middle-class academic curriculum over anything 'vocational' has ensured the second-best label attached to technical education or training. This has been constantly reinforced by the institutional split between education and training and the relative absence of educationalists in the training debate until the 1970s. This is perpetuated by the academic research community in so far as individuals tend either to be interested in education or training, but rarely knowledgeable in both.

Thus the absence of a positive training culture is reinforced on all sides. The consequences of this are now being more widely acknowledged both in terms of past performance and future economic survival. As earlier chapters in this volume indicate, all predictions about the future shape and character of the labour force and the nature of work suggest that the pace of technological change means that people will not typically remain in the same job, with the same skills, for most of their working lives. The emphasis instead will be on retraining, flexibility, multiskilling, the ability to adapt to new technologies, new work processes, and new products. Most would also now agree that the link between education and training is critical for this kind of adaptability; if people have been turned off learning at school they will be unwilling to take up training (Rigg 1989).

Many other countries recognize the need for a well educated and trained workforce as a prerequisite for economic survival. Britain is already behind in developing a VET system that enables the economy, and the individuals within it, to respond effectively to future challenges (Fonda and Hayes 1988). The possible choices have been put into stark relief by Streeck, who suggests that Britain can either attempt to upgrade its position to that of a high wage, high quality product economy based upon high skill levels, or content itself with being a low skill, low wage, mass producer (1989: 90–1).

If we are to create a VET system that meets the aspirations of individuals and the needs of the economy as a whole we must understand why persistent attempts to reform the training system have so far failed to significantly upgrade our VET capabilities. It is to this task we turn now.

VOCATIONAL EDUCATION AND TRAINING: THE BRITISH TRADITION

British governments have traditionally seen the post-school vocational education and training of young people as industry's responsibility. The chief vehicle of industrial training up to the 1960s, with the war periods apart, was the apprenticeship system. In Britain skill has mainly been used, in an industrial context, to refer to what is learnt in apprenticeships. The apprenticeship system was based on the slow accretion of skill and experience through primarily work-based training. It has always been restricted to a limited number of crafts and trades. Outside of this relatively privileged sector (of usually male apprentices) the overwhelming majority of young workers received little or no training beyond 'sitting next to nellie' in their first few days of employment.

The 1914–18 war provided the first major challenge to this state of affairs, with the state stepping in to ensure the supply of adequately trained workers for the munitions industry, but this forced intervention was not sustained as a model for peace-time organization. In the post-war period industry's priority was to return to pre-war voluntarism and the joint regulation of matters such as apprenticeship by employers and trade unions. The role of the state was limited to rehabilitation training for ex-servicemen. In the 1920s and 1930s governments' involvement in the training scene was largely limited to providing 'training' solutions to unemployment. The quality and standard of this training were poor as a primary aim was to keep the troublesome unemployed off the streets.

The Second World War saw the state step in again to ensure the supply of skilled workers for the war effort, but even here training in a Government Training Centre was never seen as anything but second best to the real thing: training in industry (Sheldrake and Vickerstaff 1987: 20–5). The post-war retreat from war-time provision was swift, a National Juvenile Employment Executive was set up under the auspices of the Ministry of Labour to oversee apprenticeships, but without any statutory powers to influence the quantity or quality of training. The voluntarist orthodoxy survived both world wars intact. The consensus of opinion was expressed at a Ministry of Labour conference in 1952: 'It is generally accepted in this country that, with or without the help of the educational institutions, voluntary organisations and Government, employers themselves bear the major responsibility for the training of their employees' (MLNS 1952: 97). This complacency was not without its critics. A report from the Youth Employment Service in 1953 noted that although some seventy industries or sections of industries had nationally agreed training schemes knowledge of these was very poor amongst employers and trade unionists (CYEE 1953: 23).

As the 1950s progressed, criticism of the prevailing system began to build up and persistent skill shortages, especially in the engineering industry, led the British Employers Confederation (BEC) to lament the problems of skills poaching. In 1956 the Carr Committee was set up by the Ministry of Labour to investigate the implications of the forthcoming bulge in the number of school-leavers. The Report, published two years later, rehearsed the by then familiar faults of the British training system: too few skilled workers, employers poaching skilled workers trained by others, the narrow and over specialized content of apprenticeships, the absence of agreed contents and standards for training; and, as an afterthought, the poverty of training for young people outside of the apprenticeship system. The Report commented: 'A boy who fails to obtain an apprenticeship has usually little chance of obtaining other systematic training in employment' (MLNS 1958: para. 73). The Report here inadvertently highlighted another feature of the traditional apprenticeship system: its overwhelming bias towards young men.

The Report did not recommend any major changes to the voluntarist system of training provision. A year later the Crowther Report *15–18*, under the auspices of the Ministry of Education (1959), dealt with similar issues. With only one member in common with the Carr Committee, the two reports were a testimony to the cleavage in the British system between education and training. The Crowther Report was rather more hard hitting in its condemnation of the British training system and argued the need for a coherent 'national system of practical education' (Ministry of Education 1959: Vol. 1, para. 533). In an appendix the report pointed to the fact that in other western European countries vocational education and training were more successsfully integrated.

Despite these mounting doubts, industry remained complacent, believing that the tradition of training was basically alright. However, in the early 1960s a growing awareness of comparative economic stagnation raised many questions about how the economy should be run, amongst which was the issue of the role of training in economic survival and growth. The culmination of this realization was the 1964 Industrial Training Act which heralded what has turned out to be three decades of repeated attempts by governments to devise policy solutions to the British training problem.

ATTEMPTS AT REFORM

In the context of wider concern about economic peformance in the early 1960s the training system came under renewed scrutiny. The 1964 Industrial Training Act marked a radical departure from previous government attitudes to training, as the first peace-time attempt by government to directly affect the quantity and quality of training. The Act, based in some measure on the French apprenticeship tax, introduced a levy/grant system in which tripartite industrial training boards (ITBs) in each industry would levy companies a percentage of their wages bill and then pay back grants to those who provided adequate training.

The aim of this was to spread the costs of training more equally across industry. It signalled an unheard of level of state intervention, although the mechanisms of intervention, the ITBs, were in industry's joint control.

The system was unpopular with small companies who regarded the levy as a tax and the ITBs as institutions dominated by the interests of large employers and trade unions. Another problem with the system was the limited coverage of the ITBs, which were concentrated in traditional industrial sectors. Educationalists were represented on the boards but had no voting rights. There was also no national co-ordinating body with statutory powers over the ITB system. A tripartite Central Training Council acted as a voluntary advisor to the Minister but had no formal powers. The system therefore tended to reinforce the sectional interests of particular industries and parts of industries rather than provide the mechanisms for addressing macro-economic training needs (Vickerstaff 1985: 53–61).

The 1973 Employment and Training Act, the next major piece of legislation in the training arena, was a political compromise between competing demands. The Act made provision for the Manpower Services Commission (MSC), the first national tripartite body with a brief to oversee the training issue; however, it also simultaneously undercut the power of this new body by changing the levy system into a levy exemption system, thereby reducing the leverage ITBs had in their industries.

The problems of a corporatist framework for co-ordinating and implementing policy on training were manifest. The CBI and TUC could not force their members to accept national strategies for training without some element of compulsion such as the levy grant system; this, however, represented an unacceptable level of state inteference as far as most employers were concerned. The MSC represented the first opportunity to initiate such strategies yet had little direct power over those responsible for delivering training on the ground. The result was the increasing retreat of the MSC into *ad hoc* special measures to shore up the failing apprenticeship system. Public expenditure on training rose but this was largely to subsidize training employers should have been providing anyway, rather than to initiate major new policies (MSC/DE 1976).

As the 1970s progressed the MSC's efforts were increasingly dominated by the need to respond to growing unemployment. Special measures which attempted to address the politically sensitive 'problem' of youth employment with the palliative of 'training' were the order of the day.

In the middle 1970s the 'Great Debate' in education was initiated by a Labour government but there was at first little spillover into the training arena. It is tempting to suggest that it was easier to point the finger at the education system than tackle the problem of how to persuade employers to increase their training effort.

In 1979 the incoming Conservative government soon established its opposition to the prevailing corporatist framework for training policy and, indeed, to state interference in training generally. The first major announcement was that the ITBs would be abolished and that there would be a return to a voluntarist system. In practice the government's desire to roll back state intervention has been severely constrained by the political problem of persistent youth unemployment. The main policy initiative in the early 1980s, the New Training Initiative (NTI), advocated free market principles for training in industry and adult retraining but significantly increased intervention in initial training through the development of the national Youth Training Scheme.

In this period government became increasingly concerned with the school/work interface, criticizing education as having failed to provide either education relevant for future work roles, or young people adequately socialized for the 'realities' of working life. As Horne has commented, the notion of the 'employability' of young people, and in particular young men, is common to both the 1930s and the 1970s and 1980s (1986: 23–4). It was to this group that the main policy developments were directed in the 1980s.

CONSERVATIVE POLICY IN THE 1980s

The attempts at reforming training practice in the 1960s and 1970s revealed the difficulty of designing and implementing successful state intervention in training. Who should define national training strategies? The corporatist frameworks of the these two decades typically left out educational and 'consumer' interests. How do you get nationally agreed policies to stick? Corporatist frameworks tend to become special interest lobbies, voluntarism doesn't work, and direct intervention through special schemes is open to abuse as employers get training on the cheap.

Conservative alternatives through the NTI focused on three areas: the development of a single national training scheme for school-leavers, the YTS; the reform of apprenticeships; and the encouragement of wider opportunities for adult retraining. The ideological rhetoric of the NTI was to free industry from state interference in the training area and allow market forces to generate a demand-led private training system. In practice, as others have pointed out (Ryan 1984), the measures were a rather contradictory mixture of free market principles and a major injection of public money. The ITBs were abandoned, and were replaced in some cases by non-statutory training organisations (NSTOs); a few were maintained under strong pressure from the industries concerned. However, in the youth training area the development of YTS marked an unprecedented level of state expenditure and involvement in initial 'skills' training. It is worth looking at the NTI aims in some detail.

The YTS and the school/work interface

As unemployment, and in particular youth unemployment, rose in the late 1970s, the MSC had developed a series of *ad hoc* policyresponses, including work experience, job creation, and youth training schemes. In 1976 a tripartite working party was established to consider the possibility of introducing a scheme that would offer all unemployed 16–18-year-olds a place on a scheme. In 1978 the Youth Opportunities Programme emerged as the most extensive programme thus far developed. In the coming years the YOP was increasingly criticized as a cheap labour, job substituion scheme. The YTS was marketed as a more comprehensive and training-focused replacement for the YOP. From the very beginning there was debate as to whether the scheme was primarily a training scheme or really a 'poor law' measure to keep unemployed youngsters off the streets.

The majority of trainee places under the scheme were employer based, confirming the traditional idea that real training happens in industry, but also more significantly leaving a large measure of control over the content of training in employers' hands. This basis for the scheme was always likely to create problems for the fulfilment of a genuinely universal, broadly based, transferable skills programme. If the control mechanisms over the content and form of the scheme became too rigid the MSC would, first, face considerable policing costs, and second, risk losing employers' support. Organizations, not surprisingly, have tended to use YTS as a vehicle for meeting their own specific, immediate, and short-term needs.

The main criticisms of YTS have been that the quality and level of training, as opposed to work experience, has been low. In depressed labour markets it has provided a source of relatively cheap and relatively unprotected labour; the emphasis here has tended to be upon the control, rather than the development, of young people. YTS has provided other organizations with a relatively cheap means of pre-screening prospective new employees. In general, it is agreed that schemes have done little to change prevailing race and gender inequalities in the labour market (Cockburn 1987; Finn 1987).

Looking at the YTS from the standpoint of the needs of the national economy it is also clear that it has not addressed areas of real skill shortages. Reliance on employers to provide places for trainees has resulted in the concentration of trainees in certain sectors and in certain jobs.

YTS has not been the only initiative at the school/work interface. The Conservative governments of the 1980s have been committed to making education and training more relevant to the needs of industry. In part this has meant education and the schools picking up the blame for inadequate training at work. In response to these perceived problems, policy in the late 1980s has increasingly encouraged industry to become more 'involved' in the definition of goals for education and in the management of schools and colleges.

Thus, reforms in the educational sphere have occurred

alongside the development of YTS and it is possible to identify a number of contradictory strands in these measures. The development of the TVEI and its subsequent extension, originally under the auspices of the MSC, attempt to front-load the YTS concept with vocational preparation at school. The wider aim of providing vocational preparation for the whole 14–18 age group is somewhat contradicted by the encouragement contained in YTS to leave full-time education in order to get a limited training allowance.

A central issue for this 'new vocationalism' (TVEI–YTS) is the extent to which it can, and has, developed the kind of training culture and social commitment that accompanies similar schemes in other countries. As Blackman (Chapter 9, this volume) suggests, it is not clear how vocational preparation fits in with the new National Curriculum, which tends to reinforce the assumption in the British education system that academic subjects traditionally examined are always, and in every case, superior to vocational education or training.

Can we identify a significant shift in attitudes towards training in the 1980s? Indicators suggest YTS has not marked a conversion on the part of either young people or their employers to the value of a broadly based foundation of VET in the transition from school to work. Young people have invariably chosen a job over a YTS place if the former is available; they have not judged the scheme to be a high quality, high status programme. In increasingly tight labour market conditions in some parts of the country it is becoming difficult to fill YTS places when jobs are available. Many employers are also willing to employ unqualified 16-year-olds to sustain workforce numbers in a tight labour market. Once the labour market conditions which gave birth to the YTS change, namely a reduction in levels of youth unemployment, it seems that conversion to the philosophy of training evaporates quite quickly.

Obviously the track record of YTS varies considerably from sector to sector, from organization to organization, and in terms of prevailing local labour market conditions. YTS remains many young people's best hope of training of any kind after leaving school. However, it doesn't seem possible to claim that the YTS and pre-vocational developments in school have really dented traditional attitudes towards the relative merits of education and training. The lack of recognized qualifications as an outcome of

YTS placements, in most cases, has served to reinforce its image as a poor substitute for a real job – it becomes a way of marking time.

On an even more pessimistic note it is possible to argue that, for many young people, YTS may have even further reinforced the poor image and value of training; where YTS has offered little by way of systematic training it may have led to the degradation of training rather than the development of a positive training culture (Lee *et al.* 1990).

Apprenticeship

A second aim of the NTI was to hasten the reform of the apprenticeship system. In reality more has probably been done to the traditional system of apprenticeship by labour market and technological changes, and to an extent by YTS, than any specific proposals aimed at apprenticeship.

There has been a continuing decline in the numbers following apprenticeships since the late 1960s. This in part reflects the fact that employment in manufacturing industries, where apprenticeships have been concentrated, has declined, but this does not explain all of the reduction; companies have also cut back on apprentice intakes in response to short-term fluctuations in the economy. Between 1979 and 1987 the number of apprenticeships in manufacturing declined from 155,000 to 58,000. In the same period the decline in craft and technician apprenticeships in engineering was down by 60 per cent. Young men still predominate overwhelmingly in apprenticeships concentrated in the traditional engineering and construction sectors (IDS 1988).

There has been progress in the reform of the structure of apprenticeships; they are now generally shorter, more standards-based than time-served, and with flexible entry requirements. YTS has taken over as the first two years of many apprenticeships. Although all of these developments are encouraging, apprenticeship is still so limited in scope that hopes for it as a source of training regeneration cannot be sustained. The sectors of significant employment growth in the last ten years, e.g. service sectors, have no tradition of apprenticeships. The progressive decline in the numbers going through aprenticeships has contributed to the persistent skill shortages reported throughout the 1980s and the forecast shortages for the 1990s.

Adult training

The weakest part of the NTI strategy has been adult retraining. There is little real agreement over who is responsible for training and retraining adults. Government maintains it is industry's job but few employers want to pay for the training of unemployed adults, which they see as the state's social responsibility (CBI 1989b: 18). Conservative governments of the 1980s have been against publicly financed schemes of training for stock similar to the Training Opportunities Schemes of the 1970s, their argument being that training for adults should be demand-led and therefore the responsibility of private organizations. Various schemes have been developed and replaced by new programmes targeted at the long-term unemployed. The Job Training Scheme, the New JTS, and now Employment Training (ET) have all aimed to provide YTS style work-based training placements for adults. None have proved very popular with the unemployed, with employers, or with trade unions.

ET is an attempt to upgrade the image of adult training with a single scheme for all unemployed 18–24-year-olds. The initial aim to provide 600,000 places has proved difficult as the scheme relies upon work placements being provided by employers. There has been a shortfall in placement offers, a relatively high drop-out rate by trainees, and indeed, in some areas, a shortage of applicants (see CAITS 1989; IDS 1989; NACRO 1989).

These schemes operate at the margins of the labour market for people in particularly depressed regions or with particular needs. They suffer from a poor image as they do not offer recognized qualifications nor guaranteed employment. Once again they are not significantly improving the stock of skills or preparing adults for the job opportunities expected to characterize the 1990s.

After almost a decade of the NTI many of the skills problems in the British economy remain stubbornly the same as they were in the early 1960s, namely, persistent skill shortages and a low level of qualification and skill in the workforce as a whole. The public profile of the training issue is certainly higher than at any previous time this century; few would disagree that training is important. However, the long awaited revolution in practice is yet to arrive. The 'new' solution proposed for the 1990s is to take privatization of training one step further by placing responsibility for the delivery of national training programmes in the hands of local employer-led Training and Enterprise Councils (TECs). We will review this development and its prospects for success in the next section.

THE RE-PRIVATIZATION OF TRAINING: THE TECs

In the late 1980s the Conservative government's desire to end state interference in the training system was taken one step further. The MSC, the last vestige of the corporatist framework for training policy, was abandoned and training is to be privatized, into the hands of the TECs. At a national level the old tripartite MSC has been replaced with an advisory National Training Task Force composed of up to twelve members of whom two-thirds are to be 'leading figures from industry and commerce' (Department of Employment 1988b). Responsibility for delivery and management of national training schemes such as YTS and ET moves to the TECs. In the words of the White Paper which heralded the new developments: 'The creation of TECs is a truly radical step. It will give leadership of the training system to employers, where it belongs' (Department of Employment 1988b: para. 5.19). This concept of a privately run, demand-led, locally delivered system, is ideologically in tune with the assumption that employers know better than anyone what VET is needed. We will assess the TEC developments from three perspectives: in terms of their composition, their organization, and the prospects for their success.

The composition of the TECs is as follows: between nine to fifteen directors, of which two-thirds, including the chairperson, must be local business leaders from the private sector, the remainder being drawn from education, the public sector, voluntary organizations, and trade unions. These requirements perpetuate the Conservative government's desire to exclude trade unions from a guaranteed role in the policy development and implementation arena. The question of the composition of TECs is, of course, a political one. Governments in the last decade have sought to marginalize the influence of the education lobby, local authorities, trade unions, and employee interests more generally. This, at the very least, raises questions about the probable support and commitment of these groups, who might be expected to be significant in bringing about a genuine revolution in attitudes to training and enterprise. In addition there is the perennial problem of the assumed coherence of employers' needs.

Much of the debate about, and criticism of, previous practice in training and education has focused around the argument that the educational system and government-led training schemes do not meet employers' needs. The key issue here is that employers needs are neither self-evident nor particularly homogeneous. As Bennett and his colleagues comment: 'There is a major difficulty for TECs that the concept and reality of local business communities in Britain are both very weakly developed' (1989, 25). This is in contrast to other countries which have locally based delivery systems in the training field, e.g. Private Industry Councils in the USA and Chambers of Commerce in West Germany (Bennett *et al.* 1989).

In Britain the likelihood is that the TECs will be dominated by the representatives of large organizations and companies. It is these which will have the stipulated stature and community standing and, perhaps more importantly, the time and resources to release senior executives to spend time working with the TECs. The outcome will be as with the ITBs; those who need them least are best placed to benefit from them. Small companies, which face very real resource constraints in the provision of training for their employees, will not have the time to devote to the considerable managerial tasks implied in the operation of the TECs. In the 1960s small employers criticized the ITBs for being run by the 'big boys for the big boys'; it is a problem the TECs will also face.

The first job for a TEC will clearly be to create agreement in its local business community about the priorities and aims of the TEC's activities. This will be easier where relatively cohesive local employer organization already exists, that is, where chambers of trade and commerce are historically strong and where Local Employer Networks (LENs) are well developed. Early evidence for this is suggested by the fact that the first TEC proposals have arisen in areas where LENs were first to develop, however the relationships between LENs and TECs are unclear. It appears that the LENs are to be abandoned in favour of the TECs, a development not welcomed by some involved:

> TECs are an unnatural grouping; one which would not normally have happened. Unlike LENs, which have evolved organically, or training boards, where there was at least a common industrial interest, TECs are to span public and private sectors, manufacturing and service industries, large established household-name firms and small entrepreneurial set-ups, and a range of other interests. There really is no common objective or purpose that might logically have brought these groups together.
>
> (Wright 1989: 45)

The ability of TECs to forge a political consensus locally is in some doubt but, even assuming agreement, a local community will contain very diverse training needs and an existing quality and quantity of provision, which takes us to the next issue of the TEC's organization.

The plan for some 100 TECs covering the country raises a number of issues about the best basis for a local delivery system. The old ITBs organized on a sectoral basis did create some problems of coverage; there were issues of duplication in skill areas common to a number of sectors and they also served to reinforce rather than break down sectoral interests in many cases. However support remains in some industries (e.g. construction) for sector-based training organizations.

The TECs assume that a regional or local labour market approach provides a better basis for developing consensus, closer contact to local providers, links to schools, colleges, etc. This makes sense; however, if one thinks of employment opportunities and travel to work areas, it is apparent that some local labour markets are reasonably wide and undifferentiated, others are extremely diverse. For example, in Kent at least four main geographically based local labour markets are identifiable with quite distinct employment bases and yet there is a single TEC. This raises the question of how priorities will be determined, especially by bodies which are not strictly representative of an area nor democratically accountable. Employer 'needs' in a region the size of Kent are extremely varied.

There are also issues of co-ordination and the management of devolved budgets. TECs will administer publicly funded schemes such as ET, but the systems for monitoring these responsibilities remain vague. TECs will operate under a 'performance contract' with the Training Agency, which will specify targets for rates and numbers of qualifications attained (DE 1988a). However, the guiding principles for the TECs are: 'decentralization, diversity, innovation and excellence' (TA 1989b).

Can a coherent national strategy emerge from the aggregated interest of individual employers in different regions, or are the TECs a recipe for disjointed incrementalism? A plethora of local initiatives is not a substitute for a national strategy. The problems are both macro and micro. However, the TEC framework focuses attention and effort on the micro level and is vague about the macro level; here the National Training Task Force will advise the Secretary of State. TECs will be responsible for delivering national schemes like YTS (now called Youth Training), but how much discretion will the TECs have? If very little, why would a local committee of business people want to administer and run a set of schemes devised elsewhere; but if discretion is allowed, how will standards and performance be measured, and how will some degree of equity be sustained from region to region?

This takes us to the issue of 'success', because it is not entirely clear what the criteria for success will be beyond relevance to local needs as defined by local businesses. An acknowledged problem with much current training activity in firms is that it is too anchored to short-term needs and that companies lack planning mechanisms to assess and forecast longer-term skill requirements. They also do not see why they should pay for training in transferable skills which may or may not bring an obvious return to them. It is not clear how TECs can avoid this familiar problem of how to convince companies to look beyond their own immediate needs; as a *Financial Times* editorial commented: 'Companies clearly can and should do much more to train their employees properly. But individual employers in a free market enterprise system do not have an incentive to provide an efficient overall level of vocational training' (6 December 1988).

Another pressing issue is the time-scale for TEC development. It is expected to take three to four years for the system to be fully operational (1993) and maybe longer where initial bids for TEC development money are slow in being put together. The skill shortages of course exist now, and in another five years the stock of skills in the workforce, in comparison to our competitors, will have fallen further behind. Evidence suggests that many countries are gearing up their VET systems now and have been for some time (Fonda and Hayes, 1988).

A free market or voluntarist system of training provision has never provided an adequate level of skills in the British economy in the past, there is no particular reason for believing it will do so now. The TEC system offers no mechanism for developing a strategy for the workforce as a whole, with the consideration of national planning requirements that implies. Yet the problems are not just local labour market ones but macro-economic issues of the possibilities for economic development and growth.

ALTERNATIVE SOLUTIONS

It is always much easier to criticize existing policies than to devise and suggest realistic alternatives; this last section will conclude by considering the policy alternatives being suggested by various groups and attempt to identify key objectives for the VET system of the 1990s and beyond.

There is clearly a need to change attitudes at all levels about the role and significance of VET in relation to individuals' aspirations, companies' strategies, and wider societal objectives. Current policy in education and training assumes that employers are the best group to spearhead this change in attitude. In particular, attention is focused upon the link between education and work, and the need to produce VET 'relevant' to industries' needs. Critics argue that employers' ambivalence over the importance of training has remained peculiarly resistant to change in the post-war period and that, from a short-term perspective, there are few incentives for individual companies to plan beyond their own immediate needs. The failure of training in Britain has been linked to the tendency for companies to view labour utilization as an operational rather than a strategic issue; the failure to forecast and plan for labour requirements and skills needs reinforces the *ad hoc* approach to training. There is little in the TECs' proposals, other than greater employer involvement, to suggest a radical change of practice.

It is equally clear that a large proportion of the British

workforce do not view continuous training as either a positive benefit or as a right. This can be explained by the traditionally low status attached to vocational training, which may have actually been reinforced in some young workers' minds by their participation in YTS/YT. Negative experiences of education turn a large proportion of the workforce off the idea of further education and training.

The need for incentives to learn, and the importance of a flexible system offering academic, technical, and vocational routes, is acknowledged in current policy but little is offered as a means to achieving it. The development of National Vocational Qualifications (NVQ) holds the prospect of a more coherent and integrated system of accreditation of vocational and educational training skills, but does not solve the problem of how to convince employees and employers of their value.

Conservative governments of the 1980s have tried to minimize their responsibility for providing and overseeing the national interest with regard to training provision, while simultaneously increasing direct intervention in the educational system. Thus the potential for a genuinely integrated system of education and training is diminished. In addition, the scope for public debate and participation in developing a VET programme that meets economic and social aspirations has been progressively narrowed in favour of market mechanisms.

The CBI has devoted increasing time and attention to training in the last twenty years and acknowledges some of these problems. The CBI has repeatedly posed the unavoidable question of who should pay for training, as it knows that its members are not likely to spend more on training without some equalization of overall costs across companies (CBI 1989b: 9). As long as firms face a significant risk that their trained workers will be poached by non-training companies the incentive to improve effort is limited. Individual organizations also do not see initial broad based training or retraining for the unemployed as their responsibility (CBI 1989a: 37). The CBI's proposals point to the inequity of government support for some post-16 education and training and not others. They suggest the provision of financial incentives to individuals through the provision of government funded credits for all 16-year-olds to meet costs associated with courses leading to NVQ level three or its academic equivalents. The argument for this is as follows: 'It forms the basis for a market for vocational education and training with the individuals as buyers and the providers competing to meet their needs. It would avoid the inadequacies of national manpower planning' (CBI 1989a: 24).

The CBI's proposals perpetuate the old dilemma it has faced over the co-ordination of employers' views on training objectives, namely, the contradiction between the collective realization that the national economy has needs for which only government can provide the framework and funding, and the individual members' opposition to any government intervention in their own training activities. The CBI's claim that a training market will provide a better substitute for national workforce planning is unconvincing. Regional disparities in training provision and employment opportunities, and a lack of market knowledge amongst young people, will not add up to a coherent national training strategy. In addition, a market-led system will not meet wider social goals (or public goods) such as the breakdown of gender and race inequalities in the labour market.

The Labour Party recognizes the need for a concerted policy in the VET area. The main policy suggestion is a National Training Fund based upon a payroll levy to spread the costs of transferable skills training more equally between companies. Regional training boards are also suggested as the delivery mechanism. Grants from the National Fund could be used to encourage enterprises to establish joint employer and union committes. A National Training Organization would oversee training standards. In addition, the Labour Party argues for the development of new four-year traineeship post-16 to encourage higher staying on rates in education. The first two years of the traineeship would be primarily education based, followed up by continuing training in employment. The Fund would meet the employment expenses of young people in the traineeship scheme. The aim would be to upgrade initial VET into a standards-based integrated qualification system (Fatchett 1989: 9–11).

The merits of these proposals are that they provide incentives to both employers and employees through a levy system and they seek to upgrade the content and status of non-academic VET.

The TUC takes some of these ideas further by suggesting the need for a set of statutory minimum rights in the training field:

> We believe there must be statutory minimum standards in training. For example, everybody ought to enter full-time work with a vocational qualification, whether they acquire that qualification through full time education or alternative programmes of on and off the job training like YTS or apprenticeships. And, for older workers, we could be looking at an entitlement, after a certain number of years employment, to paid educational leave so that they can return to learning later in life.
>
> (Willis 1989: 18–19).

This would have an impact upon our training culture putting training on a par with education as a basic right, it would also give the individual a mechanism for demanding better training.

These ideas in part mirror the proposals in the EC Draft Community Charter of Fundamental Social Rights which states:

> Every European Community worker shall have the opportunity to continue his [sic] vocational training during his working life. The public authorities, enterprises or, where appropriate, the two sides of industry, each within their own sphere of competence, shall set up continuing and permanent training systems enabling every citizen to undergo retraining, more especially through leave for training purposes, improve his skills or acquire new skills, particularly in the light of technical developments.
>
> (COM 1989: 248, emphasis in original)

The short-term imperatives for upgrading training effort are a change in attitudes towards the value of training, and a dramatic increase in investment, and thus output, of skilled, trained, and qualified workers. As we have seen from the foregoing discussion, there is little widespread agreement as to how this should be achieved.

The present author sees no short-term substitute for the need to educate and train for stock as a fundamental basis for economic regeneration. This means dramatically increasing the number of young people continuing in full time VET post-16, and public support for skills training in current and predicted shortage areas. The skills gaps exist now and government should invest in a major retraining/upgrading programme in conjunction with sector bodies like CITB and NSTOs.

The TUC's notion of certain minimum training rights should be the basis for a longer-term conversion to a positive training culture. NVQ, as a nationally recognized system of VET standards, wll serve to improve the image of training, and a proper scheme of allowances for training, collectively funded through a levy system, would provide the incentives to stay in full-time education and training, and the incentive to provide good quality training.

It is not rational market behaviour for the individual firm to pay for training in general skills. However, it should also be recognized that specific job-related skills are often best learned in the workplace. The best basis for a high wage, high quality, high skill enconomy is without doubt an extension of the VET system; this can best be achieved by recognizing the divergent immediate interests of the actors involved. Individuals need to be convinced of the value of a 'learning culture' (Streeck 1989: 93) and know that education and training will improve job opportunities and work experience. Thus apportunities in VET must be equalized and proper funding for the individual would be a necessary first step. Companies can best provide training in specific work-related skills but they can also provide valuable experience in wider training and development skills; they need to be convinced that the costs of such activities will be fairly spread across their competitors.

If economic survival, by which we mean a genuinely prosperous society without persistent social inequalities, is our collective goal then the contribution of the VET system to a healthy economy must be recognized. In the face of the prevailing assumptions of the 1980s it must be asserted that education and training are public goods that should be collectively debated, organized, and administered. Contrary to the assertions of many Conservative politicians in the late 1980s, that market forces ensure that if companies fail to train their employees it is them that will suffer, in the long term we all suffer. The last century of training history in Britain has shown, without doubt, that the free market and voluntarism does not and never will provide an adequate level and equitable distribution of education and training opportunities.

REFERENCES

Bennett, R., McCoshan, A., and Sellgren, J. (1989) *'TECs and VET'*, *Department of Geography Research Papers*, London, London School of Economics.

Central Youth Employment Executive (CYEE) (1953) *Report of the National Youth Employment Council on the Work of the Youth Employment Service 1950–53*, London, HMSO.

Centre for Alternative Industrial and Technological Systems (CAITS) (1989) *Scrounging for Skills*, London, CAITS

Cockburn, C. (1987) *Two-track Training*, London, Macmillan.

COM (1989) *Community Charter of Fundamental Social Rights Preliminary Draft*, COM (89) 248, Brussels.

Confederation of British Industry (CBI) (1989a) *Towards a Skills Revolution – A Youth Charter*, London, CBI.

—— (1989b) *TECs – The Way Forward*, London, CBI.

Department of Employment (DE) (1988a) *Training for Employment*, Cm. 316, London, HMSO.

—— (1988b) *Employment for the 1990s*, Cm 540, London, HMSO.

Fatchett, D. (1989) 'Education and training – the Labour view', *Transition*, Oct., 9–11.

Finegold, D. and Sockice, D. (1988) 'The failure of training in Britain: analysis and prescription', *Oxford Review of Economic Policy* 4 (3), 21–53.

Finn, D. (1987) *Training without Jobs: New Deals and Broken Promises*, London, Macmillan.

Fonda, N. and Hayes, C. (1988) 'Education, training and business performance', *Oxford Review of Economic Policy* 4 (3), 108–19.

Horne, J. (1986) 'Continuity and change in the state regulation and schooling of unemployed youth', in S. Walker and L. Barton (eds) *Youth, Unemployment and Schooling*, Milton Keynes, Open University Press.

Income Data Services (IDS) (1988) 'Study No. 414', London, Income Data Services.

—— (1989) Study No. 431, April, London, Income Data Services.

Lee, D., Marsden, D., Rickman, P., and Duncombe, J. (1990) *Scheming for Youth: A Study of YTS in the Enterprise Culture*, Aldershot, Gower.

Leicester, C. (1989) 'The key role of the line manager in employee development', *Personnel Management*, March, 53–7.

Manpower Services Commission (MSC)/DE (1976) *Training for Vital Skills*, London, MSC.

Ministry of Education (1959) *15–18 Report of the Central Advisory Council for Education*, London, HMSO.

Ministry of Labour and National Service (MLNS) (1952) *Report of the Human Relations Conference*, London, HMSO.

—— (1958) *Training for Skill*, London: HMSO.

National Association for the Care and Resettlement of Offenders (NACRO) (1989) *Training for a Change: ET in its First Year*, London, NACRO.

Rigg, M. (1989) *Training in Britain: Individuals' Perspectives*, London, HMSO.

Ryan, P. (1984) 'The new training initiative after two years', in *Lloyds Bank Review*, April, 31–45.

Sheldrake, J. and Vickerstaff, S. (1987) *The History of Industrial Training in Britain*, Aldershot, Gower.

Streeck, W. (1989) 'Skills and the limits of neo-liberalism: the enterprise of the future as a place of learning', *Work, Employment and Society* 3 (1), 89–104.

Training Agency (1989a) *Training in Britain*, London, HMSO.

—— (1989b)*Training and Enterprise Councils: A Prospectus for the 1990s*, Sheffield, Training Agency.

—— (1989c) *Guide to Development of TECs*, Sheffield, Training Agency.

Vickerstaff, S. (1985) 'Industrial training in Britain: the dilemmas of a neo-corporatist policy', in A. Cawson (ed.) *Organised Interests and the State*, London, Sage.

Willis, N. (1989) 'A worker's right to train', *National Westminster Bank Quarterly Review*, Feb, 13–20.

Wright, D. (1989) 'LENs in the light of TECs', in *Personnel Management*, May, 42–5.

NAME INDEX

SUBJECT INDEX